Also by David Roddis

A Slow, Painful Death Would Be Too Good for You
(and Other Observations)

SORRY LOOKING FOR NOW LOL

JESTS FOR TROUBLED TIMES

David Roddis

THE CONTENTS OF THIS BOOK, SPECIFICALLY, TEXT, IMAGES AND GRAPHIC DESIGN, ARE protected by the Canadian Copyright Act (R.S.C., 1985, c. C-42). The copyright holder and publisher is The Future Progressive (David Roddis).

You may not reproduce or distribute this content in any manner whatsoever without the express written permission of the publisher, except for the use of brief quotations in a book review or journal.

DISCLAIMER: This is a satirical work as well as a personal memoir. As satire it portrays public figures in situations which are entirely the product of the author's imagination, as well as in historical situations which are a matter of public record. These satirical essays are intended solely as entertainment, and they should not be construed as fact. As memoir, this work describes actual events; however, these have been condensed and reimagined, any dialogue recreated and identities changed.

THE ILLUSTRATIONS: Most of the digital illustrations have been created by compositing photographs and other visual elements found online. These elements have been used only in part, and/or have been substantially creatively altered in such a manner as to parody them or to comment on the text, essentially creating an original work, and without interfering with the commercial value, if any, or usability of the originals. This is consistent with exceptions outlined in the Canadian Copyright Act, Sec. 29: Fair Dealing.

"THE PIVOT CHORD" first appeared, in somewhat different form, on peacehacks.com. It is included in this collection with the kind permission of the site owner.

FIRST PUBLICATION: October, 2023

ISBN: 978-1-9995675-1-4 (Paperback)
ISBN: 978-1-9995675-2-1 (Electronic book)

BOOK TITLE:
"Sorry Looking for Now LOL"

PUBLISHER:
THE FUTURE PROGRESSIVE
392 Sherbourne Street, Unit 805
Toronto, ON, M4X 1K3
Canada

ONLINE:

slowpainful.com
futureprogressive.ca

PURCHASE ENQUIRIES: sales@slowpainful.com
PUBLISHER CONTACT: david@slowpainful.com

DEDICATION

I dedicate this book—

To all queer, transgender, gender non-conforming and intersex individuals, our new *avant-garde* in the fight for justice;

And to each and every outsider who, face-to-face with incomprehension and hatred, lives defiantly, joyfully, and without apology.

It is not enough to say, as the French do, that their nation was taken unawares. Nations and women are not forgiven the unguarded hour in which the first adventurer who came along could violate them.

— Karl Marx,
"The Eighteenth Brumaire of Louis Bonaparte" (1852)

*Again I've been just a big, sentimental fool.
It's a tendency I have.*

— Bette Davis,
as "Charlotte Vale" in "Now, Voyager" (1942)

*Time flies like an arrow.
Fruit flies like a banana.*

— Groucho Marx
(attrib.)

CONTENTS

ACKNOWLEDGMENTS • ix

PREFACE • xi

CANADIANA • xviii

Deeper Dives into David

The Birds and the Blogs • 21
Designated Adult • 29
"I Am—Ethylene Glum—!" • 39
hElTeR-sHeLtEr (Pandemic Pastimes): Coltish Captions • 45
Invocation • 51
The Limits of Funny, the Whiteness of Money • 59

Holy Sh*t-Show

Happy So-Tense-About-Saying-The-Right-Thing-idays • 71
Secret Santa, Still Stuck on the 401 Westbound • 75
Monday Man Crush: The Risen Christ • 83
Joy to the World, Unless You're Dead • 89

Terrific Tales

Queen Elizabeth II Shrinks, Gets Trodden on by Truss • 99
The Great Snail'xtinction • 109
Scary Weird Coincidence • 115
Useless Knowledge • 121
Synchroni-City • 131
So You Wanna Have a Gay Orgy? • 139
Apps in Development • 151

Pandemonium

CoronaZombies • 161
Semantic Bleaching • 171
Psychopaths with Translucent Skulls • 175
Monday Man Crush: Volodymyr Zelenskyy • 181
Night Terrors • 185

Last Liberal Standing

I Have Been Recalcitrant • 193
Ottawa Got a Little Out of Control • 205
Imaginary PR Voting Outcomes • 211
Monday Man Crush: Insurrection Shaman Dude • 217
Ministress of Silky Sheen • 221
John Tory's Heart is "Broken" • 225

Dyspeptic Digests & Loopy Listicles

Monthly Mayhem: A News Round-Up • 235
Etiquette for a New World Order • 241
Jordan Peterson's Quixotic Quest for Real Manhood • 247
A Lexicon of Conservative Invective • 257
Monthly Mayhem, Again • 269
Skipping Rhymes of Gen Z • 279
So You Wanna Be—Somebody? • 287
Angelic Visions • 295
Proverbs of Post-Truth Heaven and Hell • 298

Unhinged States of America

Refugees Are Delicious...! • 303
Putting the "Stick" in "Lipstick Lesbian" • 317
The Emotional Blackmail of Bernie's Babes • 323
Skipping Rhymes of Gen Z Redux • 329
The Poor Get Poorer, the Rich Get Kardashian • 337

Finale

The Pivot Chord • 347

ACKNOWLEDGMENTS

So many men, so little time...

Sorry, wrong acknowledgments! My bad! Oopsies!

So many *people* have been involved in the successful birthing of this book, most of them me. Then there's the guy who turned up while I was in the bath, urging me to "bear down, David, bear down!" I think that was my "midhusband" from OHIP. Is that a concept?

Still. As awesome as that is, it's not everything. Financial support is key, and my heartfelt thanks go to Michael, Aaron, Mark and Adrian for donations that helped me during the dark days of gestation.

As well, I'm super grateful to Norm R, Jonathan P and Chris U for their extra generosity in funding.

If I'm still here, thriving and giving off even the slightest whiff of integrity, it is due to Dana Oakes—generous donor, sympathetic (if bemused) listener, a loyal friend who has never questioned my abrupt changes of identity, and the person who gets my jokes better than anyone.

I'd have to publish a three-hundred-page book with nothing but *"thank you"* filling every chapter, were I to thank him properly, but I suspect he would scoff.

And *that's* everything, Murgatroyd McGraw.

PREFACE

I believe it was around, or even on, my eighth birthday—so, September 21st, 1963—when I awoke from a romantic dream about Robert Goulet (he was holding me in his arms and singing "If Ever I Would Leave You" while Julie Andrews, dressed as Mary Poppins, glared at me from her sexless void)—I awoke from that paradise of dark chin stubble and ringing baritone and thought,

"Oh, for Pete's sake. Of course! That's what they forgot to tell me.
"*I'm gay.*
"I'm a Queer. A Flamer. A Poofter, a Pansy, a Nelly, a Ponce.
"*One of those.*
"No need to pretend any more. I can own this thing! I totally identify with *Jane Eyre*, I love the men's underwear section of the Eaton's Christmas Catalogue, and if you want me to stop hogging all the attention, doll, you'd better nix the applause.

"When I put on cologne, I put on half a bottle of *Shalimar*. Seriously, what's the point of holding back? And it gets me my own seat on the school bus.

"I like hanging out with the girls during quiet time. Girls are nicer, more helpful than boys, and they appreciate my baking. Care for another date square? Charmed!

"I ♥ skin-tight and/or revealingly short clothing in, if not paisley, then either all-black or highlighter pink. Is this a crime in a world where refrigerators are harvest gold?

"No more shame about wearing those plaid shorts hiked up with the suspenders, either. Stop twirling your toe in the dirt, girl! After all, you *invented* male camel-toe. Embrace it!

"I'm constantly stressed about my unruly fly-away bangs, what self-respecting eight-year-old isn't? Pass the Dippity-Do!

"I won't deny that I tried on my sister's prom dress while she was out bowling at Whitby Plaza, but surely this proves I'm secure in my masculinity! And I suspect she was crying because I looked better in it, but I'm much too kind to say so.

"That's the other thing: *I'm kind.* When I made Tilly Pellis laugh while she was drinking chocolate milk and it came out her nose, who was there to shield her from the haters? *Moi,* that's who.

"I get it, now. That's why, when I go for a haircut, and Mario the barber presses into me as he snip snip snips away, I get that pleasurable ache in my belly that mingles with the scent of shaving cream and cigarette smoke and Barbicide—and I don't mean to be pedantic, but why doesn't that mean *"the act of killing Barbie"*?

"Freedom! No more pretending that I have a doctor's appointment once a week that gets me out of gym class when it's actually my piano lesson. I'll simply hang around the changing rooms until Coach Wessel steps out of the shower, hand him his towel, and explain that my dengue fever got cured!

"I'm done. *I'm takin' the train to Faggot Town, baby!"*

I *think* that's how it happened. And no raised eyebrows or tut-tuts about my age, either. When you're born gay, which I was, it takes a supreme act of will *not* to know, even in 1963.

So *relax*. There were no dirty uncles diddling me or strangers with candy flashing me from the driver's seat of their Chevy Corvette.

That came much later, when I was well into my twenties.

MOVING ALONG LIKE A PIECE OF DISLODGED plaque in a sclerotic artery, you're naturally burbling over with questions about my new book. Let's start with the cover I designed (*see Fig. 1, opposite*) (and please don't go all "control freak" at me. John Updike used to design his own covers, so I'm in illustrious company). First, see how I've juxtaposed—

What did you say?

Oh, it is *not*. Oh, c'mon, you're *embarrassing* me. Oh, *stop* it.

Really? You think so?

Now let's take an in-depth moment to close-read my cover design, divine the Northrup Frye-ish unity which it surely must present.

The cover shows, in the background, one of Sandro Botticelli's illustrations to Dante's "Inferno". I believe this is the seventh circle of Hell, reserved for sodomites, liars, and the guy who first put pineapple and ham

FIGURE 1:

BOTTICELLI MEETS THE
VERY PUSHY-FORWARD-TYPE GAY MEN
OF OUR 21ST CENTURY

on a pizza.

That's one out of the three, at least, that Sandro, as an Italian, would have had no affinity with, especially considering pineapples had just been invented (though, of course, ham is eternal).

(Hey, wait, I think I have a joke: "I thought sodomite was a sedimentary rock formation until I discovered Smirnoff!" OK, maybe not.)

Botticelli, a gay man in fifteenth-century Florence, had an anxious life. I know this, as one gay man knows another, down to his sweaty palms and curled toes, even across five centuries. Sure, there were lots of Florentine gay men and they were quite visibly and openly so—they say Leonardo was quite the dandy—but the winds could shift…

At any moment, out of great calm, the trees could groan, heave up their branches, and a Borgia or a Medici could decide that you were an abomination, with consequences ranging from aggravating to indescribable.

So here is Botticelli, painter of the iconic "Birth of Venus" and "Primavera", a man of exquisite sensibility and genius, filled with ambivalence as he draws what he probably believes are the torments awaiting him, his own hideous eternal punishment.

All of a sudden, like a pair of randy bovines barging into William Ashley Fine China, onto our disco floor strut the very pushy-forward-type gay men of our 21st century, camping it up in their own private Busby Berkeley routine, with no idea who Botticelli might be or why they'd want to know; who, if you told them about the seventh circle of Hell, would think,

"Seriously? Wow. What a bummer. It sounds like it's gonna be a drag, blowing all those demon dicks for eternity. I guess. Well, what can you do and in the meantime—PARTEEEE!!!"

This is by way of admitting that gay men—and of course I speak freely and with permission on behalf of every last one of them—ruin everything we stand beside, and if you tell us this one late afternoon out of anger or frustration we will look chastened for a moment, then wounded.

But after five seconds or so—having made the heroic effort to sustain an emotion that long—we'll break into a wicked smile, tell you a whimsical joke, or kiss you on the earlobe; you'll catch a whiff of hurried, early-morning sex or feel intoxicated by our Eau Sauvage and start to melt a little, thinking—

"Who needs some aerated Venus-with-a-shenis on a seashell anyway, and my gawd that hair! It just screams 'plays soprano recorder in the early music consort'! Venus may be many things, but vegan that girl is NOT—!"

You see? I've proven my thesis by ruining something, and I wasn't even trying.

• PREFACE •

SO WHAT IS MY BOOK "ABOUT"?

YOU MAY BE WONDERING ABOUT THE TITLE. ALLOW me to pull back the Oz-curtain to reveal the startling truth, the highly-strung back end, and I just wish that didn't sound the way it sounds, of the gay scene.

It's a Friday night, and you're preparing to lie face down on the living room floor in a GHB-induced coma, ready for your "date"—all that remains to do is to set that up.

You will gather from this carefree, last-minute attitude that gay dating is a very contingent, *Will-I, Won't-I, Is it raining? Can't go out, I'll melt like candy!* kind of affair.

If I'm online and some hapless newbie messages me to ask if we can meet in two days' time, I splutter with laughter because, seriously—how do I know I'll be horny in two days' time? Maybe I'll be in a Buddhist monastery. Or at my Pulitzer Prize ceremony. (Lily Pulitzer.)

I don't even know if I'll fit into any of my clothes or like any of my friends in two days' time!

Instead, once I've located a real player, someone who's been around the block, but kept their lifetime of experience perfectly self-contained and unexamined, lest it sprout even the first frail tendril of wisdom, the text conversation invariably goes (edited for brevity):

Real Player: Hey wanna hook up?
Isolated Author: *Sure, address?*
RP: 123 My Street, that's in Riverdale.
IA: *OK, I'll just hop in the shower, get dressed, get a cab, and be with you in say 30 minutes?*
RP: THIRTY MINUTES???!!!! Sorry, dude, looking for now LOL!

In other words, *any* time lapse between your last text message and arriving at their place is unacceptable. You have to be *instantly* there.

They are looking for NOW, baby, do you not *capisce* this? *Understanden Sie nicht* the *urgentesse*?

The only solution that I've been able to work out which would satisfy their surreal demand for, basically, teleportation, would be to kill myself, then get reincarnated as the infant son of some girl roommate of his, at which point I grow up in the same house for eighteen years until I'm legal.

Which would be almost the perfect strategy for a person with patience, staying power, and focus, except I am not that person.

And even if I were that person, what the other guy is saying with this is, effectively, anyone will do who is immediately available. Your hours in the gym were wasted, girl. He doesn't care about your giant biceps or your thighs like thunder. You are not his fantasy.

His fantasy is of someone who can form out of the gloopy ectoplasm the instant he's horny and wants to get off. Then, having materialized in his bed, this undifferentiated ecto-lover does something nasty to him involving double-A batteries and a black rubber sheet, then vanishes, leaving a breath mint on the bedside table.

And believe me, you'll need one, because in a ballroom filled with one thousand gay men, nine hundred and ninety-nine of them's fantasy will be, "get gangbanged by bikers, and you have to do all the inviting."

The other cockroach in the KY is my insistence on clinging to my worthless but still undeniably fabulous life. I would *never* kill myself. I'm too much of a Nosy Parker about what might happen tomorrow and wondering if it could possibly be as bad as today.

In case you were wondering but are too shy to ask: *Of course it could!* That's why I'm a considered merely a cock-eyed optimist.

OK? I'll just let you put all that in a Tupperware container for safekeeping. Don't try to figure it out, though. I didn't say gay men *made sense*. I said gay men *were fabulous*. It takes a whole lot of energy to be fabulous and we figured "making sense" was pretty much discredited as an MO anyway.

APART FROM THE SOUR DISAPPROVAL AND swoosh!-over-the-head irony of the title, this collection, like my previous one, pretends to be about current events, historical events, and philosophical questions that personkind has been asking ever since it realized that Oprah overcame the double oppressions of being Black and a woman, only to triumph by becoming a member of the despised one percent who has way too much money, way too much power and who needs to be smacked down.

Seriously, the last time I thought about shit like that, the cognitive dissonance turned my entire face into a giant hickey, just from how hard it all sucked. So, please, please exercise discretion as you read this book, and don't take on more than your two sessions of transactional analysis have prepared you for.

Little pinky-promise? Right on!

This book is really all about me, which you'll understand if you view it from a very oblique angle, and maybe squint. It's like that anamorphic painting, *"The Ambassadors"*, by Holbein.

If you stand way off to the side, so far that you can barely see the surface, you will suddenly be aware that there's a leering human skull front and centre that you couldn't see before, a *memento mori*.

No surprise there. That's what art is.

Every opinion offered to you, every story recounted, every joke executed, every bit of gossip, fairy tale or news report, is all an urgent dispatch from the front lines of someone's life. It purports to be objective. But inside that story is another story, in which a lonely voyager in a leaky vessel built for one cries, "Mayday, mayday!"

And I can't save you, nor you me, but at least we can laugh as we all sink together.

David Roddis
Toronto
October, 2023

CANADIANA

-OUR vs -OR
If you see a word like "odour", that means I forgot to spell it American-style, as "odor". If I felt all bovary about it, I'd be cramming arsenic into my mouth.

"Out and about"
No Canadian has ever uttered the phrase "out and about", nor have they pronounced it "oot and aboot". Therefore you will not find this phrase anywhere in this collection.

LCBO ("el-see-bee-oh")
The Liquor Control Board of Ontario. This was founded in the 1920s and it was the only game in town for buying liquor. Until quite recently, it worked like this: you snuck in under cover of darkness and found yourself in front of a bare counter, behind which stood a male employee with big nipples and no pupils in his eyes who waited for you to write down your sordid request on a pad of paper.

The employee then disappeared into a back area, where you could catch a glimpse of bats flying around a cobwebbed ceiling and hear the cries of the alcohol wraiths wailing at your sinfulness. The employee would then return with your relapse-in-a-bottle inside a plain, brown paper bag, ready for you to abandon your family and lie in a ditch.

These days the LCBO, still run by the government, is the world's largest purveyor of alcoholic products, and contributes billions to Ontario's universal healthcare plan. It has beautiful retail stores and a free glossy magazine.

And there's a joke that goes: "Liquor Control Board??!! I haven't even met her parents!" which is far too juvenile to repeat here.

I feel better now, knowing we understand each other.

Deeper Dives into David

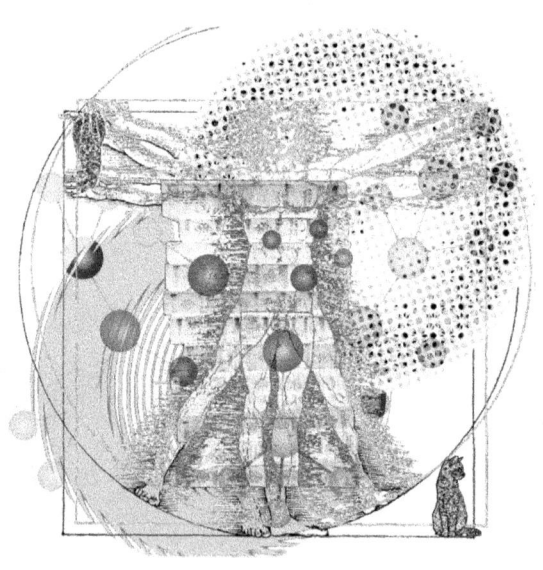

The Birds and the Blogs

J ust like 99.9% of gay men, I've always been in thrall to sex, and yet, unlike my enthusiastic co-conspirators, I was never entirely convinced that sex felt the same way about me.

Honestly, I've liked the *idea* of sex: porn fantasies that I never successfully realize, because from extensive experience I can tell you that even a threesome takes more skill at negotiation than a hostage-taking.

In real life I've found sex a little tasteless, a bit *de trop*: too hairy, smelly, rambunctious and gung-ho, and basically comical, like I should be wearing a big red nose, a fright wig, and floppy shoes shaped like pancakes. I ride down your treasure trail in a clown car, and when you cum, I get a banana-cream pie right in the kisser.

Then I honk my horn.

Sex is a vaudeville routine, in other words, once we finish with the boondoggle of romantic love, that gooey, sugary drizzle that lubricates the dry boxed cake of our self-regard. Go on, plight your troth to that guy you picked up at the Yonge-Bloor subway washroom (not that there was much choice, back in the day). As long as one of you is Abelard, the other Heloïse, you'll handily accumulate twenty-five years of dinner-on-a-tray, drag shows, dahlia beds and down-low sex, until one of you discovers the other's astounding record of infidelity.

This can only end badly, and mostly dramatically, as the injured party botches their suicide with a bottle of children's Aspirin and a Lady Schick razor; finds *Jaaaay-sus!!!;* or just crosses the floor to vote with the Liberals.

My boondoggle, which lasted about as long as it takes to unroll a condom (1980s, etc.) manifested in London, England, where for a fleeting interlude I actually met gay men my own age, gazed deeply into someone's eyes in the back alley of a dream, and experienced the sinking feeling of excitement tainted with anxiety that signaled "love".

Then I woke up, sighed with relief, and went back to the man thirty years my senior who needed to burn my body with cigarettes. (Hey, Paul, I know you're tired after work, but pencil in some time to pick up an ashtray at Habitat.)

Now sex is nothing but plumbing. I'd rather read a good book, something by me, perhaps. But what do *you* want? Typically, gay men, who are all bottoms, want some variation of the following:

"I want you to whore me out for a biker gangbang!"

Ah, yes. Every gay slut's favorite fantasy, and fantasy it shall remain in down-home Toronto, where half the gay men claim they want to be banged by bikers, and the other half have Grindr profiles that warn: *No Total Bottoms!* If you like, a bunch of us can pedal over to your condo on our CCM's from Canadian Tire then point at your balcony and laugh. Different vibe, same outcome.

"No limits guy!"

No limits. Seriously? OK. We're gonna parade you down the frozen food aisle at Loblaws dressed in nothing but a jockstrap, nipple clamps and gladiator boots, while shoppers take pictures of you on their smartphones. Oh, and we'll invite your mom and dad to a "special surprise". What's wrong? You worried someone online found out your postal code again?

MEN MAKE UNFORTUNATE LIFE choices, starting with our too quick decision on "male" that we make during our pre-birth questionnaire:

> "So ya got male or female, what's it gonna be? And hurry up, there's a bus just arrived with all the company of seraphim and cherubim, and you know how ratty they get after a long trip with bathroom breaks they didn't even need. There's infinite angelic beings after you and my manna break's overdue."

> "Well, I don't wanna hold everything up, how do I choose?"

> "So men get all the power, all the attention, all the advantages so they can maximize the power, oh and

you're physically stronger, taller, bigger body parts and also this means people cut you slack when you do shit because they're afraid of you. The only thing you don't get is, let's see, oh yeah, responsibility for life itself and something called imponderable ineffable mystery."

"What's that?"

"That's what women get that you can never have and as part of my job I'm bound to tell you that imponderable ineffable mystery means that women will drive you to acts of despair and murderous rage because you want that, too, and women don't want to give it to you. But we do give you a penis, which is a dangly body part you can play with, and here's the neat bit, it gets bigger when you're happy! It's like magic at your fingertips, twenty-four seven! Honestly, I'd recommend 'male'."

"Okey dokey male it is!!"

"Done! You're male! Please be sure to read the fine print. Next!"

The fine print says: *"Penis: excessive attention to the penis causes brain death and resentment, which can exacerbate acts of despair and murderous rage. Use only as directed."*

THERE'S THIS AD I RECENTLY SAW ONLINE, in a new kind of Craigslist-y publication catering to both straights and gays called *Locanto*. (You can also buy a used futon, find a handyman job or advertise your candle-making hobby, but seriously. It's for sex. Who am I, or they, kidding.)

I'm not going to explain why I find this fall-over-and-die funny. You'll either understand or you won't.

I *swear* this is a true story.

The ad reads, mildly paraphrased:

> *"I'm into eating poo. Looking for a male, 30's, who's willing to feed me.*
>
> *NO FAT PEOPLE."*

A QUICK SIDEBAR ABOUT my passive-reactive humor: My talents, like my personality, are basically vampiric. When you think I'm being collegial, that's just nature's way of fooling you into spending time with me so I can drain your conversation of its usefulness. So that sinking feeling you got when I walked into the room? Not your imagination!

This is why I'm so generally unloved, so that everyone shuns me and piles into the bedroom waving streamers and blowing kazoos, and shuts the door while I stay in the living room. Think Santa Claus Parade, but sponsored by Hustler or was that Hutter?

It happens like this: I've just awakened on the living room sofa bed, covered with my one clean sheet, or equally often a piece of cold French toast with syrup, or an old microwaveable container lid, anything just for basic modesty. It's early morning and my roommate has been away for a couple of days, so I can pretend I live alone again.

I've already dismissed the idea of asking over that leather queen from *Locanto*, who wants me to be kneeling, naked and blindfolded, with my back to the door, because it doesn't seem like a good idea. My back is not really all that noteworthy, I never built up any serious musculature, there's no Japanese-style tattoo with a carp, he would be stymied. My back is *plain*.

I'm only worried about his traveling a long way for a let-down. He'd probably be so disappointed, he'd forget to scream "faggot!" and bash in my head with the baseball bat he'd brought for the occasion.

OK. Confession. I did once have the leather queen from *Locanto* round, because he responded to my ad that said *whore out this no-limits guy at a biker gangbang*. He stripped, took thirty sniffs of Jungle Juice, wheezed, turned purple as he told me about his chronic asthma, then got on all fours and presented his gigantic rear end like he was Cirque du Soleil performing the USDA instructional pamphlet on artificial insemination. My illusions were, in a word, confirmed.

So I decide to have a wank, while crying, because stick with what you know, right? And I'm getting into it, maybe I've had a whiff of the ol' brown bottle, and I'm getting a bit light-headed and uninhibited. I'm running through my mental home movie of all the great sex I had thirty years ago, except in my mind they're all hung like stallions and there's more of them and they're still the same age as they were then, but now I'm the evil old guy.

Come into my parlor, twenty-something! Marvel at my hair like Einstein's, my pear-shaped body, and I'm not sure if I wiped all that carefully after going to the bathroom, which is how you start behaving when you hang around straight guys as much as I do. Old sweatshirt, no pants, but socks are non-negotiable, because my feet are so calloused and rimmed with dry skin I myself am put off me when I see them.

For some reason I say on my hook-up sites that "I'm into younger guys", which, seeing as I'm sixty-six, isn't saying anything useful. Unless I develop a hankering for terminal eighty-year-olds, or, if I miss the last subway, necrophilia, there isn't anyone who isn't a "younger guy." So, if you're forty you could easily be my son, and that's my lower limit of "young".

What am I going to talk about with a twenty-year-old who anyway just keeps checking his phone? Sorry if my penis got in the way of your third round of Candy Crush!

The last one put his phone down on my pubes and was watching Amber Ruffin while he blew me, so I had to keep encouraging him. He'd falter. But at least I was a white guy not enjoying sex because of feeling that Amber Ruffin was in the room, which I'd like to think is a kind of reparations that Black Lives Matter would tentatively approve of.

So anyway, there I am masturbating and actually having a decent time, because I'm a good conversationalist, sensitive to my needs, and, most important, I'm not shit-faced drunk for sex these days. I won't have to call anyone in the morning to ask if I had a good time. I'll totally know I was the Sunset Boulevard version of David, Salome-dancing towards the camera while everyone gasps and recoils.

Then all of a sudden my roommate arrives with guests. Fun-time is *over*. And you have to imagine that the front door opens onto a little entrance vestibule, but please don't conjure up some Martha Stewart-type scenario. It's not a Shaker coat rack covered with milk paint, masses of gerbera daisies in a pewter jug and a "Bless This House" shadowbox in *découpage*.

It's just twelve squares of dirty linoleum and a sad bag of garbage no one's taken out forever. The bag of garbage is just sitting there like an abandoned dog that's sure its master is coming back from the war any year now.

And there is no visual barrier between the door and where I'm jerking off, so you could, in fact, stand in the common hallway, prop my front door open and watch me—which, frankly, I'm not a hundred-percent sure hasn't happened at one point. There is *zero* privacy.

The door opens fast, with no warning, just the key engaging and turning in the deadlock, then a ca-CHUNK, like the supports being disengaged on a drone missile ready for deployment. My roommate switches on the hall light and I have just enough time to hurriedly throw a towel over my junk.

Young fags would stare unprotected at a solar eclipse before they'd look at the genitals of anyone over twenty.

WITH SEX NOTHING MORE THAN a fading memory, I started a blog to fill up all the spare time.

Man, did sex ever take up a lot of time! Having the fantasy, hiring the cast, buying the refreshments, both licit and il-, all that waiting while everyone you've invited texts to ask, "who else is going to be there?", which is when you realize that no one's going to come unless they know who's coming, which means no one's going to come. This constitutes the Great Paradox of Gay Sex.

Can you have an orgy of one? My answer might surprise you, except I'm going to leave you dangling. ("That's what *he* said!")

I decided my blog would be about My Life, and I will share that there is limited attention you can get with posts like "I just cleaned the mouse fluff from behind the bookcases!," especially if you're a white, senior gay male.

The next time you fill out that pre-birth questionnaire, take it from me: the only attribute I can honestly recommend from those descriptors is "gay", and even then with reservations, such as: Will you be athletic enough to run for your life by Grade 3?

MY WRITING FINALLY got into its groove. I developed a couple of personas, and my inimitable style, but before I got there, I did a lot of fobbing people off with funny cat GIFs.

There's one GIF that's just a cat sitting on a chair in front of a computer, and only its front legs are animated.

I just watch that and watch that like a developmentally-challenged Helen Keller, pre-Annie Sullivan.

There's another one of an adorable puppy crawling over a sleeping cat and sitting on its face, and the cat is like "WTF??" but does not shred the puppy like you might expect. Do you not die for that, just from my description? I could, and do, watch that cat GIF with the puppy like it was *Imitation of Life* on permanent loop.

Somehow I got sucked into believing that the world needed MY opinion on global affairs, and Canada—and above all, economics, which I crib frantically from YouTube and Stephanie Kelton.

The most advanced economic concept I've developed owes a lot to Modern Monetary Theory and goes: *Withdraw 20 dollars from the ATM five times, and that's a whole lot less than taking out one hundred dollars once."*

That's the system, by the way, that the Secretary of the US Treasury, Janet Moneyburger, borrowed from me without even a hint of a thank-you. Not even a pre-paid VISA, stupid bitch, and she tiled her bathroom with those!

In case you were wondering, there's no GIF of Thomas Piketty crawling over Paul Krugman and sitting on his face, at least a concerted search on Pornhub didn't find me any; or of Amber Ruffin sitting at a keyboard with just her arms moving. I would watch those until my head fell off.

Maureen Dowd in a fur coat, running up to a chair, doing a back flip and ending up supine with legs all akimbo?

Are you kidding?

I would never leave the house.

Designated Adult

I am scantily clad and on my hands and knees in the middle of the night, but on this particular occasion, curiously, there's no one else here saying, "Hey, pig, fancy a toot of this?" or, less encouraging, "You were a lot thinner in your pictures!"

I'm known for holding my friends, family and the world at large to the very highest standards of performance, all the while cutting myself a great, big, bleeding side of slack.

I take as my inspiration an entity such as the Acme Widget Corporation of Toronto, who sets up its customer call centre halfway around the world, in Mumbai; similarly, I effectively outsource my inevitable disappointment were the attempts at high standards mine, and give myself lots of space to refine my, I'm fairly certain, welcome feedback.

But this evening, with no one watching, swallowing my pride, I've decided to onboard Muggins McMe, here, with this "adult" agenda I keep hearing about.

I am going to, as they say, *own this.*

That's why, at two AM, I'm on all fours, wearing nothing but a baby blue bath towel and accessorized with a simple, large-yet-tasteful bucket of scalding hot water and lavender-scented Pine-Sol, would you excuse me for a sec?—

—Hi mom! Are you listening? They have Pine-Sol in flavors now! And I'm so glad you died because that means I didn't have to! —

—as I was saying: A bucket of scalding hot water and Pine-Sol, plus, from The Little Bee—my local convenience store—the cheapest available sponge, which bears about as much relation to a once-living creature from a coral reef as does a politician compare to the dimply, cooing ingenuousness of their two-year-old former self, before they learned to hide the peas by stuffing them up their nostrils then denying they ever got served peas.

And I'm scouring and scrubbing my kitchen floor, an unlovely checkerboard of once-white tiles flecked with black, in a dogged, circular motion. I suppose the white flecked with black was meant to suggest Carrara marble to people who've never seen it, but as the tiles were left unsealed this has allowed them to soak up every splotch of ketchup, every dollop of pesto or splash of coffee, every dribble from my bursting bladder relieved in the sink, damn the fine china, I've got anti-bacterial Palmolive.

My kitchen floor is a grimy palimpsest of sixteen-year-old condiment spills, pretentious dinner parties and avoidable crises.

THREE WOMEN

I'M THINKING OF MY FAVORITE Kate Bush song as I scrub: "Mrs Bartolozzi," from 2005's concept album "Aerial," treating as it does of a forlorn housekeeper wiping up mud from boots and dutifully, wearily, scrubbing the floor "until it sparkled..."

Although my adoration of Ms. Bush only grows year by year, it is despite, not because of, her poetry, which I usually find too reminiscent of a cliché teenage girl's lyrical diary ("It was just so beautiful, it was just so beautiful, it was just—so —beau-ti-ful!" are the words which nearly cause me to run screaming from the room and ruin the second half of "Aerial" for me) but this song is different.

This song, a haunting piano ballad, is full of pregnant pauses, this song has a perfect and serene depiction of the *washing machine, washing machine* and its soothing mechanical splishy-sploshing as it gets "the dirty shirty clean;" the aching emotions—loneliness, sorrow, yearning—of its *ritornello* transport you to every moment you've ever spent doing work you detest, every moment when you wished your life away.

This song is not really about the never-ending drudgery of daily life, that unending cycle of banal routines that I endlessly chafe at.

It is about the ripple, the dazzle, the shimmer; the unveiled reality that suddenly manifests and evokes our gasp of recognition.

Mrs. Bartolozzi has a laundry epiphany:

>..."*I watched them go 'round and 'round*

My blouse wrapping itself in your trousers
Oh the waves are going out
My skirt floating up around my waist
As I wade out into the surf..."

— Kate Bush, "Mrs. Bartolozzi", from Aerial (2005)

And a shirt on the washing line, waving in the breeze, becomes the arms of—who is it? Lover, husband, son? *"And it looks—so alive..."*

I'm the kind of guy who attempts to infect as many people as possible with his quirky enthusiasms. Once, during the early morning hours when my apartment had been invaded by an entitlement of millennials—I tried, I really did, to come up with a different collective noun, please believe me—I mentioned "Kate Bush" to a boozy babe and was rewarded with a blank stare.

Boozy Babe had already had the once-over from me as I met her and her male companions—my friends—at the entrance to my building to let them in.

As we took the elevator to my eighth-floor slum-in-the-sky, I didn't even attempt to suppress my scowl of disapproval bordering on disgust.

She was wearing her "waitressing uniform:" a leather micro-skirt that I had first mistaken for a large belt, and a sloppy T-shirt that stopped just below her big naturals, baring a roll of belly fat a twenty-something had no business flaunting. Her face was red and sweaty as a coal miner's and her skin exuded a nasty odor of ketosis that enraged me.

And at some point during the next three hours I mentioned Kate Bush, got the blank stare, and proceeded to give her a Boomer 101 music appreciation lecture, starting with "Wuthering Heights" and touching all the major pit stops up to "Aerial."

As the boys polished off the remaining food and beers and packed up to leave, and my impromptu torture session drew to a close, Boozy Babe seemed to experience an atavistic memory: the dim recall, I'm guessing, of a parental figure admonishing her always to express gratitude when adults go the extra mile with our ponderous, guilt-inducing diatribes.

As she stumbled towards the front door, she turned to me and, with the excruciating good manners of the insincere, blurted out: "Thanks for telling me about The Lady."

Kate Bush—The Lady—utterly feminine in the way she celebrates both her sexual appetite and her power—understands how not to be a lady; she's not afraid to handle the soiled linens that once touched someone's body. She understands that a strangled cry at a phantom on the washing line, or a guttural growl of Wow, are necessary colors in the singer's spectrum.

And it's just—so—beautiful.

ALICE MUNRO, ONE OF THE greatest living writers of short fiction, is Canadian. She won the Nobel Prize in Literature in 2013, and I imagine she must have an awards room, the way Imelda Marcos had a separate building for her shoes, so many has she received. So you could say, without much fear of contradiction, that Alice Munro is world-renowned, a household name, even, to those who read and revere literature.

The other day I asked a young man if he liked her stories, and he said, "Who's Alice Munro?"

Who's Alice Munro...

If this were Japan, Alice Munro would be like Mount Fuji, or the person who invented life-sized sex dolls, or the one remaining Buddhist monk who can explain how to dye silk using vegetables according to a one-thousand-year-old method.

She would be made a "Living Treasure," an icon, a superhuman repository of culture. Every Canadian would be proud of Alice Munro; we would have read all of her stories, voluntarily, and stage adaptations would be common. We'd attend the premieres of these plays, and afterwards go to a coffee shop and argue about how faithful it was to the original.

We'd wear Alice Munro T-shirts while gardening, and we would understand how Munro has recorded a uniquely Canadian take on life, in which the ordinary is illuminated with lightning flashes of the sublime and the characters downplay their crises with irony and wry humor.

On the day the Nobel Prize was announced a national celebration would have occurred. Children would have been given the day out of school; window washers and bankers and kids on skateboards and those down on their luck, and everyone's wife and boss, if they had these, would have had a holiday, too.

Alice Munro would have been the centerpiece of a grand parade, with her own float, a parade heading from Christie Pits, all along Bloor Street then down Yonge and ending up in Nathan Phillips Square. Little girls dressed in white would have accompanied her, throwing flowers at the crowd as she passed by.

She would sit on her special throne on the float, wearing bright-colored slacks, Spectator pumps and a plain white blouse with a big bow in the front. Her silver hair would be beautifully layered. She would look genuinely pretty, with a touch of coral lipstick her only make-up.

She would look like the first generation of women who called themselves "liberated" (which they were only in comparison to their mothers); the first generation to dare to wear pantsuits to work, where they worked mainly if they wanted to, or even to make a point, but not always because they had to.

She would smile rather shyly and wave at the crowd with sincere affection and you would sense she might want to cry from overwhelming emotion, but would not indulge herself; you would understand that she is a writer and would be observing the occasion a little more than she would be participating.

You would sense that she was deeply honored and aware of her responsibility to her fans, but also thinking, "I'll be glad when this is over and I can go home and take off these damn shoes."

That evening, in Nathan Phillips Square, after the fireworks display, she reads her latest story, broadcast nationwide. The audience listens in enthralled silence; children are told, "You'll remember this when you grow up!" At the end of the story grandfathers wipe the tears from their eyes; women weep openly.

Then a great roar of appreciation and hats in the air: Our greatest living writer!

When she appeared in public wearing her kimono we would rush up to her giggling and prostrate ourselves, and she would laugh and say, "Who do you think you are? Arise!" And when she passed on, which could be tomorrow, because she's really old now, we would go into mourning nationally and cry uncontrollably, like the traumatized Parisians watching Notre-Dame's spire collapse in flames, and we'd be given time off work to deal with our collective grief.

But this is not Japan. This is Toronto, the city without a soul, where we say, "The Arts generate a lot of money! That's why they're important!" in a really chirpy voice, while condo developers roll their eyes then check the latest stock prices.

GLENDA JACKSON[1] IS ANOTHER cast member in the ongoing

---

1 I chose not to update this piece from 2019; Glenda Jackson died on June 15, 2023, at the age of 87.

sixty-four-part epic, eclectic cultural survey and revamped Mickey Mouse Club that is my life; another name that evokes blank stares from Young People whenever I try to explain who she is and what she did, why they should care even though they won't, and how she underpins my favorite movie: Ken Russell's masterpiece, "Women in Love."

Women in Love may very well be a movie that's actually greater than the book on which it's based, or, alright, then, if you must, as great as.

Glenda Jackson's presence is elemental in that movie, her voice like the chalumeau register of a clarinet, measured, honeyed, even as she torments Oliver Reed (as Gerald Crich, a wealthy mine owner who's besotted with her); torments and goads and degrades him until, nullified, he curls up in the snow under a brilliant, indifferent Alpine sun. Only suicide in the icy embrace of Mother Nature can numb the agony of his emasculation.

Jackson as Gudrun Brangwen is the quintessential *femme fatale* but translated into Anglo-Saxon terms, torturing her hapless male, despising his servitude yet refusing to leave until his destruction is complete.

One of the most vivid and astonishing scenes takes place during a garden party on the Crich estate. Gudrun and her sister Ursula (portrayed by the exquisite Jennie Linden) ask Gerald Crich if they can escape the crowd; he sees they are provided with a picnic basket and the women find a secluded spot. All is peaceful English pastoral until the two women are suddenly menaced by a herd of bulls.

What happens next is unforgettable: Gudrun confronts the beasts, enchants them and chases them off with a transcendent, improvised dance that is a celebration of female mystery and power. Jackson invests what could have been laughable with such conviction that we believe in her magic. The message is clear: male energy is plodding, boorish, anxious, all blustery show; female energy is mercurial, teasing, unpredictable, hornet-like. No contest. The bulls scatter, a ton of trouble conquered by a wisp of a girl.

As she half swoons in a kind of spent, solipsistic afterglow, Gerald rushes up to save her. But he's too late and already irrelevant; she's drunk with her victory.

"How are they your cattle," she says, with palpable contempt; "Did you swallow them?"

She gives his face a swift, unexpected smack with the back of her hand, and the gesture is all the more demeaning for its spontaneity. It's the way you'd brush away an annoying insect, without any energetic investment or sense of struggle.

Women in Love, from 1970, presents Jackson in her youth; last week, I called up the New York Times online to read about her celebrated turn as King Lear (she's returned to acting in her eighties, after twenty years in the British House of Commons as Labour MP for Hampstead and Highgate) and I experienced the shock of seeing her for the first time as an elderly woman.

Glenda Jackson's unconventional but undeniable beauty, in her twenties composed of equal parts dewy English rose and bovine sensuality, has contracted, no doubt due at least in part to her smoking habit, into a loose, sagging face that's an accretion of wrinkles.

With most people you can trace how they've traveled from there to here, still unearth the familiar features, but Glenda Jackson is unrecognizable in a way that defies all my attempts to connect my youthful memory of her and how age has since worked her over.

Her face is a desert scored by cracks and fissures, an arid landscape Edward Burtynsky might photograph; an apple that you've stuck in the fridge and forgotten, retrieving it a year later to find it brown and withered; and from that face she peers at us with an expression that is part amazement, part defiance.

I'd give anything to see her turn on Broadway as Lear, but I'm afraid. I'm afraid of her voice of righteous anger, in full throttle arguably the least comforting sound ever to issue from a woman's body. I'm afraid of what she has told me about how the most beautiful can turn monstrous and alien under the pressure of time.

I am sad about Glenda Jackson, and you will not need your psychology degree to understand that that is another, less blatantly self-interested way of saying I'm sad for myself, about getting old.

You looked a lot thinner in your pictures.

THAT'S WHY I CONTINUE SCRUBBING THE FLOOR, in a dogged, circular motion, with my sponge dipped in near-scalding water and lavender-scented Pine-Sol and my soul dipped in regret for every moment lost. I will redeem myself. I will persist at this chore that I previously despised and I will prove my housekeeping critics wrong. I will get this done.

How should I spend the rest of my life? The question now haunts me. I'd been a blissed-out swimmer in a sparkling endless ocean of allotted time. I hadn't noticed until recently the thin mark of the shoreline on the horizon as I drift towards a destination I never chose.

Every minute now is consciously spent or squandered. Housekeeping or writing? Practising the piano or caulking the bathtub? Why would I watch Game of Thrones when I've never read "In Search of Lost Time"?

When I'm on my deathbed—

—a rather extravagant, even cinematic, concept that assumes I don't plunge to my death upside down in a Boeing 757 with someone's vegetarian meal shoved up my nose—

—whatever happens, if I have the time to fade away graciously (I'm thinking Melanie in Gone With the Wind for the total ninny factor), I'm fairly sure I won't be clutching my lace handkerchief and thinking *I'm glad I washed the kitchen floor.*

I'll be thinking:

I'm glad I wrote a book that made people laugh. Maybe slightly less than they might have had I not explained all the jokes to them for two years, but, in the end, laughed.

I'm glad I took beautiful pictures, and so what if they turned out to be placemats.

I'm glad I learned to play Beethoven's Bagatelles, Opus 126, in my dotage, impressing beyond all description my houseful of young thugs who'd never heard anything but rap.

I'm glad I said kind words when I could have said unkind ones, and instead wrote down the unkind words for worldwide publication and universal consumption.

I'm glad I forgave again and again, because you never quite know how much forgiveness you'll need for yourself. Think of the people you forgive as your forgiveness bank account.

Sincerity? As if!

I reckon I'm a good twenty years from that tasteful cough and final exhale. Right now, tonight, I'm on my hands and knees at two AM, alone, in my kitchen, cleaning up my mess.

No one told me to do this. There's no one to criticize me, or pat me on the head. There's no one here to help me; no lover to give me an excuse to procrastinate, no one to kiss, no one to entertain or comfort or argue with. It's taken sixty-four years, but I'm finally the designated adult.

Under my right knee is a sliver of glass or possibly a very hard English muffin crumb. A cockroach, the first I've seen in months, scurries along the baseboard and slips into a crack that's thinner than a hair. My hands sting when I plunge them into the hot water and Pine-Sol, the fumes make me squint.

Splishy-sploshy wishy-washy. Scrubbing the kitchen floor is not a task I'm engaged in until real life comes along; it *is* real life, every sweat-stained second of it.

The kitchen floor will be clean and sparkling, so that everyone will notice it and say, "That is, unmistakably, David's floor."

I'm determined to be ready for that unspecified day fast approaching when I'm not around to defend myself.

"I Am—Ethylene Glum—!"

"Testing, testing... zing, string, zing, string... testing, testing... Ahem. This is Judy Garland, OK? and I'm running outta time. So, listen up, future husbands, fags and father-figures,

and, yes, I know there's some overlap, category-wise. This may be the last chance I get to talk. I'm being held here against my will, in a state of complete consciousness, and my Flying Monkey Overlords could return at any moment.

I especially dread the one that looks like Liza and goes *Mamma! Mamma!* I have to keep reminding myself, "It's just a flying monkey, it's just a flying monkey."

And I'm hiding under the duvet, so apologies if I sound bat-shit crazy.

I know you were all told I died on the toilet in some hotel bathroom... Where was I? Australia? Very possibly. I do recall that at some point in the previous month I went for a slash on a private jet, nodded off for a second, and woke up on stage at the Sydney Opera House, with everyone pelting me with Anzac cookies.

Wait—Ssshhh! Did you hear that? I could have sworn I heard Liza flapping her monkey wings... *zing, string, zing, string, hellooooo?*

I just wish I knew what country I was in. Things were easier with a husband, which is why I so regret pissing off Mark, was he number eight? I wrote it down somewhere.

First off, he didn't realize I was so much older, thanks to those MGM tips I learned, like splashing my face with ice water every morning, and having Liza turn up for our dates instead of me.

Then, I mistakenly served him Luft's divorce papers instead of handing him the caterer's estimate for the wedding reception. Which, frankly, saved so much time, I'm gonna mash up the wedding reception and the divorce permanently from now on.

Our wedding night didn't go as expected. I let him remove the three hundred yards of bandage that were holding me in place while I slowly spun around, a sexy trick I learned from Marlene. Then, when I collapsed into a pile of dust, Mark stormed out, leaving me to cry and settle on the furniture alone.

Mark was becoming more faggoty and distant. I was so worried about losing him and his erectile dysfunction before we had a chance to divorce, then, joy of joys, I started ballooning out of all proportion—I naturally assumed I was expecting. Cue to double down on the eating for two!

As the months dragged on, I became completely exhausted. At one point, I so desperately needed a good night's sleep, I called up Radio City Music Hall, offered them eight shows a week for two weeks, which sold out instantly, then canceled. That was June, I think. Or December.

All I needed after that epic shut-eye was the occasional couple hours sitting on a bar stool in front of a jazz trio at Johnny's Blue Note, New Jersey, with my head slumped on my chest. Beats me how I got there from Australia.

SO MUCH HINGES ON A WORD MISSPOKEN, a suggestion misconstrued. I don't blame the old film crews or legendary moguls. When I was nine, Irving Thalberg asked me what I wanted and I said, "A funny Barbie doll!" I thought that was reasonably clear, but what with all the noise and distraction on set, he got his wires crossed and gave me an ongoing renewable script for Phenobarbitol instead.

I'm not complaining! That little bit of heaven came in mighty handy when I was yearning for a near-death experience, especially after twenty-four hours underneath Mickey Rooney, or the odd occasion when I'd sneak in a discreet power nap, face-planted onstage at Talk of The Town, with Princess Margaret in attendance.

Zing, string, zing, string... Is this thing still on? Someone get Mister Mayer! Tell him his little hunchback's on the line!

So, where was I? Oh yeah, expecting. So one day, all of a sudden I come-to sitting on the john in, let me guess, was it backstage at Wigmore Hall? Beats me how I got there!

The contractions get more violent, I'm in labor for eight agonizing hours, I'm totally alone, Mark's not even in the audience, there's no one but Princess Margaret occasionally bringing me a phone call from Liza.

"*Mamma, Mamma!*" she sobs, then hangs up.

I must have passed out, because next thing I know I'm at the Palace and it's a foggy day in London town. But no new little nine-pound bundle of joy. False alarm! Turns out it was just the senna pods from 1953 finally working their Wizardy magic. But that was only half the story.

The other half would be—how the hell did I get back to Claridge's? And where was Mark?

Unable to cope with the shame, I bribed the chambermaid, disguised myself as someone responsible, then snuck out while monkey-wing Liza flew through the lobby as a distraction.

It was Princess Margaret who said to me, "When you're a has-been and everyone's losing patience, often the best way to proceed is to fake your own death then return as a hot-mess former child star named—Ethylene Glum."

And she was absolutely spot-on.

YOU KNOW, I WASN'T THE FIRST choice for "Dorothy", and certainly not as long as Shirley Temple could draw breath. Victor Fleming wouldn't let me wear my glasses, which meant I stumbled over some munchkins during the preliminary phone audition.

So, the munchkins were lodging with me at the time! Let's not get all faggoty about it, OK?

Disaster by rotary-dialer! I'd prepared an ace version of "Jitterbug," rehearsing day and night with my Lesbian mentor Kay Thompson, vocal coach to the stars, and horsey-faced author of those children's books about a little girl Lesbian who lives at the Plaza Hotel.

I ask you: What's not to identify with?

So you can imagine my distress when my three o'clock amphetamine injection was interrupted with the news that she'd seized up during a photo shoot with Richard Avedon and couldn't be pried off her brass bed frame.

But—she could move her eyes!

Brave, foolish Kay! Saved by her desperate need to turn every waking moment into a dazzling display of over-confidence!

Charlie—the lead munchkin in the Lollipop Guild number, and Academy Award nominee for "Best Background Actor with a Clean Syringe"—was so relieved on my behalf, he immediately upped my dose to thirty cc's before ripping off my panties with his teeth.

Rehearsals for my audition resumed, and with just a glance here or a glance there, Kay communicated everything she knew: how to flail my arms if I forgot what nightclub I was at, and how to just stand with my legs apart and talk through a song if I had that urge to rip off my bra and show Mr Mayer my tits instead of singing.

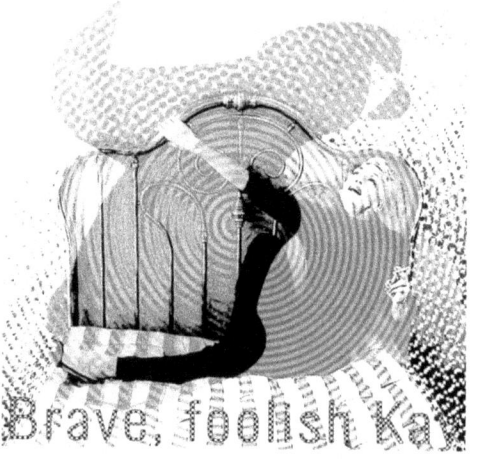

So, like, either everything she knew, or maybe just both things. Kay was truly one-of-a-kind: a stick-thin, shifty-eyed Lesbian vocal coach attached to a bed frame.

If that weren't just the very nadir of the *tragique*, a teenage tap-dance injury resulting from a badly-mixed Canadian Club and soda made it awkward for me to click my heels together more than twice, and as you know everything works in threes.

Ruby red heel-clicking. Sneaking out of the Plaza Hotel. Freaky amphetamine sex with munchkins.

If only, if only. I lie awake at nights reliving the humiliation of that little-people pile-on, blaming myself for my failure instead of, for example, blaming you, or, really, just any old random person who springs to mind.

If only I'd stuck with the Mateus rosé. If only I'd opted for the Lasix surgery limited-time offer. If only Charlie had had that chancre looked at.

Ah, well. The world is a cruel, harsh place, a vale of sorrows, but what's the alternative? Live with your faggoty agent?

As if. Even a spacious Bel Air mansion can only accommodate, say, fifteen wannabes, twenty tops if they clear out a shoe closet. Still, I'd line up around the block in a heartbeat if it weren't for my recurring phantom ectopic pregnancy gives me swollen calves.

Also, I'm not a wannabe. I'm a Definitely Am. Definitely Am Scared of All the Secret Cameras Filming Me 24/7. It's tragic when your star fades. Not as tragic as running out of Barbies, though.

AND I HESITATED ABOUT TELLING YOU all of this, knowing you'd never again be able to watch Ethylene Glum singing, "I Wish I Were a Sad-Eyed Puppy GIF" without feeling a pang of betrayal and like your life had been built on a lie.

Ethylene understands! Indulge yourself with, maybe, a petulant toss of those silk throw-cushions you had re-covered in a Pantone Color of the Year—was it Elegant-Piss Yellow? or Hideous to be Poor Greige?

They tell me that newcomer, what is it, Julie Android, tops the poll for sappiest crowd-killer with that ditty from "The Sound of Gumption", about raindrops on roses and whiskers on kittens.

Bully for you, Miss *Hashtag Gay Icon FAIL!* You know what's *my* favorite thing? A big bunch of sour grapes served ice-cold in an old-fashioned glass, while Charlie jerks off with my panties.

Victor Fleming called me the day after the audition with the unexpected news that I'd got the part: I was Dorothy! But it was gonna be a tough slog until that glorious awards ceremony decades later when I took home the Special Juvenile Oscar for "A Star Is Born."

"Just remember," George Cukor said, as we wrapped on the principal photography. "You gotta fall on your face at least once before you can make a comeback. Generally speaking, men don't make passes at girls who wear glasses, but with James Mason? Take it from me:

"You'd be wise to wear protection."

◘

hEITeR-sHeLtEr (Pandemic Pastimes): Coltish Captions

I trust it will not be a huge surprise to you if I confess that—and, I beg you, please, stand another six feet away from your priceless collection of carnival glass, lest your startle reflex should cause you to knock over the display cabinet—I'm kind of lazy.

Yeah, majorly. We're talking Governor General's Award for Lazy, a Genie and a Gemini, a Lazy Webby, maybe even a Pulitzer (i.e., Lily). In fact, with my level of expertise, I can do diddley-squat all day with both ambitions tied behind my back and without even a statutory lunch break.

Which makes perfect sense seeing as doing diddley-squat all day *is* my statutory lunch break.

Yet once every decade or so, give or take, a morning dawns when I find myself inexplicably filled with pee, vee and spunk—should one of those guys from Leolist ever turn up, maybe even drenched in them—and ready to prove there's a reason, even just a biological one, for me to exist.

On such an auspicious morning of robins and daffodils, I might awaken—or, "come to" as I like to characterize it—as I did this morning: still wearing yesterday's clothes, a litre of Kawartha Dairy strawberry ice cream leaking into the pillows, butter tart crumbs clinging to the corners of my mouth, and with a scratchy, oily sensation in my lower back which I at first assumed was an outbreak of atopic dermatitis, but turned out to be a grilled cheese sandwich that I made around 4 AM then didn't eat because I dozed off. ("Dinner.")

Never mind—it's a new morning! The sun turns its hot, shining face to me like a woman in the desperate throes of menopause, my heart sings an entire Handel opera, including the soprano and counter-tenor roles, all the repeats in the *da capo* arias and a couple of encores; and I even manage to find a sock; only the one, please note, and why it's dangling from a denuded branch of the Christmas tree I leave up all year so it's ready for decorating on Boxing Day (see *lazy*, above), I really couldn't say.

Betimes, as I sip my coffee and reminisce about those adventure vacations in the rain forests of Gstaad, it may transpire that I get ambitious and think of posting a new piece on my blog, the entity I spend most time with, which is why I think of it as my bitch-mistress—(bastard-master?)—of eight years.

But before I can close the curtains—after briefly opening them to check whether it's really daytime or if, in fact, I've only been unconscious for five minutes; rev up the Bodum and commit to yet another three thousand words of idiosyncratic, bolshie, left-wing political commentary, or snarky take-down of some Hollywood star now familiar only to myself and a few geriatric cases receiving end-of-life care—my Buddhist training kicks in.

Enlightenment cracks open my skull with a cast-iron dongle, and I think: "Fuck it. Fob them off with the captions thingy."

Whoah! Thanks, Enlightenment! That was close!

Here, then, is "Honey, I Mixed Up the Captions!", an almost offensively puerile game I devised for myself way back when I was desperate to avoid any practical activity, for example, leaving the apartment to earn money, and around the time I was starting to admit that just staring slack-jawed into space while chain-smoking was not quite fulfilling its promise as a life strategy the way I had anticipated.

At the very least, I hope this brainless diversion will see you through yet another twenty-four hours of coronavirus lockdown; or, as the Canadian media, the Prime Minister and our Chief Public Health Officer gently explain, "The way your remaining allotted days are always going to be from now on until you die of sorrow."

Playing this game is simple. Find one of those websites that purveys gossip, or aggregates weird stories, the kind of site where the headline is something like "Twenty Most Awful Lands That You Should Never Travel To Number Six Will Make You Gasp;" and underneath are linked images, as though for related, "you might also like…" articles, one of which is always about Princess Diana and/or her wedding dress—but these are not, in fact, articles.

These, like the Twenty Most Awful Lands, are "sponsored," meaning they are only there to stay out of the rain and sell you stuff, i.e., clickbait. And because you have the attention span of boiled rigatoni, you start engaging with the clickbait.

And now you find yourself transported to a magical dream world that out-nevers the most pixie-dusted, Tinkerbell'd Neverland that Disney's fevered imagination could conjure up.

Here is an alternative universe where Susan Boyle's new career as stick-thin, platinum blond porn princess is not only the next, eagerly anticipated step along her life's path, but its most happy culmination; you are newly fascinated by the tacky marital dramas of long-forgotten soap opera stars the way Madame Curie was once fascinated by isotopes; and all of your internal organs have turned into a southern-style Bar-B-Q of pre-cancerous tissue for the parasites harbored by the *ten foods you must stop eating right away* THEY ARE KILLING YOU.

Now the game potential reveals itself, for as you examine the images and captions more closely—eureka!

By the simple exercise of switching the captions around, you are crying hot salty tears of hysterical laughter, because, seriously. Right?

It's like shooting whales in a bidet.

I want to make this more challenging (I'm so very much all about respecting your intelligence), but because I am a late-stage boomer who caught the tail end of the Summer of Love—which means whenever I see a Young Person wearing bell bottoms, a paisley shirt from GAP and a tie-dye headband, I hear my mother shrieking "Roll up the windows!" then briefly pass out—I rebel against rules, albeit in a helpful, fawning way. So I suggest the following parameters:

- Use the images and captions from that one page only;
- Don't use any image or caption more than once.
- Extra brownie points for the most salacious and/or sophomoric laughs you can provoke.

But you don't have to use up all of the pictures and captions on the page—it doesn't matter if you have some orphans left over. It doesn't have to work out exactly, like, it's not chess or a Rubik's cube or something.

Jeezus! Who are you, the Caption Game Hall Monitor? Lighten *up*, Mistress Suck-Out-All-The-Fun!

Take a look at my results for today (*pp 48-49*), and *enjoy*.

If that's—even a word.

Honey, I Mixed Up the Captions!

The Queen Has Just Banned Prince Harry
from Doing This

Cheetah and Puppy Met As Babies,
See Them Now

When These Gay Twins Came Out To Their Dad, They
Didn't Expect This Reaction

Princess Margaret's Wedding in 1960:
Start of a Doomed Marriage

Oprah Winfrey Archie First Birthday
Gift Book Club Duck! Rabbit!

Man Thinks He Sees A Huge Beaver In The Creek,
Pulls It Up and Realizes Big Mistake

Cross-Species Animal Friendships That Are
Sure to Melt Your Heart

Invocation

Hail Minerva, Full of Grace
Goddess of Disappointment
Petty Theft and
Flaked Tuna in Broth:

It's Dave. Remember me?
Eighth floor?

From the depths of my
Shame and squalor
Largely self-induced, but whatever,
I cry to thee.

Restore to me
What I have lost

Generally, my innocence, but
Specifically, my smartphone,
Which I may have forgotten to charge.

I know, I know.
You don't have to tell me.

I have followed too much
My desire for devices,

Purchasing today
The identical twin of
What I already own
Priced a thousand dollars more,
And minus the headphone jack.

I always kind of enjoyed the headphone jack,
And I can only surmise
That someone knows better
And removed it for my own good.

So—thanks.
I guess.

It was The Early Adopter, the Evil One
Who tempted me, this time
With a three-lens
Camera, which merely enlarged
The scope of my incompetence
To twenty-four millimeters.

Forgive me the sin of pride
For I have taken billboard-sized jpegs
Of undistinguished architecture
Just because I could;
Standing one hundred feet away
Bouncing flash off the clouds;

I have snapped the sunrise
And the sunset
Confusing effort expended
With quality achieved;

For their crepuscular variety cannot be expressed by
What appears to be

An orange rectangle on top of
A black rectangle,

So that I have to explain,
"That's a picture of the sunrise."

Taken aback, they pause,
Then, with flat affect
and a deadness in their eyes,
Whisper, "It's lovely."

It really isn't much, but god knows
It gets me through the day.

Blessed Minerva
Patroness of Lost Hope
Baroness Apathy
Keeper of the Curled-Up Luncheon Meat

Grant me your indulgence

For I have walked, trembling and distracted,
With the unrighteous slackers
Through shadow-valleys of
Soiled bath towels
Clutching a pressure-sensitive tablet

And I weep,
For in thy ineffable wisdom thou hast
Snatched from my hand
The stylus
Which is, apparently, gone forever

Gone with the unholy tribes of Ninevah!
Gone with the bakers of raisin pies!
Gone with the summer sunshine of my youth
Filtering through clouds of pot smoke
On Yorkville Avenue!

I just remembered—
There's something else.

Oh, is that a *problem?*

So, yeah, I'm a little high-maintenance today.
Suck it up, Fish Fingers.

I mean, it's not like you're
Fending off crowds of acolytes with a stick,
Miss Seen-Better-Days
Downgraded Member of the
Roman Pantheon;
"Where is she now,
The Broad with the Can—?"

Right? So listen up.

O Minerva,
I grow old, miserable offender,
And my usefulness is sore diminished.
For if fifty is the new forty
Then sixty-five is the new
Cryogenically frozen.

Give me my due:
A time somewhere between
Afternoon roll call and
Cinq à sept when I can

Unload my hard-earned wisdom,
Such as it is,
Onto the fledgling generation
Who will quaff the nectar of my words
And buzz off well advisèd.

No more for me
False witnesses who cry

"I'm listening, old man!"
As they continue editing

Their fourteenth
Tik-Tok classic of the day
And I enlighten the
Indifferent tops of heads.

Crush them beneath thy feet,
Those feckless ones!

For their names are cursèd in Willowdale,
Their counsels unheeded in Mississauga!

Great Minerva—
I think that's all
Thanks a bunch for listening
Even though you or some other
Deity with a warped sense of humour
Still have my stylus.

But maybe you needed it
More than me,
Perhaps it gives You
An obscure pleasure.

Hey, I can let it go.
Sometimes all I need is
To unburden myself—
and I have.

Now back to your real job—
Taking care of dolphins
Flaking tuna

And reminding people that
The Trident,
Formerly the weapon of
That old trout,
Poseidon—and please, do give Him my regards—
Is now the name

Of a sugarless gum
Made for our chewing pleasure.

Sicut erat in principio, et nunc, et semper!
As it was in the beginning, is now, and ever shall be!

I've never thought about them before,
The words of the doxology,

And this is a real trip, but—
That's what I always say:

"The first ten minutes tell you everything."

"The first **ten minutes** tell you **everything."**

The Limits of Funny, the Whiteness of Money

No one is ever going to cancel me. Ever. How can I be so sure? Well, first, I'm a white male, albeit fairly bursting with, I hope, controversial opinions (I could use the publicity, and what is a controversy? Just publicity that smoked a spliff and got delusions of grandeur).

Second, you will learn during the life-enhancing journey of wide-eyed wonder that is this, my second collection and gift to the five people left who still read—and if you move your lips, big deal, so you move your lips, I'm not fussy at this point—that no one has ever been canceled, ever, at any time. It's all a big, stinky red herring.

I repeat: *no one has been canceled.* Not that neoliberal who complains about socialists and deficits to his three million subscribers, not that avatar of toxic masculinity who teaches incels how to pick up chicks. Not even, or maybe especially, Jordy Peterson. Nope.

(Speaking of picking up chicks: even though I'm gayer than a leather queen at the opening night of "Parsifal," I'm going to share with you my business idea for helping shy guys meet girls. Are you ready?

(Get yourself some golden lab puppies, then rent them out to your introverted dudes. They take the puppy to the local park, girls run up to them shrieking OH my GOD he's just DARLING OOOJA BOOJA, WOOJA SHNICKUMS!!! at which point he blurts out, *"W-w-w-w-anna fuck?"*

(Good, eh? Maybe more like an unpolished diamond of an idea, but still. Feel free to co-opt and attract seed funding for this, because the moment has passed for me; also I haven't left the house since 2014.)

"Being canceled" is a popular choice these days. It's like a badge of honor for all the conservative trolls whose reptilian brain stems cannot cope with the concept that so-called freedom of speech is a two-way kind of affair.

You can freely, sweetly or offensively broadcast your ideas and opinions. *No one will stop you.* In response, I can applaud you, heckle you, walk out of your lecture, not invite you to lecture in the first place, decide you're annoying the people I'd like to have as customers and withdraw my advertising dollars, sue you for defamation of character, burn your stupid book in the town square, start a fan club, or simply shut down YouTube.

That's *my* "freedom of speech" (or, as we call it in Canada, "freedom of expression"). Freedom of expression does not create an obligation to provide you with a forum or endure listening to your bullshit.

Has Dave Chappelle been canceled? is the question I've decided to circle around, the way a seagull at the beach circles around your French fries, then takes a swift, opportunistic stab at them.

But before I squawk and fly away, I need to disclose the shameful secret that I haven't seen his latest show, "The Closer".

And I have absolutely no intention of seeing it. Go ahead, throw everything at me. I don't freakin' care.

So here we go.

AS A GAY MAN WHO'S KNOWN HE was gay from the age of eight, believe me, I've had some emotional abuse in my life. Some of it—and I sincerely regret bringing this up, even as I bring it up—some of that abuse came from, well.

Christians.

And I don't want to make this tiny admission into a "thing." Like, a resentment. Or god forbid, because god apparently is kind of the driver of all of this, an accusation.

And as abuse goes, it wasn't all that bad or that much, really. I'd already got used to the general disapproving looks, nasty slurs and rejection, starting from the day I first lip-sync'd Joan Sutherland singing "Casta Diva" while wearing my mother's brown chiffon cocktail dress, with matching cocktail booties that had little pom-poms of mink.

And I tell, ya, this eight-year-old *rocked* that cocktail dress.

No, I learned to endure just the standard disapproval and pursed lips, except on the rare occasions it was fire and damnation.

Just enough Christian abuse to be the size of, say, a small, nicely groomed, keeping-to-itself sort of, you know.

Elephant in the room.

Lately, I've started paying more attention to the trauma I've experienced as a gay man just living his life and being himself. Because I fit into that Quentin Crisp category: Not a closet case. An out, in your face queer. The type who goes through hell, but only inside; and on the outside puts on a brave face, firmly insisting on being who I am, however excruciating that might be to others, but mainly to me. I didn't really feel I had a choice, though, in fact, like every other gay man, I did.

I could have opted for invisibility, which would have meant accepting that I, the real me, had no right to exist. That I was a mistake. A bad arrangement of genes, or the product of my own perverse, defiant refusal to conform.

I'm starting to understand that a lifetime of negation, free-floating anxiety, and condemnation, leading to constant feelings of worthlessness—an atmosphere of judgement that was all-enveloping yet mostly unspoken—a spiritual miasma I had no choice but to breathe—is not such a minor complaint.

I'll tell you honestly. I'm not just pissed off about it. I'm *enraged*.

And though my memory tells me most of my oppression came from just random bigots, maybe that's because, in my small town and later in a bigger town, there really weren't a lot of Christians in my line of sight, the product, surely, of my family being Anglican, a subset of Christianity whose adherents feel that to speak of "God" or "Jesus" or "The Lord" is really kind of, well, lacking good taste.

Not to mention confusing, seeing as the real "Lord" of Anglicanism would be, not Jesus, but Henry VIII, who started the Church of England after a tiff with the Pope.

And maybe the non-Anglican Christians were just otherwise occupied, their calendars too full to put in the necessary effort into making me feel I was a failed human, a vicious, willful sinner destined for eternal agony.

"Iron the altar cloth, make the ambrosia salad for the social, oppress a sinful homosexual.... OK, scrap that last one until I learn to play 'Jesus loves me, this I know...' for this week's Sunday School." They had *stuff to do*.

The "making a child feel worthless" thing got, you know, bumped.

WANDA SYKES FOR ME EMBODIES THE best of that uniquely American genre of stand-up comedy. And not "best Black stand-up" or "best Female stand-up" both of which qualifiers would subtly mean "macaroni picture", which is to say, good, for a (insert identifier here). No, just best.

I feel this way because, well, Wanda's a dyke, but that doesn't mean she doesn't make fun of, say, gay men. Her stories about coming out and being invited on gay cruises poke wicked fun at the scene.

But she's speaking from personal experience, pointing out the hilarity of the situation, and she's basically dishing. She's like your cool sister, laughing with you.

She doesn't hold back on white people, either. She can be caustic enough to make me stare down at my shoes when she hits home. But she's got empathy. She's not extrapolating her experience to make bizarre analogies or pontificate, or to insist that her opinions are automatically facts.

Well, of course she isn't. She's not a man. Women dish. Men pontificate.

Wanda Sykes is hilarious without being malicious or abusing the power that comes with a public platform. She sticks to what she knows. She understands what she's doing, in other words, she has mastery. She's fearless.

She would never, I sense, end up eating a great, big, sour, ineptitude pickle the size of the one that's gagging Dave Chappelle.

In her special "Imma Be Me" Sykes makes a startling assertion. "It's harder to be gay than to be Black," she says, about her coming out. "After all, I didn't have to come out as Black!" She then riffs on this by playing a fantasy scene in which she "comes out as Black" to her shocked parents. It's to-die funny.

And it's very sweet of her to say, but it's not true. It cannot be true. Because of the history of Black Americans as enslaved people, and the bloody and deadly struggle for civil rights which they have fought for over two hundred years—because of the burning of white supremacy into the neurons of white Americans and its subsequent embedding in the very structures of society—it *cannot* be true.

The reason is simple. I, gay people, we queer folx, invisible, hiding-in-plain-sight, *don't exist until we choose to make ourselves exist*. If some bigots think being gay is a "choice," that is the only sense in which they're more or less correct.

Being visible is the choice. That's what "coming out" entails, and it's a struggle, for sure. In my youth, it was understood we were outlaws, and if visible we were certain to get beat up, publicly humiliated, jailed or even killed. Housing and jobs were denied us (we were immoral or a security risk!), and even to hint about a same-sex relationship was unthinkable.[1]

---

1   North American queers tend to think that the world enjoys the same privileges as we do, but these dangers are still very much the reality in countries such as Uganda, Nigeria, Poland, Russia and Indonesia.

Even now we're assumed to be second class citizens, having had to fight for the right to marry and to raise kids. We are branded, especially gay men, as child molesters or "groomers" (which is the calling card of QAnon and the lie that never dies).

Just the other day Pete Buttigieg, US Secretary of Transportation, was called a pedophile on Twitter for holding one of his adopted babies in his arms.

So, there's definitely a struggle. But, honestly. I can't look a Black man or woman in the eye and say it's harder to be gay than Black. I would be ashamed to say that.

It's not harder. It's just plain, old, bog-standard, fucking hard.

I'M NOW THINKING OF ANOTHER BLACK female stand-up comic and damned if I can find her on YouTube, or remember her name. I probably wiped it from my mental hard drive.

I was thoroughly enjoying her raucous, raunchy performance, which had been recorded in a grand-looking old-timey theatre somewhere in the US, and, as far as I could make out from the occasional long camera shot, for the enjoyment of a predominantly Black female audience, when her material took a nasty and viciously homophobic turn.

Enough to say that it riffed on anal sex (always and forever supposedly the invention of, and copyrighted by, gay men), and how you could tell if your man was on the down-low by his campy gestures, his suspicious habits and the sorry state of his underwear.

The audience went approximately nuts.

And I felt my face going red with that involuntary rush of fear, shame and self-loathing so familiar to me, that inner sense of threat and exposure that can only come from a thousand people reducing you to a sexual stereotype, a laughingstock, and a target of unalloyed disgust.

PROGRESSIVES, ONE OF WHICH I consider myself to be, drone earnestly on about intersectionality, those shifting nodes of privilege and oppression, which codify the idea, which you could corroborate by spending five minutes on social media, that everyone needs a punching bag.

Someone to be the target of your barely suppressed anger and resentment. Someone you can point at and say, I'm oppressed, but you? You're just indefensible.

Intersectionality, so I thought in my naïve, old-white-dude way, told us that we're all oppressors and all oppressed. It's like a three-dimensional chess game, or one of those drawings by Max Escher, the staircase that's also a wall if you squint.

I'm white (privilege) male (more privilege) gay (oppressed). You can calculate your own score. Now you see the oppressor, squint, now you see the oppressed. No one is immune. We're all in this together. We all have innate prejudices to deal with and we all have to acknowledge that, and, in the end, we've got to stay humble, feel some empathy, listen to and love and take care of each other.

Oh, boy. What a steaming crock of horse doody *that* exercise has turned out to be.

We, I mean progressives, put on our magic intersectionality goggles when we need a way of viewing society that is closer to the truth than the standard narrative: that *everyone starts with an equal chance and so what if you experience some prejudice? That didn't stop Herschel Walker!* We already know the standard narrative is merely the hectoring voice of the dominant group.

The dominant group tells a narrative that bolsters their belief in their superiority, even as they twirl their toe in the dirt, and coyly insist that anyone with determination could succeed just as well. "Oh, it was nothing, really!" It's just poor luck, they insist, that some days there's no determination left in the determination barrel.

In fact, they're the gatekeepers: these white, heterosexual males who are the most coddled, most entitled, most fragile (and therefore most dangerous) creatures on the planet.

Seriously. Those dudes are frailer than a preemie with coronavirus in a crowded ICU. We give them all the power (or else they'd grab our toys and run off with them anyway, so it's easier to just give in) and we wipe their noses when they've done too much blow and soothe their diaper rash with whiny-baby powder and we cook their meals and tell them how big and strong they are. They have the rest of the world jumping to their feet and saluting should they even break wind. So you think they'd be happy.

Nah. A happy straight white dude would just sit contentedly in the corner, gazing with love at his shrively white penis and marveling at its power (until a woman laughs at it, which is why women have to be kept in purdah.) The only attention he'd be getting would be his own, and that's a given.

And what's worse than an attention whore without attention? Exactly right. Nothing on gawd's gang-raped and abandoned Earth is more insufferable.

No, white straight guys are unhappy. Forever. Not content with their wealth, and their power, and their shrively white penises, they need more. So, restless and dissatisfied, they turn their attention to what you've got that they should have, too.

They need to control what women do (so as to not get laughed at, and so they know that another shrively white penis hasn't invaded their private property and spawned bastard babies) so they take a hard line about abortion, in relation to which they are in the position of, legally, having no standing.

Their involvement in the miracle of life lasts approximately five seconds. They are exempt from having their body co-opted by incarnadine Mother Nature as an incubator for an alien being who might just eviscerate you on the way out.

And their misogyny has, throughout history, singled out women's bodies as disgusting. ("We are born between feces and urine," as Saint Augustine phrased it, which as a grim reveal of his joyless attitude to life, even for a Christian saint, makes him the Rodney Dangerfield of the beatified set.)

Straight men cannot think of menstruation, especially, and the whole mysterious Rube Goldberg-via-David-Cronenberg contraption that is the female reproductive system, without emotions ranging from confusion to revulsion.

Curiouser and curiouser: Straight men are simultaneously afraid of and disgusted by and in thrall to vaginas. Straight men are so conflicted about vaginas, I don't know how they manage to be straight. It's mind-boggling.

And they are insane about LGBTQ2+ people. They never stop obsessing about us! Once a year, at Pride, they find the attention has been directed elsewhere, and then, with all the stoic maturity of a child with oppositional defiance, they shout over us, demanding to know when straight pride will be held! (Answer: 24/7/364, dudes.)

And anyway, gay men? It's just—dudes taking it up the ass! Gross! Straight white men can't understand how anyone could do that! Straight white men don't even *wipe* their ass! And if you don't believe me, honey, blow a straight white dude one day. You'll understand why women cry.

Now, along with all that, there's an interesting effect of money. You see, we've all known that money talks, lately in the form of Dave Chappelle on Netflix, more on that in a mo, but here's something amazing: Money is magic. Money can make you into a straight white dude.

Just let that sink in for moment. I know, right? Is that deep or what?

Like Dorothy's ruby red slippers, the simple escape route from your oppression, great oodles of money, has been right there in front of you all along! Couldn't you just kick yourself, you female or gay or black or poor or trans or—or any combo of the above, with or without fries—person?

Because if there's one thing we revere even more than straight male whiteness, it's great container ships full of cash, mountains of freshly minted, new-car smelling, petroleum-drenched, diamond-mined, crypto-change-o money.

Mmmmm! Freshly minted money!

Well, I want to propose an exercise. Let's put on our magic intersectionality goggles and examine us some Dave Chappelle.

IT MUST BE OBVIOUS BY NOW THAT when we put on our magic intersectionality goggles and gaze at Dave Chappelle, whose deal with Netflix alone was worth twenty-four million bucks, we see—ta-da! Well, brain me with a cotton gin if it ain't a straight white dude!

Tinkerbell'd by the glitter dust of money, Dave's Blackness magically disappears. Poof!

Netflix gives its imprimatur to Dave's "edgy", "non-pc" humor. It's a no-brainer. He validates the ignorance and intolerance of white—and Black—audiences who just darn well want to believe that "there's only two genders"; his stratospheric earnings validate the lie that "people just gotta pull their socks up".

White audiences can point to Dave Chappelle and say, "Look! *He* made it!", choosing to ignore the inconvenient reality that his talent is beside the point: "he made it" because white gatekeepers let him through the gate.

They let him through the gate, and not because of his "Black humor". I suggest the opposite: Dave Chappelle's earliest mega success was always based on his willingness to filter his comedy through white sensibilities until it was just acceptably "edgy". He played up to and embodied the reassuring tropes of the non-threatening Black man that exist in white folks' brains, until, as he explained to Oprah, he found he was aware of being laughed at, not with.

That's why he took that little ten-year sabbatical and walked away from a $50m contract. It's not hard to infer that, when he returned to stand-up, he was going to do it on his own terms; he would call the shots.

This makes it even more depressing that, instead of taking the truly radical position of a Black man advocating for gay and trans people, he flipped into the cheapest form of "non-PC": perpetuating the noxious stereotypes of *another* oppressed group.

His stance is analogous to that of the MAGA voter who *just can't understand* why confederate statues and flags have to come down, why army bases need to honor honorable people, not white supremacists. Or the social media trolls like Jordan Peterson who *just don't get* why gay people have to prance around one month a year, being "proud" (one of those seven deadly sins, don'tcha know!).

Here's a thought, guys: Instead of shaking your little white head in confusion, why not friggin' ASK a POC what's hurtful about the statue?

Why not ASK a gay man or trans woman why Pride, being visible, is like the difference between life and death?

You'd almost get the idea that they don't actually care what the reasons are. It's different? It doesn't foreground white men? It requires societal change and treating marginalized people with respect? Shut it down! *Save the children!*

As the cult of Trump shows us, the only point of being racialized white is to be able to say: *Fuck you. I can do and say anything I want, and any protest against that is just the radical woke agenda.*

Dave Chappelle, already softened up through years of giving white audiences safe "Black" humor, took the obvious and easy route back to the A-list.

LUCKILY FOR ME, MAGIC MONEY and my intersectionality goggles have erased the divide between Black humor and white humor. Dave, a Black man, has opinions in lieu of facts, just like straight white dudes. He just out and out thinks that being trans is exactly like—well, "blackface."

Yep. He really, unbelievably, said that.

It's like, so he explains—and if you can imagine anything more idiotic or inappropriate or just downright hateful, send it to me on a postcard and I'll eat a pound of boot polish—waking up one morning and deciding you're Chinese, and walking around making a racist stereotypical Chinese face, and when people call you out on that, you simply say, "Hey, this is what I feel like inside!"

Dave. *Dave.* Now, first of all, if my experience of Black straight guys is anything to go by, I know you've had yourself some down-low sex with a dude. Don't pretend you haven't. C'mon...

Besides, if you know what goes on in a trans person's head, then I know what you've been doing with your baseball bat. OK? Fair's fair.

Here's the thing: *Why do you imagine we would give a running, jumping or standing toss what you believe about trans people?* What could you possibly know about their lives and loves, hopes and fears?

I gladly and willingly allow that I will never, as a white man, ever understand what it means to be Black in a white supremacist culture; that

I have never experienced, nor will I ever experience, racism. I have to learn about it, listen with humility to those who *have* experienced it, grasp my part in that oppression, and, painful as it is, imperfect and inept as I may appear, try my best to be a good ally.

So what is this free *sneer at a trans* card that you awarded yourself when you could not possibly know what is their experience?

Why do you use your platform to weaponize your ignorance and transphobia?

Why do you risk trans lives by punching down a vulnerable minority, and supporting the perception that all they deserve is scorn?

Stand-up comedy occurs in a sandboxed arena designed and understood by both performer and audience as a place for airing outrageous, even taboo, concepts. We cut performers a lot of slack in this arena. But there are still unspoken rules.

You mock upwards, your oppressors.

You mock sideways, your peer group.

But, baby, you never, ever mock down.

You never openly mock and oppress a vulnerable group, because—for heaven's sake, do I really have to explain why?

To get your credibility back, Dave Chappelle, you will need to humble yourself.

You'll need to admit you don't know every damn thing, and particularly any damn thing about being trans.

Shut your fresh mouth about trans people and, maybe for the first time in your privileged life,

stop talking and start listening.

Holy Sh*t-Show

Happy So-Tense-About-Saying-The-Right-Thing-idays

And lo, it came to pass, in this season of ill will and bad faith, that a primary school teacher somewhere not terribly far from Des Moines banned candy canes "because they form the letter 'j' and that stands for Jesus."

I checked it out on Snopes, the site that I decided to trust because they promise to determine what's true and not true when lefties or righties make outlandish claims—that everyone in the White House is a Russian operative (lefties); or that George Soros hired all those Central Americans to come and overthrow Texas, armed with all those feisty brown kids and some tropical fruit (righties). You can imagine the carnage, as they lob their avocado pits at the five thousand troops!

Commies, Christians, illegals! Ya can't live with 'em and ya can't live without 'em!

Well, Snopes tells me it's true about the teacher and the candy canes. Just what we libtards needed, to go with our lumps of coal. Thanks, Cindy! That's what I'm calling her, Cindy, and damn it if I'm playing to stereotypes, here. I just don't see an Amanda or a Beatrice or a Patricia getting so granular about the whole Xmas thing.

This is Cindy material. Cindy's well-meaning but tends to get too intense when she thinks she understands something.

This is perfect, because now conservatards, latching onto this one person out of three hundred million people, one overly-earnest Cindy who went a little too far and got a little too zealous about the inclusiveness thing, can stick out their chests and say, "crazy dumb-ass freakazoid Liberals, the people who banned CANDY CANES!"

You know what I'd like for the holidays? I'd like conservatives to relax, enjoy their power and superiority, and just stop saying "war on Christmas," because, once again, there isn't one. Christmas is still there, in our faces, always jingling and Kris Kringling, always promising a Silent Night but never delivering.

There is no war on Christmas just because we have decided to recognize all of the other bat-shit crazy religions. It's analogous to the non-existent War on Men that is not happening just because women are tired of being assaulted and saying so. Lots of bat-shit crazy religions, lots of women not being assaulted—these things are, in order of mention, tolerable and desirable.

Besides, Christmas wouldn't get the hint if we torched every crèche and carpet bombed the Santa Claus parade. Christmas is even more numb in the skull than Joe Whitie-McButtpincher, who, despite a Mormon Tabernacle Choir's worth of the well-behaved begging him to go away, is too busy ordering a sex droid from Japan to pay attention.

Liberals being what we are, neither is there war on anything that might actually merit one: poverty or racism or the attempt to disenfranchise everyone who isn't a Republican; no war on anything, because Liberals and Progressives, believing that we are so obviously right that we shouldn't have to convince anyone, are perpetually sideswiped by unrelenting conservative zeal and gob-smacked into pouty indignation by every conservative schoolyard taunt. Someone who crumples up from being called "snowflake" is just not angry enough; anyone who's reacting is not leading.

No one's bowl of wassail is empty, all the mangers and chimney-hung stockings are filled to capacity. It's oh so very freakin' much Christmas, everywhere, until at least the twenty-sixth of December. The Gospels are strangely silent about snow, but whatever.

Behold in the West! The Three Wise Kardashians cometh, bearing their gifts of vulgarity and irrelevance! RELAX, conservatives! All is for the best in the best of all possible worlds, at least for you!

Conservatives love to play the disingenuous, "what little ol' me?" role. They're Just Simple Folk. They pretend not to know that the Happy Holidays generic greeting is a *public stance*.

It's the stance of governments, who, apart from theocracies (which we claim to abhor), have no mandate to promote one religion; it's a recognition that Canadians and Americans are celebrating a veritable figgy pudding of different celebrations. All are citizens; all are equal. So, like a wise mom giving all her kids the same toys, public institutions try not to play favorites.

Likewise, businesses, who never met a cultural practice they couldn't appropriate, ruin, then monetize, have an interest in welcoming all. Happy Holidays!

But in private, we do and say and wish what we like. Public versus private. This is not a difficult concept.

Happy Holidays is not "Politically Correct." It is *neutral*. It's not aiming to not offend; it's aiming to include. How did inclusion, making people feel welcome, become controversial?

Politically correct is a term that was passé thirty years ago, but those on the right find it useful because it shuts down conversations about privilege and societal change which they find threatening. Conservatives insist on clinging to their power, yet they can't just come out and admit, "We'd like to say 'n***er' again."

"We'd like to say *cripple* and *faggot* and *women's libbers* again because when we could say those things we were certain we'd won the lottery."

Is that what conservatives want, instead of so-called political correctness? The freedom to say "*n***er*" again? At the very least, what would Miss Manners think?

What the right snorts at in derision as politically correct is simply, in all cases, the attempt to speak of, and to, others in a way that acknowledges their humanity, their equality and their dignity.

Words are performative: To utter the word "faggot" causes a human to assume a new skin, that of a despised outcast. A word uttered empowers or stultifies; humanizes or degrades.

For the sake of society, civility and getting along, let's raise the tone a little. As a minimum standard, let's show a bit of class. I define "class" as: *not doing that thing you feel you have every right to do.*

Now get out there and enjoy the winter solstice, as appropriated by the Christian Church.

Light your apple-cinnamon scented candles, blow all your credit, deck your balls with holly and erect your phallic pagan tree.

It's Christmas Eve. I'm going to listen to some John Rutter, bake some shortbread and smoke a joint. Thank you, Jesus!

I mean, Justin.

Secret Santa, Still Stuck on the 401 Westbound

I t's the most wonderful time of year, and I want to make extra sure I've addressed everyone's concerns, neuroses and conspiracy theories, because I really, really want you to get just what you asked for.

(Or, as expressed by H. L. Mencken: "Democracy is the theory that the common people know what they want, and deserve to get it good and hard." You know, like that.)

To kick off, have we all had our annual gobsmacked day of incredulity that there's snow, in Canada, in winter? In my era, when millionaires cried if you didn't tax them enough, cars were bigger than a studio apartment, and kids got swaddled in snowsuits so thickly padded they were unable to flex their elbows or knees between October and April, heavy snow squalls were eagerly anticipated by young and old.

What we now regard as an apocalypse that someone forgot to add to our calendar was innocently called *White Christmas* and generally agreed to be Hallmark-card levels of picturesque and desirable, even singable if you're Bing Crosby.

We're a cranky lot these days, though. Snow, in Canada a truly indulgent weather event consisting of billions of ice crystals swirling in a gale-force wind, lowers the ambient and body temperatures a fair degree, and there's famously no one to complain to who can make it stop if you decide it's not really high on your bucket list.

("Out of our comfort zone" is a concept now best reserved for people like J.K. Rowling, the gal who invented an entire fantasy world of fledgling witches and wizards, but who desperately refuses to accept that transgender folx could ever exist, no matter how many actual transgender folx keep smiling and waving at her.)

Snow is no longer picturesque. It is quite simply shivery and inconvenient, and means Uber Eats can't get to you with your iced coffee and grass-fed macaroni and cheese in under forty minutes. This is unacceptable. It's *sorry looking for now*, but with Gen Z's and food.

The sheer offensiveness of snow in winter boils down to the difficulties it poses to people driving cars. Please remember that drivers are the most important people in the world, and only grudgingly accept us pedestrians and cyclists because it gives them something amusing to aim at and hopefully kill when they're bored. Driving cars without impediment is the ultimate measure of all things.

(Shall we have a green belt around the city to buy us one more day on sinking ship Earth? Will I have to walk to the convenience store? Pave that sucker NOW!)

I never have understood why drivers, who are as addicted to their cars as junkies are to smack, to the degree that living underwater during the remaining two decades before our extinction is a fate the rest of us just have to accept, always seem to find driving their cars a nightmare of effort and tedium.

You're basically sitting in an armchair, flying above a paved highway that was engineered for your safety and comfort, pushing your right foot down and holding an Italian deli meat sandwich in the hand that's not turning the steering wheel half an inch in each direction, while listening to Carly Simon.

Why are you moaning about "the long trek", like you're some desperate refugee trudging barefoot through Islington with all your worldly belongings in a President's Choice bag, when all you have to do is sit resentfully in your air-conditioned flying armchair as it conveys itself from Royal York Road to Bloor and Yonge?

"Oh, but you're so far away!" Yes, bitch, that's the problem that the automobile *solves*, as opposed to people spontaneously bursting into flames during the summer, which is the problem it creates.

Next on Santa's list: it's OK to say "Merry Christmas", or at least I'm so assured by a US Senator on Twitter—name of Kennedy, apparently just coincidentally named after that great statesmanly family of visionary Marilyn-bangers—which is a welcome relief, because I was just about to message "Hail, Satan!" to my entire address book because of all that unrelenting social pressure.

Moving along, in a display of bile surprising no one, US Republicans and right-wing pundits, basically the only people left on Twitter, expressed their stern disapproval about the super secretively-executed, but otherwise eagerly-anticipated, visit of Ukraine's President, Volodymyr Zelenskyy, to address Congress:

Tucker Carlson: "Zelensky has declared war on Christianity." (But, according to Tucker, so has your grandmother by giving out Quality Street hard candies on Hallowe'en).

Donald Trump Jr. : "Zelensky is basically an ungrateful international welfare queen." (Does this mean Franken-forehead would be OK with an international welfare queen if they expressed gratitude? Maybe it's unreasonable to expect subtle shadings of meaning from a guy who proudly wears his special Friday-night shirt, unbuttoned to the navel, made out of the American flag.)

Josh Hammer: "Raise your hand if you are personally DONE with the Ukraine gravy train." (If by "Ukraine gravy train" you mean "billionaire tax cuts and corporate entitlements", hell, yeah!)

Benny Johnson: "This ungrateful piece of sh*t does not have the decency to wear a suit to the White House—no respect the country [sic] that is funding his survival. Track suit wearing eastern european con-man mafia. Our leaders fell for it. They have disgraced us all. What an incredible insult." (Umm, Benny, darling, he *literally* just came from active combat in a war zone, fuckface, and please do note that I frequently use that as a term of endearment.)

I know that you know that in conservative-land, since a long long time, up is down, might is right, and everything you know to be factually true is really just the smoke and mirrors of the Deep State.

If you're my age, you lived through the Cold War under your desk at school, heard Ronald Reagan inveigh against the USSR as "the evil empire", and cautiously celebrated Mikhail Gorbachev's policies of "glasnost" (openness) and "perestroika" (restructuring) signaling the gradual opening up of the Soviet Union to the reality of democracy.

Hardly daring to trust our eyes or ears, we witnessed the subsequent fall of the Berlin Wall and communist autocracy in 1989, to the sounds of Leonard Bernstein conducting the finale of Beethoven's Ninth Symphony, whose text by Schiller he rewrote for the occasion to make it an Ode to "Freiheit", freedom, instead of the original "Freude", joy.

The collective psychic tremor was so unexpected, so intoxicating, we might even have believed, just for a reeling-drunk moment, that the reverberations of Beethoven's modernist masterpiece were the new trumpets of Jericho, blasting into dust every dictatorship of the Eastern Bloc.

We had experienced an entire thrilling story arc from oppression to liberation. It chokes me up even now to recall the youth of Berlin tearing down the wall with their bare hands, to recall my awestruck realization that our righteous optimism had not been in vain and that the world was returning to the path of justice, jolted back into its proper and eternal orbit. *"Alle Menschen werden Brüder..."* All humanity united in brotherhood.

And now?

Now we find that we lived through those decades of agony and ecstasy, of terror and transfiguration, so that, in 2022, the President of the former USSR (now the Russian Federation but lipstick on the same old pig), an insecure, power-mad autocrat with a short fuse, would be the good guy, the guy you root for.

Why? Because Republicans, disenchanted with democracy and the rule of law, now insist that Goliath must be our hero, not David, because Goliath is big. Strong. Power is no longer the means to an end, it's the end itself.

Republicans, historically the most vociferous in condemning the Soviet Union, now actually support Putin, a marauding psychotic and former KGB operative, over Zelenskyy, arguably the world's most inspiring leader at this moment.

It is common knowledge that Putin was the architect of Trump's 2016 victory, so perhaps Republican support is inevitable. But an American political party supporting Putin in his terrorism against the people of Ukraine is nothing less than an outrage.

This would be obvious in an ecosystem of truth-telling and shared values. Instead, after the slow-mo implosion of common-sense conservatism, we're no longer even surprised that extremist Republicans and alt-right hoodlums would revile Zelenskyy—a Jew who they smear as a "Nazi", in a twist of repugnant but weirdly predictable illogic that justifies their opposition and the Russian invasion.

They revile him for uniting and leading a terrorized population determined, man, woman and child, to fight to the bitter end for their freedom—a word I might have heard a couple of times out of the mouths of right-wingers.

Conservatives apparently wanted more than anything to gaslight us for eighty years. Done! I give you my exhausted incomprehension, tied up with a satin ribbon, and it's so very much not a beautiful thing.

And as a stocking stuffer, note the level of discourse: these days, thanks to the miracle of Trump + technology, when you disagree with a world leader, you just out-and-out call them "a piece of shit" in a public forum, with no shame and no substance, in front of millions of people. The concept of saying nothing is dead, because facts are important and your opinion is a fact.

Trump's legacy is far from settled, but it will surely include the death of civility: the dismantling of any tiresome inhibitions we might have had around sounding like thugs in a back alley, or hurting people's feelings, or being incorrigible, defiant liars. Trump showed us how to remove the filter; the algorithms remind us that the more obnoxious your opinion, the more traction it gets. That will go nicely with the Terry's Chocolate Orange that the cat loves to play with.

Anyone else? Oh yes, the people in Toronto—but, and here's the interesting bit, not *from* Toronto—marching with signs that insist "Trudeau must go."

And why is that? I'm not sure they themselves know, or surely they would have asked us Trudeau-stans who live here for permission to clog up our roadways with their Mars Bar wrappers and GO train stubs and puffer jackets.

These are the *lumpenproletariat* of suburban Ontario, marching in lockstep with Doug Ford, our premier (think governor); if I identify him as a conservative of the new ilk you may already have all the information you need, save that these followers, his base, are cultishly referred to as "Fordnation" (even Doug Ford's Twitter handle uses that moniker).

You'll already know that, like all conservatives world-wide, they are neoliberal to the core: they're not seeking freedom from all government interference, but the active intervention by government in order to substitute market forces for democratic norms.

It is surely just coincidence that, in Doug Ford's case, market forces and his own personal financial interests so frequently, exquisitely coincide.

You won't need to waste time reading any white paper to know what his economic policies or "platform" will be.

I now present for your delectation the complete, hard-core conservative playbook. Having established that "the market", strolling down the red carpet which they've rolled out for it, will determine not just the cost of toothpaste, but what actually constitutes an economically just society, they proudly trot out the only two ideas they ever have: *Lower taxes, tough on crime.*

Go on, I dare you. Show me a conservative who has any other idea, any solution to any social ill or inequality, and I'll eat a hardcover edition of *Das Kapital,* including the frontispiece and the linen boards.

It's the Chanel of conservatism; their little-black-dress-with-string-of-pearls of policy. Goes absolutely *everywhere*, darling, and they always feel so unaccountably pretty when they throw it on.

So. Fordnation on the march! They're still whining about mask mandates, even as public health professionals urge us once again to kit up, as though even the suggestion of wearing a mask, even to express solidarity with their community, is like being hooded and shipped to Guantánamo Bay for water-boarding.

They're still calling Justin "a dictator" even though he didn't actually issue the public health directives; still characterizing his brief but decisive use of the draconian Emergencies Act to end the chaos of the "Freedom Convoy" (and who else was taking action?) as an unbearable assault on the rule of law.

But even a cursory look at the video record online shows how completely and how swiftly their protest against wholly uncontroversial public health measures took a sinister turn, degenerating into an invasion of our capital city with the stated goal of overthrowing a democratically elected government. The mob abused the forbearing locals with misogynist and homophobic taunts, physical violence and wanton vandalism.

They blame Trudeau for—well, fill in the blank, but this time it's inflation, when inflation is a worldwide concern right now and largely fueled by corporate greed. They don't understand economics, but definitely hate the money Trudeau pumped into the economy at the very start of the pandemic; with a wildly popular benefit—two thousand dollars per person per month, no questions asked— that ensured that there would be a functioning Toronto to protest in. Money without which they'd all be out of work and living on the streets, having lost their homes, but, Trudeau.

They are sad they didn't get their way, because what can you do when your guy isn't elected? Look to the US for the answer. The people—just not all, or even most of, the people—will take matters into their own tyrannical hands.

Hey, Fordnation, you know what your present is, and shame on you for peeking: Doug Ford, Premier of Ontario, who never met a senior he didn't want to shove into a long-term care facility at random and feed "bio-similar" drugs or a developer whose ass he didn't want to cover with kisses.

You stole our city when we amalgamated with the 'burbs, by sheer weight of your hockey bags and SUN newspapers; we knew it would be forevermore suburbanites against townies, drivers against sustainability, "taxpayers" against "freeloaders," teachers against parents, because being the leader of everybody, not just your supporters, your lobbyists or the people you "like", is not part of the conservative ethic of winners and losers.

So, in Toronto, Canada's largest city and the country's financial engine, we wake up bleary-eyed and weary of soul to yet another day fighting yet another fight for basic human rights like paid sick days and decent wages for unionized public employees; fighting the never-ending fight against privatization of our waterfront and the principle that there's such as thing as the commons: Ontario Place, parks, Green Belt, wetlands. These are things of which Doug Ford, a sleazy, corrupt businessman kitted up like a leader, knows the price, but not the value.

Here, I'm gifting you the grifter, the contemptible collectible: Doug Ford, sour sprite of suburban spite in quasi-human form. Save the bow and paper for next year's right-wing, frat-boy version of Winter Carnival.

JUSTIN TRUDEAU, OUR BELEAGUERED prime minister, tired of constant petty bickering by the Conservative Party of Canada (who just kicked out their leader, Erin O'Toole, because he wasn't bigoted enough—I wish I was joking), sauntered over to "Invisibility Corner", this being where Jagmeet Singh, leader of the New Democratic Party (NDP), is sent when he's in danger of being noticed.

Jagmeet Singh is charismatic, charming, smart, savvy, and supports everything that a champagne socialist should support. He leads our underdog of a party and he has not a hope in hell of ever becoming Prime Minister until we reform our first-past-the-post voting system.

The NDP has never held power federally. Never. Which is why it made perfect sense that Justin would head right over to Jagmeet and give him a little taste of power, like a tempting cube of cheese on a cracker offered in passing at the supermarket.

Before you knew it, they had a deal: The NDP would vote with Justin's Liberals until the next election, effectively giving them a majority in Parliament until 2025, and guaranteeing no votes of no confidence could pass.

It's a beautiful thing, this partnership between the two hottest progressive leaders in Canadian political history: the Sikh with the bespoke suits, crimson BMW, and pink turban; and our love-him-or-hate-him laid-back PM, with the flawless political pedigree and surprisingly steely spine.

The Conservatives are apoplectic, which is MY present.

Monday Man Crush: The Risen Christ

Inside the gloomy sepulchre, sometime around unto the third hour on Easter Sunday, Jesus squinted at his day planner—which didn't even say "Easter Sunday," heads were gonna roll over *that* little slip-up—and sighed with frustration.

Three days in this stupid cave, absolutely splitting headache, stigmata throbbing like the dickens, the Stone Angel's late again—and not even an out-of-date copy of National Geographic or Puzzler to relieve the tedium.

Honestly, he thought, this was so typical of good old Galilee-with-a-G, the Backwater-with-a-B! You were expecting maybe entertainment? Fat chance. You had one option—Mary Magdalene, that was it, dude. And after your first five visits, even she was like, "All right, boychik, time we switched things up. Just close your eyes and, umm, I dunno—think of Bathsheba!"

Why had he let himself get sucked into this whole incarnation trip? "You're gonna love being human!" they'd insisted at Word Made Flesh, the travel agency of record for the heavenly in-crowd.

"On Earth, it's all about the binary, dude. You'll be a *man*, like, male human, but don't worry, you'll still be God. But not God. More than God... OK, let's take a deep breath, drop those shoulders and put that on the back burner for a minute.

"Soooo, you'll also, now hear me out, *occasionally* manifest as an annoying dove that appears with a circle of gold rays around its head. That's—you see—hmm. You know, don't try and figure it out," Archangel Michael reassured him.

"And genitals!" he continued. "This is gonna sound weird, but they're bits of your body that most of the time just dangle between your legs, but listen to this: they change shape when you're happy! In fact, they're so sensitive, we petitioned The Big Kahuna to make them retractable, but no cigar, so instead, He just made using them at all a mortal sin. Of course, that was a HUGE success!

"And if you're into the whole networking, LinkedIn-type schmozzle, you'll meet all sorts of interesting and influential people like…. let's see, there's Lucifer, John the Baptist, Pontius Pilate, Mary the Big-Tittied Slut, you name it, talk about lovable eccentrics! Great nosh, you heard of the Mediterranean diet? Cause that's all there is, and sunshine day after day after day after… Me, I prefer a nice infinity pool and air-conditioning on "high", to each his own, eh? So, how's about it? Sign here, not valid with any other offer."

Jesus, quite eager by now, signed on the dotted line, at which point Archangel Michael added breathlessly, "Oh, by the way, you read the small print? No?

"OK, couple things: You're going to be an influencer, develop a following, get popular for a bit, then the Romans and the Jewish High Priests decide you're a troublemaker, at which point things go south a little, so, you'll be an outcast, get betrayed by Judas, that's one of your followers, at Passover — I know, absolute *worst* timing *ever* but what can you do?

"Let's see, oh, yeah, arrested as a political prisoner, humiliated, whipped and crucified, then rise from the dead and end up on TV as some chick named Tammy Faye Bakker, which involves a lot of mascara running down your face. I think that's everything. OK? By-eee!"

And he was gone with that grating little twang of sound like a chord played on a Wurlitzer organ and the sprinkling of angel dust that always accompanied his arrivals and departures.

Bait and switch. That's what this whole earthly stint amounted to. Restless and bored, Jesus flipped ahead to see what was on his plate in the coming week. With all the Friday kerfuffle he'd endured—

—hangin' with the two low-lifes on either side for a conversation he frankly would have passed on given the choice, and an especially messy deposition, his earthly mom, Ave Maria, all weepy and tragic for the media but still somehow managing to hold back her sobs long enough to squeeze in a "Pietà" photo-op, how many times did he roll off her lap? —

—he'd forgotten that Bed, Bath & Beyond was holding a major going-out-of-business sale starting tomorrow.

But would he have time to step out of his tomb, unwind the shroud, pick the cloves and coriander seeds out of his split ends and find the right escalator? And would slow cookers still be on special?

Would he be able to schedule a well-deserved chillaxing chamomile foam bath? And maybe Down-Low John The Beloved Boychik would be free for one of his famous rub-downs. The first time had been a revelation—!

He still had to deal with manifesting as the Holy Ghost all over the map and scaring the pants off his earthly bros—(reminder: determine location of Emmaus, he scribbled, or just Google it)— and the final straw? Given the last-second choice of Carry the Cross? Carry the sunscreen? he'd figured it came down to optics.

Honestly. This whole weekend was just turning into a black hole of stress, stress, stress.

His stomach was growling with hunger. "Verily," Jesus muttered, "I sayeth unto Zion: When, as is foretold in the scriptures, it shall come to pass that I ascend to the many-roomed mansion of my heavenly father, should a serving dude offereth unto me even one more plate of stale freakin' hummus—t'would be better had that man never been born..."

HI THERE. I KNOW THAT I MISSED MONDAY yet again, but at least give me credit that I'm hitting some high spots. I mean I'm early, this time. Or maybe late. Anyway.

Why this petty insistence on that hobgoblin of small minds, consistency? I can only think you must be new. My regular readers come here for something they can't get anywhere else: straight dudes ribbed and served with their morning coffee at unpredictable intervals.

Today's #MondayManCrush is a hymn to Him that strays beyond the boundaries into blasphemy, but seriously? Jesus turned water into wine, which shows more than a little mischievousness. To quote him directly:

> "To women caught in adultery, I say: No way you should get stoned. A glass of Manischewitz, maybe."

The story goes that later that same day he bumped into Mary Magdalene who, hungry for something a little exotic, had ordered some take-out from "Auntie Boo-Boo's Yummy Gentile Snack Cart." Jesus raised an eyebrow at her choice, and was about to reprimand her, but she cut him short.

"Look," she said, "I know it's not kosher. But seriously, I'm a whore. They're gonna stone me anyway, sooner or later. So fuck it, I might as well have the BLT!"

So now I'm supposed to elaborate what makes Jesus so tantalizing and appealing, even though he's a straight dude. That is, after all, the whole point of Monday Man Crush: making straight dudes uncomfortable but hopefully in such a way that they have to laugh it off and not publicly come out all homophobic.

Since Jesus never said anything about gay dudes, and, significantly, surrounded himself with hunky guy-acolytes, it suggests he was maybe a bit shifty-slidey about the whole man-to-man love situation. Stranger things have happened.

On a different note, he also said, "Suffer the little children to come unto me," which taken at face value is straightforward. But taken another way by Catholic priests, it's problematic, seeing as the dudes in the dog collars, after those years of seminary deprivation—and accidentally, I'm sure—misread that a little too much to their advantage.

What a *shanda for the goyim*, right? With the slight problem that Jesus isn't perceived as a Jew, and wasn't even a Christian yet because, Easter. It took a few generations for the goyim, that's me, to come up with that Hail Mary/How's It Hangin' Alice? boondoggle.

Anyway, Jesus—who it turns out *is* white, by the way; sorry, guys, but photos don't lie—dresses in super-cool sixties hippie clothes, has lush, curly long hair that smells like Old Spice body wash and fairly screams "Social Worker with a Garage Band"; appears in at least two Broadway musicals; and is not unfamiliar with how sensual a pair of stigmata-hobbled feet can look when encased in a pair of those handmade sandals they used to have at PayLess—the ones with the thin straps that wrap around the ankle and which easily last a couple of months if you're carried everywhere in a sedan chair.

If you need further proof of JC's *savoir-faire* under stress, check out that runway spectacle of the Grand Entrance into Jerusalem.

Minerva! This guy knows his PR backwards. No falling down on the catwalk for this canny martyr to fashion—He rides ass like a pro! Jesus, I kiss your dusty Nazarene toes. Ditch that Magdalene bitch and make with the switch, bubbaleh!

And speaking of switches: crucified, mocked or whipped under pressure and sprayed from a can, our Ghost Buddy from the Great Beyond knows that, like an adult movie starlet wearing drop earrings from Birk's, lucite-soled stiletto's, and nothing but air in between, it's the come-hither drape of a loincloth and what's left to the imagination that sets a body lusting for the falafel that can never be yours.

Yet, somehow, I don't feel awful about the falafel. Hit me with another Vinegar-On-the-Rocks-of-Golgotha, garçon!

Here's how I like to think of it: Jesus is just like you and me, in other words, human, but really more like the Royal Family: human but undoubtedly better than human.

To be more specific, there's really no comparison between a Meghan Markle and anyone else's California-tanned trophy bride. Yours is a real housewife, so, just human; Prince Harry's is bestowed by God, whose wisdom cannot be questioned, so better than human.

That's why we love Meghan and want to shelter her from hurt. It wasn't her choice to be bestowed by God! Let up on the pressure, world!

And, just like Jesus, if you love her enough—Meghan will deliver the goods.

Joy to the World, Unless You're Dead

Merry Coronadays, readers! Are you dead yet? No? What's holding you up, and what can I do to encourage you? Because the latest stats show that you should be, with a standard deviation of ±3 percentage points.

Get with the program and do your part, so everyone can be right about something.

In the good old days, when the bubonic plague boogied its way through Europe, the usual social niceties, like wearing clothes and not engaging in sex with your close relatives, broke down.

Boccaccio recounts, in his introduction to the "Decameron"—which consists of stories told to pass the time by a group of aristocrats who've fled from the plague-ridden city of Florence to a more salubrious country estate—that formerly chaste women were emboldened by the need to show off their symptoms to "doctors" and their proof of vaccination (large, unsightly pustules) to the hostess at the Keg, and soon got the taste for enforced exhibitionism.

So they just kept showing off like Real Housewives of the Plague: on the High Street, at the Mall, at trendy witch burnings, wherever their fancy dictated. After all, it was the end of the world, why not maximize your sin during history's first Black Friday Sale? Just shoehorn a confession into your final moments and it's all good. (Christianity is very transactional.)

God, in yet another whimsical about-face, had withheld His protection, because, you know, god, and was obviously isolating along with the rich people, out of town, in a gated community, with cucumber slices over His eyes, which get tired from watching 3.5 billion penises 24/7.

I only hope He stockpiled Visine!

Partying till you drop during a fashionable plague is a strategy not lost on the Toronto gay community or our social hubs, like Spa Excess, the bathhouse down the road from me. They've thought hard about this and have developed some of the strictest protocols in the block of Carlton Street between Mutual and Jarvis.

Not the usual protocols, like their screening device that flashes "NOT HOT ENOUGH!" or "TOO OLD!" or "ASIAN!" when you pass through it, which triggers an air-raid siren and three bouncers who toss you down the stairs. That's a given.

No, this rigidly enforced protocol demands that you wear a mask while cruising the hallways. You may only remove your mask when it's safe to do so, like when you blow three strangers through a glory-hole, or if your breathing is otherwise contained by, for example, a twink sitting on your face.

Believe you me, when it comes to health, safety and social responsibility, gay men mean business and then some.

Torontonians in general are weary and cynical about this virus ever being contained, which is natural given the messaging of *"this Omicron variant is different and less serious but more transmissible but actually we're not sure."*

And of course, anti-vaxxers and freedom nerds, who are hugely responsible for the never-ending waves of infections and hospitalizations, are saying "I told you so," and don't you just hate it when stupid people think they've been proved correct even though it's just randomness and self-fulfilling prophecy?

(Yes, I know we hate stupid people whatever they're doing, but when that gets same-y you can always drill down.)

Health experts in Toronto are now suggesting that a fourth shot, or second booster if you want to give the medical community every possible break, will help in the fight against the Covid upgrade. Cases are spiraling out of control and are currently at a level not seen since the last time!

We know we're in trouble because our relatives are all in hospital after our defiant "no bureaucrat's gonna tell me what to do!" Christmas family reunion dinner for one hundred in a crowded, hermetically-sealed living room.

Grandma, who thinks she will cure her pink-eye by harvesting her saliva immediately after awakening ("virgin spittle") then rubbing it directly on her cornea, licked the spoon for the cranberry sauce then put it back in the bowl. Then, after dessert, feeling tipsy from five mils of Dry Sack

Sherry, she put on her car coat and scarf and kissed everyone good night, full on the mouth, while coughing.

But still. This variant is diabolical! How could we ever hope to evade its grasp?

THE WORLD CONTINUES TO SCRATCH ITS HEAD as it tries to figure out why four people own everything and still get tax breaks, while the rest of us exchange mimeographed copies of "Three Hundred Days of Kraft Dinner But You Only Get to Eat After You've Done Monsanto's Recycling For Them."

Wealth inequality is mirrored in vaccination availability, with much of the developed world at 90% vaccinated, but African nations at only 8.9%.

The Pope, looking fab in a hand-embroidered Alexander McQueen gown covered in gold leaf and some amusing shades by Balenciaga addressed the issue in his yearly homily from the balcony of some church we forgot to burn down.

"I just hope that god or Elon Musk or someone will provide enough vaccine doses for the poor Black persons of African origin! *In nomine Dei patris!*" he prayed, his words only slightly drowned out by the platinum cuffs studded with square-cut emeralds clanking down his forearms.

"We're working hard behind the scenes here at Vatican City," he continued, "scouring our budget in a desperate attempt to find a few extra pennies here and there but seriously, do you know how much a good Chianti costs these days?"

The homily closed with a reading of "The Fine Art of Not Giving A F*ck" but without the asterisk in the title.

In Quebec, a perfectly secular French society showed its *laïcité* by early-Xmas gifting a young Muslim school teacher with unemployment for wearing a hijab, and its lack of irony by making her temporarily part of the administrative staff of the diversity and inclusion programme. *C'est drôle, ça !*

Never mind that it's perfectly legal to wear the headscarf on the street. Once you cross the threshold into a classroom full of kids, that headscarf becomes a forbidden symbol of religion so potent it will cause the breakdown of society and poison young minds.

Instead, let's poison young minds with the concepts that it's OK for the government to determine what women may wear, that Islam is weird and scary, and that you punish minorities for being different instead of accepting them. This, handily, makes your life as a student easier because you don't learn anything.

Expressing his regret over the unfortunate impasse between tolerance and the *pure laine* purity of the Quebec bloodlines, Premier François Legault remarked, "She should never have been hired in the first place," adding, "the law was approved by a majority of Quebeckers."

You're all heart, François. And thanks for reminding us that having a majority of people agreeing on something—that Muslims are terrorists, that gay men are pedophiles, that Black people are subhuman and that Jews drink the blood of gentile babes, to name four historically popular points of majority agreement—is forever proof that you're morally right.

Justin Trudeau, who I'm starting to believe really is the love child of anyone but Pierre, his distinguished father, "did not rule out" stepping in to resolve the problem this law creates—blatant discrimination clearly in violation of Canada's Charter of Rights and Freedoms, resulting in someone who just happens to be female and Muslim losing their job over an item of clothing—but expressed how pleased he was in the meantime to see every leader from the Mayor of Toronto up, in fact most of English Canada, petitioning to have this law struck down; in other words, delegating the task of governing to us ordinary citizens who thought we'd elected him to do it.

Justin, *Justin*. Let's rehearse:

> Canada: "Prime Minister, just how far are you willing to go with standing up to Québec's refusal to honor Canadian values of inclusion?"
>
> JT: "Just watch me."

No. I can't see it, either.

IN THE UNITED STATES, MORE XMAS wars and bald-faced lies, and what, after all, is a lie? Just a disadvantaged actual truth that didn't get its chance to happen! Give it the opportunity and, unlike poor people, at least it won't buy smoked salmon with food stamps YOU paid for.

Making sad, bullied lies into happy, well-adjusted could-be truths is just a question of having the right attitude and a bit of get up and go.

As if designed to prove the point, there came the arson upon the Fox News Christmas Tree, obviously perpetrated by a homeless, crack-addicted liberal terrorist, maybe even Hillary Clinton, because why not. Clinton, or her proxy, had perhaps mistaken the gorgeously festooned fir tree for big-haired Fox host Jeanine Pirro—who crushes the stereotype that "strident" must always be followed by "feminist"—while under the influence.

Ms Pirro, who could strip paint by just shouting a little louder, is one of several Fox hosts being sued by Dominion, the voting machine company whose reputation has been tarnished by the lie that their machines were agents of fraud, either through lack of sufficient security, or actively primed to fake votes.

Does she—did she—actually believe the lie? It's impossible to credit that a lawyer who was also a public prosecutor would be so lax about demanding proof of the claims of widespread voter fraud.

In fact, most of you will know by now that the January 6th Committee uncovered text messages sent by Sean Hannity and other major Fox hosts, as well as Don Junior and other family members, to the President while the Capitol riot was taking place, asking him to intervene lest his "legacy" be tarnished. At the very same time, they were telling viewers that "antifa" and Black Lives Matter were behind the riot.

Could there be a better example of the contempt that Fox has for its audience? Trump, clearly understanding that the Capitol riot and everything leading up to it IS his legacy, declined to intervene for several hours, while his lapdogs propagated more disinformation.

Speaking of inappropriate H-word analogies, how about Herr Doktor Fauci, Public Enemy Number One? People who've never even seen a Jew instantly recognized him as the reincarnation of the truly monstrous Joseph Mengele and did not hesitate to call him on it, even while insisting that the Holocaust is a hoax on a grand scale never equaled except for 9/11 and climate change.

This is the great thing about being post-truth: it's just more in keeping with the spirit of individualism. Everyone can have their own truth, bespoke, instead of that boring old hand-me-down truth that's all baggy in the ass and feels scratchy on a hot day.

And because your truth is, by definition, well, true, you don't have to worry about things like actual facts or falling in line with the group, which is clearly what Stalin would have wanted. (Hey, I gave up the German Guy, I didn't say anything about Soviets.)

Anything with "group" is wrong, for that's how Communism takes root. It starts innocently enough with agreeing on a collective truth, and before you know it you're all driving Polski Fiats and singing Shostakovich *a cappella*.

Dr Fauci, who should get a ticker-tape parade to and from work every day for his decades of service to the US in public health research, and who accomplishes more in twenty-four hours than most people do in their entire lives, does have a problem. He insists on believing that he's talking to adults when he gives advice, rather than realizing that his critics are under-educated trolls whose mental development stopped at the point where they're just dumb enough to survive, thus proving one of the core tenets of natural selection.

Science, you see, doesn't claim to have all the answers, forever. Science creates the best explanations it can, given the data it has at the moment. Best, because the explanations come from the entire scientific community, with everyone eager to poke holes in your hypothesis. Science, therefore scientists, adjust the explanation as new data is produced.

This is not proof of shiftiness, it's proof that you can trust science not to fool itself. His critics, on the other hand, want advice based on 100% certainty, which is advice that's like the stopped clock—correct twice a day; or like religion—correct never.

Incidentally, Ghana, one of those poor African countries, has been ecstatic over the development of a malaria vaccine, which will probably mark the historical moment when malaria is consigned to the dustbin. Oddly, rather than getting all antsy about people taking away their choice to have malaria, should they want malaria, the people of Ghana are actually grateful for and eager to receive this vaccine. Can you imagine anything more backward?

The silver lining of course is that North Americans and Europeans can hang onto their prize for world's luckiest ingrates.

SINCE YOU ASKED, I SPENT XMAS DAY EVENING with my straight friend, to prove how broad-minded I am. I keep suggesting he take the cure, but, like all white straight guys, he knows best, right? Sigh!

We feasted on chicken breast with stuffing, raised cruelty-free at the President's Choice chicken breast farm, and my homemade desserts, leaving out, in the manner of little boys, all things yucky and plant-based that might come between chicken with stuffing and dessert.

Then we watched David Cronenberg's "Naked Lunch," Canada's traditional holiday movie. Judy Davis is heartbreaking in her role as William Burroughs' overly-trusting wife, and Peter Weller demonstrates an interesting but ultimately overly specialized acting technique in which you say your lines without actually moving any facial muscles or producing any sound.

Cronenberg's fascination with physical horror is embodied by gigantic bugs who talk through disgusting sphincters on their backs, which might trigger you if you have any conservative relatives.

My buddy's tiny apartment is immaculately tidy and clean and decorated to the hilt with seasonal cheer, making it a nicer place to hang out compared to my bigger apartment, a shambolic victim of housecleaning neglect bordering on abuse. My aerial slum could easily have given Cronenberg the concept of a writer who mainlines cockroach powder while deploying a typewriter that secretes clear mucus from a semi-tumescent phallus.

In a further display of one-upmanship, my friend had displayed about three hundred Xmas cards on his special Xmas card display table.

"Look at your cards!" I said, putting maybe a little more emphasis than necessary into my resentful tone. "I only got one!"

My friend always tries to make me feel better, and I do the same back, except for today.

"Oh, those!" he said. "Those aren't from this year. Those are all the Xmas cards I've ever received."

Aspirational types, take note.

Terrific Tales

Queen Elizabeth II Shrinks, Gets Trodden on by Truss

The entire world that lives in London, SW7, is in shock after it was announced yesterday that Queen Elizabeth II had finally kicked the gold-plated bucket at the ripe old age of ninety-six.

The shy girl of German ancestry who bravely sacrificed her personal life in exchange for being the world's wealthiest woman, the winner of the birth lottery who was unaccountably put in charge of everything before giving her name to a hundred cruise ships, had, during her reign of seventy years, gradually shrunk to almost nothing, only to be accidentally stepped on in her eleventh hour by rookie PM and former anti-monarchist, but who gives a toss as long as you get elected, Liz Truss.

The accident had been a long time coming, but was almost universally seen as inevitable, considering that the mini-monarch had been noticeably shrinking since she assumed the throne in nineteen fifty-three.

At first this was no more than a couple of centimeters per year, which her doctors attributed to her heavy schedule attending African banquets, which tend to be dehydrating, or evenings at the Royal Opera House, Covent Garden, during which the weight of precious stones covering her evening dress gradually compressed her spine.

As the years passed, however, the subtle smallification had taken a drastic turn, to the point that the late Prince Philip had had to walk beside her in a specially-dug trench so as not to tower over her.

By 1992, an entire miniature replica of Buckingham Palace had been constructed so that the Queen, who at that point was eighteen inches high and losing ground by the day, could appear to be living her normal life of unabashed luxury interspersed with charitable works such as helping the poor, as long as it didn't entail giving up one iota of privilege and had her name all over it so people could be suitably grateful.

A LIFE OF SERVICE

ELIZABETH II WAS BORN MITZI SALZBURG von Schleswig-Holstein in a huge, listed Georgian mansion in London's tony Mayfair district. Once safely arrived, she was kept in the nursery by a carefully-vetted army of white nursemaids, governesses, and nannies, while her parents remained on the first three floors with the doors locked so they could enjoy adult conversation.

This upbringing, common to the English upper crust, ensured that Mitzi (who assumed the name "Elizabeth Mountbatten-Windsor" after the checkout girls at Tesco started saying things like, "I mean she's just a bloody Kraut, needn't give 'erself airs, that's why we fought the bloody war, innit?") would grow up into the sort of stoic, emotionless misfit destined to rule a global rag-tag assortment of loyal subjects.

As former-Mitzi-now-Elizabeth expressed it shortly before her coronation: "It's not the *wealth* one minds so much as the *common* part."

Her seemingly endless reign was marked by constant travels as she sought to provide comfort and aid to every country where Britain had colonized the people and stolen the resources, which is why they needed comfort and aid in the first place.

As she once famously remarked:

> "From Rwanda to Rawalpindi, one is touched beyond measure when one finally reaches the safety of the local Four Seasons hotel, changes into one's second-best tiara, and has a Pimm's.
>
> Once the chauffeur has scraped the donkey excrement off the bonnet of the Rolls-Royce, it's off one goes to the banquet with the braised armadillo followed by the dusky-skinned dancers.
>
> It certainly would be a dismal life without banquets, one fears, and thank god for Susan, umm, sorry, The Duke, who always reads the program beforehand, frankly it's all just a blur to one.
>
> If it's Tuesday it must be Zambia, as one says!"

Her rapidly increasing shrinkage was finally a matter of record after the shocking death of Diana, Princess of Wales, in a car crash in Paris, in 1997. While the nation mourned the People's Princess, Buckingham Palace remained tight-lipped.

The public, hysterical with grief, begged the royals for a word, a wave, anything to demonstrate they had normal feelings like the rest of us, or even just a bladder. But nothing. Crowds thronged outside the gates to the palace, where they would occasionally spot lilliputian Liz on a window ledge, peeking through the net curtains, before being whisked away and placed in a Peek Freans biscuit tin for safe-keeping by a lady-in-waiting.

Further inflaming the situation was the awkward moment when a couple of American tourists walking through Kensington Gardens spotted the Queen, incognito, riding side-saddle on a corgi, proving that it was life as usual for the unfeeling Royals.

Our microscopic Ma'am finally pulled herself together and rescued the situation with an impassioned speech given inside a specially outfitted Barbie Dream Home, from which venue she reassured her subjects:

> "You know, if one thinks of it, which, frankly, one would prefer not to, one is really jolly sad after last Sunday's dreadful news about, you know, whatsername. Thing. The Sloanie—Yes, that's the one.
>
> I mean, let's be honest, it's not the worst news one had all day.
>
> But still.
>
> And "convincing" Elton John to attend and perform is going to absolutely blow the budget, one would prefer to use the money to make charitable donations to third-world countries who wouldn't need charitable donations if it weren't for us in the first place.
>
> But taking all things into account, one was, in the end, quite, umm, fond of her, if one thought of her at all, and if "fond" means that ghastly thing where you start to notice other people.
>
> So, there we have it and how is one doing? Oh, jolly good, well, enjoy the funeral everyone, send us a

postcard or something. Occupant, Buckingham Palace. One just throws them in the dustbin but *you'll* probably feel better.

OK then. Talley-ho. Pip pip.

Bloody hell, well that's over and not a minute too soon. Fond, indeed! Now, will one of you overpaid prats please take away the body mic and I suppose one must ask to be given another eyedropper of Ribena—oh, sod, is one still broadcasting..?"

THE MODERN MEDIA QUEEN

ELIZABETH MASTERED THE ART OF SAYING nothing of any import whatsoever in ostentatiously palatial surroundings, to an ever-widening audience, beginning with her first interview with the BBC:

Tell us about your typical day.

Well, if I don't have any charitable engagements with poor people or third-world countries filled with dusky natives, I find it jolly amusing to make Susan—oh, dear, well, that's what I call The Duke behind his back, so you see it's bound to slip out in public sometimes—I like to make Susan dress up like a lady-in-waiting and serve me tea and dry toast points in bed.

Charming! And then...?

What d'you mean, "and then"? That's the whole typical day. Silly man!

Favorite foods?

One is not fussy, anything served on a Spode plate by an inferior.

Any modern trends you deplore?

This frightful new thing for teeth. One doesn't quite know what to make of it. Queen Mum was always happy with just a bit of white cardboard with a few squares painted in black magic marker. An occasional rinse with Bombay Sapphire gin and you're good to go.

What do you see as your role in a world where economic inequality is increasingly a cause for concern?

I see oneself as a beacon of hope that one day, one, too, will be able to wear a sparkly dress by Norman Hartnell or live in gilded palatial surroundings entirely due to an accident of birth. Oh, wait, if you see me wearing the sparkly dress, you're already born—so much for hope! HAW HAW HAW! That was a little joke, did you like it? Think carefully before you answer.

Her Royal Tininess's uneasy relationship with the media was once more highlighted by the impending birth of her great-grandson Archie, when his mother, Meghan, Duchess of Tantrum, revealed that someone had made racist remarks about the potential color of his skin, which made Oprah's jaw drop slightly less than when the flamboyant friend of Dorothy in charge of her soothing facial creams asked for a raise.

Meghan did not hold back, revealing, "I won't say who, and maybe she's known as The Rottweiler and maybe she isn't, but how do you think I felt when this unknown Camilla person remarked, 'Well, for the love of Mike, I mean, enough is enough, there's no precedent, I mean, is the cuck's sprog a wog, or an n-word?'

"I mean, I'm only just beige and it won't even help if Harry spends five minutes in the California sun, he'll simply have the same bright purply-red skin tone he inherited from his dad plus the effects of knocking back a two-four before lunch. It's still *all about me.*"

ACCIDENT OF BIRTH

ELIZABETH CAME FROM A LONG LINE OF RANDOM ancestors who, by an accident of birth, got to behave as monstrously as they liked and to remain at a level of emotional maturity that would get a Neanderthal a prescription for lithium.

Notable examples include:
- the fun-loving, boisterous Henry VIII, who had his second wife's head chopped off in public because she didn't know

how to tell her body to make male babies, a crime currently being revived as Bill 24 in the US state of Mississippi; and who popularized an early game-show prototype called "unwind the intestines of that person you don't like very much on a wheel;"

- her namesake, Elizabeth I, who brought the so-called Elizabethan period to a glorious flowering of exquisite culture, alternating with unwinding the intestines of people she didn't like very much on a wheel; and

- Victoria, who allowed child slave labor and was so sexually repressed she had to cover the legs of her piano lest she get "that funny feeling we don't like very much that our intestines are being unwound on a wheel. Do you get that, too?"

. . .

THE QUEEN'S BEDROOM, APRIL 9TH, 2021. EARLY MORNING.

CECILY, LADY IN WAITING: *Your Majesty.*

ELIZABETH: (removing the gel pack from her eyes) What—?

Sorry to waken you, Your Majesty, but I'm afraid I have some terrible news —

Oh, no, Cecily. Please don't tell me—

I'm afraid so, Your Majesty.

Well, identify the useless twat who keeps burning the toast and give them the sack!

It's not the toast this time.

Oh, bloody hell. It's Susan, is it? Susan's gone? Kicked the bucket?

Please don't call him that, Ma'am.

No? Shan't I? Cecily, listen to me: Greece and Denmark. Hmm?

Well, I do see your point, but—

Seventy years of "Just close your eyes and think of

Snowden!" Simply ghastly! It's a wonder we managed the four. No magic purple pills in those days, my dear. We understood duty back then. Just hiked up our farthingales and got on with it — !

Yes, Ma'am.

Well, so he's shuffled off, had to happen sooner or later, poor old sod. Hangin' by a thread and packet of Boots panty pads. Give me a sec while I spread out… Bit more room now—oh, that's the stuff, the sheets are lovely and cool! Fancy, Cecily, I can touch the cool bits with my toes—!

Ma'am, please! I know you must be in shock, but you must try to pull yourself together—

Oh, dear, you're right. You're absolutely right, I'm avoiding. Thank you for pointing that out, Cecily. Yes, well. Ahem. Susan's gone—sorry, HRH the Duke, and I'm all alone in this great cruise ship of a bed, and it's all frightfully sad, and… and life just isn't going to be the same. Is it. Kind of thing—?

I'm—so very sorry, Your Majesty. About the Duke—

Never you mind! Can't be helped! Pshaw! Now, dry your eyes, Cecily, because for the rest of the week I think I'll take a jolly old jaunt up to Balmoral, waste a few deer, what do you think? Second-best Range Rover? Hmmm? Keep the old pecker up, no point getting all down in the mouth—oooh, don't forget to call the BBC—

We've already notified them, and then there's—the funeral arrangements—

Oh, yes. There's a thought. Dear, dear. Well, how about find that Stella McCartney I wore to Tonga and dye it black. No point shelling out for something new, wear it once and off it goes to the Science Museum! Or dig up that number I wore for Diana, it'll stink to high heaven of mothballs but just run it up a flagpole or something, give it a good airing. Unless it's in the V & A?

You had Missus Parker-Bowles shred it and Purolator it to The Earl Spencer, if you recall, Ma'am.

Yes, indeed I did, and what fun! Cecily, you're an absolute poppet, you always know what to say to cheer me up! Now, moving forward. It's a new day, my dear! Tell the footman I'm ready for brekkies, and can he please leave the bag *in* this time. And extra Cooper's Oxford for the toast.

Very well, Ma'am.

Oh, and Cecily — ?

Ma'am — ?

Just the one spoon, though.

. . .

FINISHED OFF BY TRUSS

IN A MOMENT OF IRONY YOU WOULD ACTUALLY pay good money to view, it was left to Liz Truss, the temporary Prime Minister of Great Britain and former vociferous critic of the monarchy as an institution, to finish the Queen off.

No sooner had Boris Johnson's hair, which had just resigned, rushed *out of* the reception room at Balmoral, when Liz, overcome with excitement at her election win, rushed *into* the reception room at Balmoral, but failed to see the tiny queen tottering towards her on her cane.

A sickening crunch, a quick look at the bottom of her pumps... "Never trust an ambitious woman, chaps," she muttered as a tiny, hysterical lady-in-waiting fainted dead away onto the tartan carpet.

She wiped what remained of Mitzi Salzburg von Schleswig-Holstein off her shoe with a look of disgust, adjusted her pencil skirt, and, clearing her throat for her first press conference, stepped out into the light.

. . .

In other news: Don't worry, Meghan is OK. Thank *God*.

Dark

Victory

The Great Snail'xtinction

Achatinella apexfulva, known by those closest to him simply and unpretentiously as "George the Snail," is dead. He was 14, and the last remaining of his species. Achatinella Apexfulva is now extinct.

In human terms: It's like, there will be no more teenage boy Biff Apexfulva's begging to borrow the keys to the car so they can drunk drive and boy-bond and pick up girls; no more teenaged girl Cindy Apexfulva's staying out later than her Dad's deadline, to make out after Prom and leave pink lipstick and a promise on a shirt-collar.

But, let's face it: The human terms are just to get you more invested in what is probably, to you, and probably always will be, a non-event, because you just don't care. It's all bullshit, because George was a SNAIL, OK? And snails do not drunk drive. These are the lengths I go to in order to pander to your attenuated concentration levels. Yeah, uh-huh, is that so, and don't nod at me and pretend to listen while you stare at your device.

George (145,000,000 B.C.E.—2019 C.E.), who started life as a simple tree snail but who leveraged his rarity, whimsical antlers and ability to leave a slimy trail on any hard surface to become one of history's rarest and most beloved gastropods, slipped away into coily-shelled heaven on January 1st, 2019 on the Hawaiian island of Oahu, where he had spent his retirement in contemplative solitude.

Described variously as "a real card," "don't let him anywhere near your prize Dahlia beds" and *"a thumbnail-size whorl of dark brown and tan... like a swirled scoop of mocha fudge"* (JULIA JACOBS, NEW YORK TIMES, JANUARY 10TH, 2019), George appeared unprepossessing, even repugnant, to the casual observer.

Yet underneath that "Everysnail" persona beat a heart, or whatever snails have to pump the sticky, silvery viscous fluid around, of a prophet, and from his tender throat, or whatever snails have that represents the beginning of the digestive tract, if they even have one, erupted the angry voice of doomed but defiant snaildom.

George was found slumped over a plate of his favorite leaf fungus, and in a long, sticky, silvery viscous trail that extended from his glass tank and covered the walls of the Snail Extinction Project's offices, he'd written a disgustingly moist yet poignant farewell note:

"CAN'T TAKE THE LONELINESS ANYMORE. Ten years of solitary confinement, thanks to you cocksuckers, *homo sapiens*.

"I survived *The Great Snail'xtinction*. That's what we named it that very first night. They found us huddling together, dangling from the branches like clusters of grapes ready to drop, and before we knew it, everything went dark, then light again, and we were here.

"They meant well, but—we'd rather die at home, you know, instead of living longer in a place where there's nothing to live for. We never wanted to be rescued so the twenty people who could probably feel guilty about needing to rescue us could feel a little less guilty.

"As soon as the green-colored tube-suns had set, we tried to comfort each other, whisper all kinds of soothing lies:

"We'll escape one day; we'll overpower the guards and make an exquisitely-slow three-week slither for it!"

"Which was our peak of enthusiasm. I didn't have the heart, or whatever we snails have that yada, yada, to explain that this was it, dudes; the end of the silvery, viscous trail.

"Sapiens! That's rich!

"Here's what it felt like if it had been you, OK?

"It's like... some Sunday afternoon in July, and you're at home in Etobicoke, with your friends and relatives over for a big celebration, and you're grilling meat patties and drinking imitation beer and playing Frisbee and everyone's having a really laid back awesome time.

"What you no longer worry about is that the ozone layer is so fucked up you're all developing skin cancer; or the pollution count is off the charts which is why most of you have asthma, then emphysema, and crops are failing and the ones that don't fail are laced with pesticides; and you're rationed fresh water once every three days unless you're elderly or sick.

"And somewhere, some aliens have taken pity on you and decided you need rescuing because otherwise you'll all die.

"You know that already, but you try not to think about it, just like you don't think about those new blue-black spots on your skin since yesterday or how you're always parched and thirsty, how your rumbling stomach is always sour.

"All of a sudden the sky goes dark and giant alien hands reach for you, grab you, throw you into a giant plastic Tilt-a-Whirl and when you come to, you realize you're being transported, flying through the air. So much time seems to have passed, hours? Or days? And you're at your destination, and they dump all of you—the whole party—into some sterile panic room with glass walls.

"Something will go wrong, some miscommunication. It's inevitable. Maybe they'll keep the men but eat the women, stir them up alive in their alien blender for protein and extra fat and electrolytes, or keep the adults and eat the babies. Something off-kilter in their understanding. They'll have heard all the urban myths, so they'll tear off a leg, maybe, thinking it will grow back.

"Or your teeth will fall out because they won't know about Vitamin C, oh sure, they'll know how to travel a billion light years to the Milky Way, but they'll miss that one little detail and theirs is a world without Tang. Plus, they don't have faces or eat solid food, which is why the toothless thing is kind of whoosh over their heads.

"So there you are in your panic room, and this effort to save you is not going well, because in a couple of days, everyone is sick. It's some catastrophic virus, like the Spanish flu, and it carries off every single one of your relatives, friends, neighbours and kids—everyone except you. You're the lucky one!

"Nothing but lukewarm water and Swanson TV dinners for the rest of your life, watched over and prodded and interrogated, but when, you can never predict. Mr. Very Last Human, just you and some Man Meals the aliens managed to extract from a landfill, dumped on a paper plate. No presentation, no Coke Zero, the Salisbury steak overdone and the apple crumble still cold. Same old story.

"Welcome to my final decade, dudes. Just munch, digest, slimy trail, rinse, repeat for ten long years. You're it. The last of your kind.

"I mean, if this is a rescue, gimme extinction!

"And you think, Aww, he's just a snail, right? Can a snail run a savings bank, play in a band, build houses, drunk drive? You forget one thing, that we're a hundred and forty-five million years of evolution apart. *I came first*, then you. Without me, you would never have happened.

"Tonight's the night and here's how I'm gonna go, guys: Give thanks, finish my last dinner, then mate. Not with a whimper, but a bang! Yep. I'm hermaphrodite. What will you do to pass the time in your panic room?

"I'm gonna go to that great big fungus patch in the rainforest sky filled with luscious moist writhings and suckings of snailfuck, wrapped in my own seductive, soft body, little popping wet explosions, pow pow pow, with God watching me, laughing with cosmic black-holed horniness in His eyes, at the beauty of the evolution He designed, the random perverse allsexness of male and non-male and non-female and female, and a do-si-do, rolled and roiled and stuck in and stuck to and plopping out wet and trembling and dripping and all of it together— and He sees that it's good. Hermaphrodite snail-sex.

"Snails understand. Like, snails get it. Why can't you guys?

"Honestly, God's feeling a little, shall we say, inauthentic, to use the current buzz. It's eating at Him. All His brand equity is tied up in this "all-perfect, all-knowing, all-the-time" thing, hard enough to maintain, right? And it's getting a little bit uncomfortable because He realizes He made this one unmistakable mistake, or sin, to use the traditional oojamacallit.

"Of course, when God prays to be forgiven for His one, terrible sin, it's like, Research In Motion drops the Blackberry ball on security, right? Game over! Nice idea while it lasted! Humongous God-oopsies!

"*Homo sapiens*... God the narcissist had to look in the reflecting pool of the Universe and see His human face stare back at Him. He moulds a little clay, extracts a little rib... Big sin of Pride.

"So He prays for forgiveness... *but to whom...?*

"So tired... It's getting dark. And I'll tell you something, Ed... Either I'm going to slither up that tree trunk...

"...or Max Steiner is going to slither up that tree trunk...

"...but I'll be God-DAMNED... if Max Steiner and I...

"...are going to slither up...
"...that tree trunk...
"...to... geth... er...

"

I ASKED SOME RANDOM GUY on the street for his thoughts on the demise of George, the extinction of Achatinella apexfulva, and of snails in general.

"Garlic butter," he replied, with no hesitation and a gourmand's glint in his eye. "Garlic butter. With lots of finely minced parsley.

"And a nice Chardonnay."

Scary Weird Coincidence

So I managed to fool someone, via photographs from 1982, into thinking I'm young and handsome and desirable and that they should spend the better part of a sultry night caressing my eyebrows,

following my treasure trail—currently overgrown and littered with cigarette butts and empty Coke cans—and exclaiming with delight, either real or feigned, I'm not fussy, when they reach the pot of baby-batter at the end of that slightly frayed-around-the-edges *homosexual* rainbow.

Whoever is making those gagging noises: I didn't say you had to *visualize* it. Jeezus. Have a little empathy, or, failing that, a Manhattan cocktail garnished with one of those Bing cherries you preserved in Marsala, using a canning method regarded as dangerous by the USDA.

Which you were going to do anyway, weren't you, cupcake?

And while we're taking a detour: The word "homosexual."

Does not the word "homosexual" come conveniently packaged with its own dispenser of hand sanitizer, a pair of tweezers, and pristine surgical gloves that haters pretending not to be haters can slip on as they roll those five plummy yet sibilant syllables around their mouth like something they ate on a dare and are just waiting to spew out again?

"Homosexual" was the ersatz medical word invented because "invert" was sounding a tad Krafft-Ebbing, or was it Kraft Cheese Slices, I always get them mixed up; and just coming out and saying "nancy-boy" or "poofter" didn't have that Harvard Med School cachet, though they got the point across.

"Homosexual" wasn't a description or an identity. It was a *diagnosis*.

I'm thinking about this word partly because of a gripping and unsettling YouTube documentary on the celebrated and still polarizing British painter Francis Bacon: *"A Brush with Violence."* (It's free, I do recommend you look it up.)

This stellar doc consists entirely of reminiscences of friends and colleagues, whose patchwork of stories gradually coalesces to illuminate the ghastly and terrifying work of this prime practitioner of art as theatre of cruelty.

And as part of the experience, we are treated right off the bat, and then some, to the analyses and observations of an American art critic, Annalyn Swan, who sports hair pulled back into a bun designed by a consortium of librarians, and a voice like your bratty cousin on your mother's side who sticks her hand way *way* up when the teacher asks a question and rats you out if you copied someone else's homework.

The redoubtable Ms Swan proceeds to play mouth billiards with the word "homosexual," blushing slightly and almost barely breaking into a nervous smile each time she explains how Francis used to get it on with the stable boys, and how, as an asthmatic, he was unable to take part in manly, hetero-building pastimes.

Well, you know what? She's so utterly annoying and indefensible that, I must confess, it was all I could do to stop myself looking her up in Who's Who, putting on my best pair of black winkle-picker boots, then flying down to whatever part of Connecticut she haunts, walking right up to her, then picking her winkle. Right then and there, on the spot.

No one says "homosexual" anymore, and anyone who does is just using it to stir up the unconscious idea that being gay is a pathology.

It's official: Being gay is neither pathological or cause for pity, except when bigots make it that way for us.

Bacon's severe, cold (even by British standards) and snobby upbringing, his clueless stiff upper lip father who rejected him, and the grimly repressed post-war society at the time all conspired to force his desires underground and fill him with a self-loathing and internalized homophobia so extreme he was incapable of intimacy with a loving partner.

His eventual callous rejection of his "bit of rough," working-class lover-lad and Kray Brothers hanger-on George Dyer, drove Dyer to suicide—and imagine believing that the only way to get Bacon's attention was to kill himself mere hours before Bacon's first great triumph, a major retrospective at the Grand Palais in Paris; imagine the bitterness fueling that act of sabotage.

(Making a desperate and shockingly self-serving decision, Bacon and his entourage, even the hotel manager, conspired to hide the fact of Dyer's death, deliberately and almost certainly criminally failing to report his suicide until the glitzy reception was over.)

"Homosexual." Even saying the word was unthinkable. Imagine a sense of self-worth so degraded that Bacon needed to arrange his own gay-bashings with violent men. His first lover, Peter Lacy, was a vicious, bona fide sadist who beat Bacon mercilessly and once threw him through a plate-glass window; Francis sustained appalling injuries to his face. Then he went back for more.

I wonder what work he might have achieved had he not had to spend his life alternately loathing and punishing himself. I found myself once again stunned by the work and sad beyond description, sad that a sensitive gay man, born to frigid, remote parents and at a time which offered only the extreme tool of sadomasochism with which to act out his confusion, had to sacrifice his life and mental health to produce these nightmares in paint.

I despise the way Ms Swan wants us to sense how brave and forbearing she is for even talking about disgusting gay sex, but it's Francis Bacon, she has to. She sounds like she wants to slip into a Chanel biohazard suit every time she smirks out "hummosssexual." Her disgust and distaste are palpable.

And we're supposed to be all integrated and no big deal anymore, we "gays"! Imagine how she would have handled "gender dysphoria"!

She probably would have giggled and puked at the same time, which would be unexpected for someone of her obvious stature, but, hey—if you choke to death on your own vomit, you choke to death on your own vomit. It's no big deal, there's other critics!

And if you, my readers, haven't figured it out yet: Trans persons are now in the place that gay men were in circa 1970. Outed, visible, but with few people who care to understand what they experience; so vulnerable and so discriminated against, so loathed and considered subhuman by some, even, that our parliament felt it necessary to enshrine their human rights specifically in legislation. That's where they are, right now.

You know what else? I bet Annalyn Swan even has Cabbage Patch Doll ankles, like stove pipes. Yes, I'm shallow and cruel but you made me this way.

WHERE WAS I? OH, YES. Back to my date. Not to doxx anyone, but my date's address is germane to the story, which is why I've included it below. More precisely, the *number* is included, but I've obviously changed the name to 'Whatever Street' in order to veil the innocent.

Innocent for believing in the photographs and being unaware of the possibly terminal door-shock he soon will suffer when he sees the "after" version of this forty-year "before and after" make-over.

Anyway, I pile into the cab—I can't really afford a cab, not all the way to Whatever Street, but a sixty-six-in-less-than-two-months guy doesn't always have a lot to enjoy in the ways of the flesh, and, as Stephen Sondheim said, "A girl ought to celebrate what passes by." She should know, little Tony-award monopolizer.

Is there an award for "Best Least-Popular Broadway Musical"? Maybe it should be called the "Toni-*est* Award"!

I scrabble around in my knapsack—which should be, if there's any justice, a sack to carry your knaps in—for the piece of 17 x 22" onion skin tracing paper, which was the only piece of paper I could find, on which I've written the address in red Crayola, which was the only, etc. etc.

"Three one nine six Whatever Street, please," I tell the driver.

And the driver turns round with a peculiar expression on his face.

"Are you sure," he says. "Because that's my cab number. *Are you sure?*"

I look at the license info on the back of the front passenger seat. Then I look again at my red crayon handwriting on the tracing paper.

And as crazy as it sounds, I kid you not: *The number of the cab is 3196.*

So that's how I ended up spending the night being verbally abused by Satanic bikers in the parking lot of the Summerhill LCBO.

Worth every friggin' penny.

kray twins and george dyer

Useless Knowledge

In her final work, "Dark Age Ahead," the great Jane Jacobs lamented the rise of what she called "credentialing vs. education."

In this model, a university degree is now considered necessary for decent, well-paid employment, but not because it is evidence of the highest levels of learning and expertise in a particular field of study.

Instead, it is simply a credential that proves to a prospective employer that the degree-holding graduate has jumped through the necessary hoops and shown that her values and skills are in alignment with those of the company. By graduating, she is by definition reliable, honest, able to turn up on time, work well with others and finish projects efficiently and on-budget.

Paraphrased, it doesn't matter so very much what you've studied, but it does matter that you've been mixed, rolled and stamped out with the cookie cutter of compliance. Universities are just a pre-filtering step in the assembly-line process of creating corporate workers. Go ahead and finish your thesis on Lesbian Cave Poetry of the Early Neanderthal—what's really important is you can work until midnight without complaining. Go team, go!

We are in thrall to the concept of "efficiency." Getting the most end product from just the right amount of input of time and resources, which boils down to maximising profit by minimizing, or, even better, externalizing expenses (getting others to foot the bill).

What do you acquire at university? Useless knowledge. Knowledge without "practical" application.

. . .

IN 1854, SELF-TAUGHT ENGLISH MATHEMATICIAN George Boole had the inventive notion to apply the rigorous procedures of algebra to logical thought, and by doing so made possible a digital revolution that would occur one hundred and fifty years later.

Boole's concept was a set of operations that, working with propositions instead of real numbers, and using only three operators, AND, OR and NOT, could determine their truth or otherwise (a proposition is a simple declarative statement that is either true or false, but not both; for example: "the window is open" or "all boys like hockey").

This method of treating logical propositions with a scientific method and the stringency of mathematics became known eventually as Boolean algebra.

And, brilliant an insight as it was recognized to be, no one knew what to do with it. So there it sat, interesting but effectively useless, a brilliant abstraction, and without any practical application, for eighty years.

Mary, George's wife—also a self-taught mathematician, a species which was apparently raging through academia like crabgrass during the early nineteenth century—was not necessarily impressed.

Fun Fact: Mary was a believer in homeopathy, the cretinous quackery that takes as its gimmick the doctrine that a substance causing symptoms of a disease in healthy people would cure similar symptoms in sick people, or *"similia similibus curantur"*, like cures like.

Which effectively means curing by placebo, as there is literally nothing in homeopathic medicines.

At any rate, George walked home in the rain one day after a hard day's AND, OR and NOT-ing at the Uni, and subsequently caught a severe chill. That might have been the end of it had Mary not gone all homeopathic and covered him with sheets soaked in ice-cold water.

He died a week or so later, or, "like *kills* like."

Mary's reaction was not recorded. Personally, I think she should have been publicly stoned for being an airhead.

AT HOME WITH GEORGE AND MARY BOOLE: AN IMAGINARY EVENING MEAL

MARY: Hello, dear, nice day at the University of Cork, Ireland, as its first mathematics professor, even though you didn't even go to university yourself?

GEORGE: Pretty good. Any more biscuits or did you and your bridge club scarf the lot?

MARY: What did you do today? Any more ponderous speeches to the students about their loose morals? That's rich coming from you, pumpkin!

GEORGE: If you must know, as a matter of fact I discovered Boolean operators, which I've named after me, obviously, and which can be employed to determine the truth or falsehood of logi—

MARY: Tripe?

GEORGE: Well, really, Mary! At least hear me out before you start tearing everything—

MARY: No, no, darling, PASS the tripe, please. Thank you. And the potatoes, if you'd be so kind.

GEORGE: Oh, rather. At any rate, then in the afternoon Harry, Algernon and I chatted up that new strumpet who's been hanging about at the Royal Society meeting rooms, then we took her for a spin, kicked the tyres, saw what's under the bonnet, if you see my meaning... why are you laughing, for heaven's sake?

MARY: Well, you see—IF (George with strumpet NOT lady boy) AND (tells me about it) THEN (hard to take) OR IF (George catches cold from walking in the rain) AND (given ice bath by me NOT hot cocoa) THEN (sudden death of George from pneumonia). AND (at least I'll have your insurance policy)!

GEORGE: My word, you picked that up fast! Jolly impressive!

GEORGE KNEW THAT HIS BOOLEAN ALGEBRA had major significance, but was understandably shaky about its possible applications. Boole had simply come up with an interesting but random idea, like a Cockney barrow boy who'd dreamed something up in his spare time when he should have been shoveling coal or selling cherries from a cart in Covent Garden.

Fast forward: In the 1930's, Claude Shannon, an American mathematician, had a flash of insight. It was a world-changing moment. He realized that these binary variables could be used to represent the low- and high-voltage states of electric circuits, or OFF and ON.

Zero and one...

Boolean algebra applied to the switching of electric circuits! These switches, the zeros and ones, are the machine language of computers, and Boolean algebra would provide the conceptual and practical basis for our entire technological world. Unprepossessing George Boole became the architect of a digital age which he could barely imagine; though he spoke of his most important work with a touching sense of purpose.

Reading an excerpt from a letter to a colleague in 1851, you can sense his pride and barely contained excitement about the work he was about to commence:

> *... I am now about to set seriously to work upon preparing for the press an account of my theory of Logic and Probabilities which in its present state I look upon as the most valuable if not the only valuable contribution that I have made or am likely to make to Science and the thing by which I would desire if at all to be remembered hereafter ...*
>
> — George Boole, letter of 1851, referring to his groundbreaking *"An investigation into the Laws of Thought, on Which are founded the Mathematical Theories of Logic and Probabilities"* (1854)

But the results of his work really started life as a *succès d'estime*. In other words, useless knowledge.

AUGUSTA ADA KING (1815 -1852) WAS THE daughter of Lord Byron and his only "legitimate" child. He adored Baby "if my name were Ada, I'd be Ada, even backwards I'd be" Ada, but nonetheless abandoned her after four months to the care of her mother and continued gallivanting around the eastern Mediterranean, writing the occasional epic poem for posterity and gifting his magnificent body, lily-of-the-valley eau de Cologne and epicene facial features to all and sundry.

He did manage to squeeze out the word "Ada" with his dying breath. Jeepers. There's nothing like the devotion of an obsessive helicopter dad, right?

Ada King was wealthy and grand and eccentric enough that she was able to devote herself to her preferred useless pastime, which was—no, Murgatroyd McGraw, not needlepoint or home production of quince jelly, but mathematics.

Mathematics, the only perfect language humankind has discovered apart from music. I think it's possible she may also have dabbled in watercolors, invented ciphers and then written secret messages in her journal and even tinkered a bit at the old Joanna, as they say, but math was her "thing."

Everyone who wasn't of the aristocracy believed that the aristocracy were just a bunch of useless tits, so nobody got on Ada's case about "doing something meaningful" or how she was wanting "something for nothing". They never expected anything meaningful from a countess to begin with.

Of course, there was at the root of this disdain her unfortunate choice of being a woman in an era when women were believed to be barely above cattle in terms of intelligence and common sense. And so this particular useless tit had lots of "me" time.

Now, under normal circumstances, Ada's wealth could have funded a typical, tastefully extravagant and useless aristocratic life. Parties, balls, more parties, dancing lessons (the quadrille was big at the time), evenings at the Royal Opera House, a fashionable jaunt to see the Coliseum and the Pyramids, then back to more parties and more balls.

Not Ada. Instead, Ada spent her time becoming a mathematical genius. This girl did equations like an Olympic gold medalist does press-ups and chin-ups (unlike yours truly's attempts at algebra, where one more resembles a Diane Arbus photograph of special education students being group-punished in an asylum).

Ada's training proves my hypothesis that real freedom—have you heard, apparently there is a type that involves more than one option to choose from, who the hell knew?—is, after all, everything to do with money.

Money buys you two extremely valuable commodities: leisure and privacy.

Leisure: You can pay to outsource every single tiresome thing except eating, breathing, defecation and peeing.

Privacy: Freed from the boring and the distasteful, you can now talk endlessly about the one or two things you're obsessed with. Your new glass plate photography kit or your experiments calling up the dead with a ouija board, or building a full-scale replica of the Trianon in the backyard. This yields privacy because this is not easy to be around.

The lifelong process by which Ada took her above-average intelligence burger and, with extra privacy and leisure on the side, and maybe a dill pickle, supersized it to genius, also proves my theory that genius would probably arise more commonly if we all had Universal Basic Income so we could sit around staring into space.

I do this already, so, like, *hellooooo*, genius, but if you could give it at least a try? We might want to start getting somewhere eventually. The rest of us would appreciate it.

SO IT CAME TO PASS THAT ADA, AT THE AGE of seventeen, met Charles Babbage (1791-1871), an English mathematician who, you guessed it, taught himself algebra and calculus while in his teens, and went on to great achievements at Trinity College, Cambridge, where he was made Lucasian Professor of Mathematics at the age of twenty-five. (Sir Isaac Newton and Stephen Hawking also held this professorship.)

Babbage was, it is fair to say, no slouch with his math abilities, which is understandable considering every person he'd ever met was a self-taught mathematician.

Unfortunately he had what I would delicately call, so as not to offend any touchy old people hanging around, "a shitty personality."

Call it "shitty personality," call it borderline; Chuck was a tad difficult to get along with and this would have what we call "far-reaching consequences."

Enter Ada, whose mother had insisted on her rigorous education in mathematics so she wouldn't turn out "crazy, like her father" (crazy was the current psychiatric term for bisexual).

So by the age of seventeen, Ada was a true débutante: accomplished at just about everything, charming in that "I've got more brains than you" way,

and discussing Bernoulli numbers as casually as you and I discuss what mattress cover we're planning to order from Wayfair, or whether Kamala just forgot to be Black enough or if it's a strategy and she's in cahoots with Trump to blow the whole thing.

Bernoulli numbers. Just saying "Bernoulli numbers" makes me feel smarter! Even though I couldn't tell a Bernoulli number from a pile of lukewarm fettuccine, with sauce.

Anyway. Babbage got funding for his Difference Engine, a mechanical, room-sized calculator using punch cards that was not programmable. It got partially built but then Babbage's shitty personality kicked in. He had a major fight with his head engineer, and suddenly his investors couldn't see the point of all this "new-fangled stuff"—also because this was England, so, all together now: "Why would you ever want to change anything?"

With the Difference Engine still unfinished, and with his investors becoming less and less sympathetic to his project and refusing to fund him any further, he started designing his Analytical Engine. This was even grander and more complex than the first, and now its architecture included the feature of conditional branching, meaning that, in hindsight, it was a digital, programmable and Turing-complete computer.

But it was Ada, not Babbage, who had this flash of insight.

In her words:

> "[The Analytical Engine] might act upon other things besides number, were objects found whose mutual fundamental relations could be expressed by those of the abstract science of operations, and which should be also susceptible of adaptations to the action of the operating notation and mechanism of the engine...
>
> ...Supposing, for instance, that the fundamental relations of pitched sounds in the science of harmony and of musical composition were susceptible of such expression and adaptations, the engine might compose elaborate and scientific pieces of music of any degree of complexity or extent."

Not just numbers, but numbers that symbolically represented other values. Musical notes; letters of the alphabet... a universal computer.

But she had one final trick up her satin sleeves. In her notes to a seminar Babbage was giving at the University of Turin—in typical smart-alecky smart girl fashion, her notes to the lecture were longer than the lecture, and are the chief reason for her fame—she added an algorithm for the Analytical Engine to compute, yes, Bernoulli numbers. She is cited as the first computer programmer for this reason.

The Analytical Engine was finally built according to Babbage's specifications in 1991 (if my memory serves me correctly, though you should take my confident air with a grain of salt, here...I was pretty drunk throughout the nineties. Like, there are big patches of vodka and tonic.). The Analytical Engine, once built, worked.

The first ENIAC computers from the forties, handy for home use if you had your own power plant and a garage the size of an airplane hangar, were less Turing-complete. The architecture from the Analytical Engine would have come in mighty handy, and the engineer of the ENIAC is said to have wept when he saw it, but the Engine had been obscured by the misty mists of time.

Babbage's remarkable work is rightly celebrated. But Ada's partnership and contributions were not, until very recently. In two pages of search results for Babbage, and in one lengthy article from Stanford University discussing his life and influence, Ada King, the young woman who had the genius to see his earthbound cogs and gears and imagine them creating an enthralling music of the future, is not mentioned once.

Ada King, Countess of Lovelace, died at the age of thirty-seven, of uterine cancer, and was buried beside Lord Byron, the father she had never met, whose dying wish was to see his beloved Ada again.

WE COULD HAVE HAD COMPUTERS IN THE 1840's. And as we design computers in a lackadaisical way then build on top of the shoddy architecture forever, they would have retained their Victorian aesthetic.

The Babbage Remarkable Machine! Eight thousand parts, weighing four tons. Encased in oak—sturdy beams of oak. Big oak computers in our homes and offices and stock markets and banks. You know that they would never have basically changed, right? With double opt-in, it would take a week to sign up for someone's marketing campaign, which would be delivered to your door by an employee of the Babbage Company.

We'd feed our oak computers punch cards to tip off the telegraph operator, Pippa, that we needed to access our bank accounts and then keep the punch cards locked up in case of identity theft.

Every Babbage Remarkable Machine would still have a built-in umbrella stand, a stereoscopic viewer, a make-up mirror for the ladies' toilette, and a fold-out tray for the teapot.

When you shut the Babbage down, it would play "Rule, Britannia!"

Synchroni-City

Saturday: an ex-roommate drops by with a friend who's in town to see the Raptors play. (I'm not sure, but I think the Raptors are some kind of sports team.)

My ex-roommate installs the handsome Raptors fan in my armchair, offers me a doggie-bagged hamburger, then flits about, wreaking delightful sketchy havoc.

He scrummages through another friend's personal effects (some of which he appropriates—he's a bit of a kleptomaniac), tidies the kitchen, messes up the bathroom, and gives me news of someone, let's call him "Ben," whom I haven't seen in nearly two years.

Ben and I are estranged because of my big mouth and my snippy tactlessness and my sour, flippant remarks about his abusive passive-aggressive female partner, whom he endlessly complained about but couldn't seem to break free of. Ben took offense at my unasked-for advice, which admittedly was a little brusque, and stormed off in a straight-guy huff.

This is because straight guys pretend they're manly and strong, but in fact, compared to gay men, they are as fruit flies to our turkey vultures, so spindly and ephemeral is their sense of self-worth. Straight men are used to being coddled and kow-towed to, and receiving the world's deference and the security blanket scented with Febreze, so they are soft and frail.

Gay men, by contrast, eat rock-hard shit for breakfast and halt juggernauts of bigotry with our bare hands, all while dancing backwards in Louboutin cocktail booties, lashes mascara'd so thickly our eyelids glue shut, and wearing a print dress from the Sally Ann that someone's grandmother died in, so we're ready to take whatever you care to throw at us.

Like, "Hey, faggot!" for example.

Then we laugh our silvery, ironic laugh, shove a butt-plug up our hole and head to the office.

You know. *Tough.*

Straight men are all about the masculinity and the deference, but their masculinity is butterfly-fragile, so that if you so much as brush its powdery wing they are irrevocably maimed. And trust me when I tell you that they will exhibit their stigmata with a stoic, martyred acceptance that is worse than any accusation, like those portrayals of saints holding out their lopped-off body parts on a tray or having their entrails slowly wound up on a wheel.

They will pull on the sweat-stained track suit of their straight-guy pride, they will draw themselves up to their full height and they will take their elevated chin, their grim *have a nice life, dude,* expression and their affronted, bruised ego out the door, pulling their ruined masculinity behind them like a stuffed toy rabbit on a string.

Still. Ben was handsome and slim-muscular, refined and smart and soft-spoken, with a hint of Barbadian accent, and he let down the straight-guy façade every so often and we'd mud-wrestle, winner take all, quite effectively. So I feel wistful about Ben, wishing we could be friends once more, although I'm not so wistful as to think my comments were unjustified. Just badly timed, and with a little too much emphasis, perhaps, on the words "co-dependent" and "dysfunctional".

You know, and can I just say, seriously. I mean, someone's gotta cut me a great, big bleeding side of slack, and it might as well be me.

And, in case you're wondering: When we mud-wrestled? I *always* made sure I lost.

MONDAY: I ARRANGE A HOOK-UP with a guy in North York. For an elite downtowner, as our bloated odious demagogue premier, Doug Ford, would call me, this might as well be the moons of Jupiter.

As I rarely travel north of Bloor Street, and start bleeding from the ears somewhere around St. Clair, I pack with a vengeance, remembering that it is food and its availability that determines the outer boundaries of possible interplanetary travel.

Book for the subway ride (Resident Alien: The New York Diaries, by Quentin Crisp, who I am trying to become), shoulder bag with cigarettes poached from the Mohawk nation, lighter, butane. An apple, culled from my roommate's sock drawer and slightly mummified, in case I get peckish, a sweater in case it's cold up there, sunglasses for viewing any displays of the aurora borealis.

Hey, Cortana: What's his particular corner of North York called? *Willowdale?*
You can't be serious, girl.

Phone charger. I will definitely need the phone charger cause my phone's at twenty-eight percent, but I figure I'll plug it in at the hook-up's place before plugging the hook-up into me. Yowza!

And I have five dollars and some change. A subway ride is three dollars twenty-five cents, but because I'm providing a little government-sanctioned legal *cannabis sativa*, I figure I'll touch him for a subway token to get me home, if I'm still able to walk to the subway, that is.

I am placing a heavy burden and high hopes on this hook-up. And I haven't even met his boyfriend yet!

I'VE BEEN ON THE NORTHBOUND TRAIN for twenty minutes. As the subway leaves York Mills station, my hook-up texts me: "When you arrive at Sheppard, go upstairs to the mall, find the Shopper's Drug Mart and wait for me there."

At Sheppard Station, I head up the escalator and look for any random exit because it is all the same to me, and it is not immediately apparent what the mall means, because that is what North York is.

One big mall.

I have no idea where I am in relation to the mall, the exits were designed by Max Escher and a sign says "take this stairway down to the first level" while displaying an arrow that points to the ceiling. The sign is in front of another escalator.

I take this escalator back down to where I started and follow a TTC worker, who leads me into a cul-de-sac where she disappears through a door marked "Employees Only." I backtrack. I take another escalator up and this time I exit to the street, where the people, who are all teenagers, look different and full of cares and have diametrically opposed interests to me, and I look across Yonge Street and I see the words "Harcross Centre" on the front of what looks like a mall.

It looks like a mall because everything looks like a mall. This particular mall does not have a Shopper's Drug Mart, but it has a fine-looking Rexall.

I'm glad I brought the sweater because it is freezing cold on the street corner. I text the hook-up: "Hi! I've arrived and taken the wrong exit, is it OK if we meet in front of the Rexall Drug Store instead of Shopper's?! LOL!"

I'm unsure which way is north and which way is south. Perhaps this does not matter in North York, where you can just say *the mall* to indicate directions. I cross the street to the Harcross Centre, sit outside on a granite bench and vape.

I wait and vape, vape and wait. I wonder if the teenagers in North York are property speculating and driving up housing prices, and how they manage generally without adult supervision. I'm convinced the teenagers are looking at me with stern disapproval, the way the people looked at me in Flatbush, New York, when I was running around looking for a pay phone wearing a semi-transparent Indian hippy shirt, tight, white hot pants from Joe Fresh and sandals, which would not be a positive thing. Or perhaps they haven't seen an adult in a while. The vape produces impressive clouds of pipe-tobacco-y sweet smoke, but makes me cough like I'm going to hack up my remaining functional alveoli.

I text, "Hi, I'm wearing blue shorts, sandals, a jean jacket and I'm reading!"

I text, "Hi, I'm still waiting for you in front of the Harcross Centre! Sure hope you're getting these!"

I text, "I'd feel a lot better if you were responding!"

I text, "I'm waiting fifteen more minutes! LOL!"

My phone has just shut itself off with a little Bronx cheer, like, "I'm on strike for better working conditions, loser. You might at least charge me." I turn it on again. The screen is on power-saver mode, like, "I'm working to rule, buddy. And you call *me* dim!"

I call the hook-up. A voice says, "The wireless customer you are trying to reach is not available at this time." I have two dollars and fifty cents, in dimes, and I'm realizing that the hook-up has come out without his phone, or the hook-up doesn't have a phone plan but is using an app—or the hook-up is a wanker who has pulled one over on me.

I WANDER ALONG THE BYWAYS AND ALLEYS OF North York, in the process walking directly into a plate glass window in a wistful attempt to re-enter the Yonge-Sheppard Centre, the mall that is the wrong mall (because for reasons of late-blooming vanity I stopped wearing my glasses about a year ago. This helps me look better except when walking into plate glass windows, when I look as dumb as I did when wearing glasses).

In the mall that is the wrong mall I effortlessly find, now that there is no reason to find, the Shopper's Drug Mart, where I wait for the historical thrill of knowing my hook-up had waited there, and for the practical matter of charging my phone via a socket located on a nearby pillar—which turns out to be just a decorative gew-gaw socket installed merely for its visual flair and architectural irony and which does not charge my phone.

I take my uncharged phone and myself up the escalator with the sign that points down and emerge once again street level. Twilight has faded into night in North York, probably because of the higher latitude, and I have that rising panic I feel in dreams where I suddenly realize there will be a terrible gut-wrenching eternal calamity if I don't get on the train that will take me to that clandestine meeting at Wembley Arena with Justin and Chrystia Freeland and my high school Phys Ed teacher, and I must persist despite the annoying inconveniences that I'm wearing only my underpants and pushing a Steinway concert grand in front of me on a luggage trolley.

Crazily, because I don't know his address, only the street and that it is "directly across from the station," I decide to try and find the hook-up's apartment building. I wander along the back alley behind another mall onto a residential street.

Here I spot a young Asian dad and his son, the only pedestrians I've seen so far who are not teenagers, and I slink up behind them silently like a ghost cat approaching its prey, so that they shriek and jump in the air when I say excuse me. After they've calmed down, they point me to Yonge Street, which means I've asked, for example, someone in Times Square if they could point me to 42nd Street.

Then it hits me: I only know my hook-up by his screen name, and I did not envision myself, in the movie of the week that will be my lasting contribution to Canadian culture, asking random residents of the building, as they exited or entered, "Excuse me, do you happen to know in which apartment Big-Hung-Bubble-Butt-4U might be found?"

I did not see myself doing that with anything like nonchalance.

I DECIDE TO GIVE UP AND HEAD back to civilization, or, in a pinch, just absolutely anywhere that's not North York. I don't have enough to make the subway fare, which is not usually a problem at this hour, when the TTC ticket booth guys abandon the booth to go for haircuts or play Parcheesi behind the doors marked "Employees Only."

However, this is North York. The normal laws of physics do not apply. When I reach Sheppard Station I find that in this wacky topsy-turvy mall desert of furrow-browed teenagers the ticket booth guy is clearly visible, looking work-ethical and fierce, bristling with multiculturalism and wiry, fiery red hair.

I consider just dumping the inadequate handful of dimes into the fare box and striding away, but that's like fare-dodging and I could be arrested, though this rarely happens.

I am the adult in the room and I am nothing if not compliant. My fare-dodging strategy will be to age myself to "golden oldie" status, a little white lie which requires the addition of three years.

This is a concession which I would not, before today, have considered psychologically safe, but I have been beaten on the anvil of desire and tempered in the purifying crucible of rejection and I no longer care. I will pretend I am disoriented and in the throes of early-onset senile dementia, which I now view less as a tragedy and more like a coping mechanism.

I approach the booth.

"Excuse me, do you have a seniors' fare?" I make my voice querulous and raspy, as though I have just torn out my feeding tube and fled the Sunset Lodge. I only wish I had a kerchief and shawl.

"Ten — Seniors' teeckets? Vhat? Vhat?"

"I think I'm — a little — short…"

Ticket Booth Guy looks at me like he just recently spotted something similar crawling out from under a rock.

"Jus' go troo!"

Life, they tell me, can reasonably often gift us with random moments of bliss that sneak up unexpectedly and just as quickly pass, leaving gratitude and nostalgia in their wake.

I'm not convinced about the bliss thing, but I can confidently say that humiliation this made-to-order is rarely experienced without participation in a spelling bee, awakening in a urine-soaked bed or attaching pornographic selfies to the email of recommendation you are sending to your friend's probation officer. My tender dialogue with Mister Go-Troo is humiliation perfection.

I AM ON THE SOUTHBOUND SHEPPARD-YONGE subway train. I am so freezing cold and so demoralized that I am alternately crashing asleep like a marionette with its strings cut, then waking up with an audible high-pitched yelp as the train pulls out of each station.

I left home at six-fifteen. It is ten-thirty as the subway train approaches Wellesley. Normally I get off at College, one stop further, but I am suddenly blindsided by whimsy, and I decide to get off here and walk the rest of the way.

The streets are fairly quiet on a Monday night, but it's still the gay village, or what's left of it that drugs, rising rents and quasi-equality haven't ravaged, so there are still flickers of that tawdry, hot-dogs-for-dinner, dirty-bingo, drag-queen, drunken-sex circus I sometimes guiltily, secretly miss.

Nothing disappoints quite as much as getting exactly what you asked for, and now that the larger-than-life, extravagant outlaws have been homogenized, suburbanized, deflated and dispersed, mediocrity and misery have filled the void. Goodbye, desperados and Doc Martens; hello, homelessness and heroin.

I cross Jarvis, and now I am walking past the Petro-Canada gas station with its convenience store and twenty-four hour A&W Burger.

And a voice calls out, "David? David!"

I look at the car stopped at the lights one west-bound lane away from the curb, the car in which the driver is leaning over and calling to me.

"It's Ben!" says Ben.

He drives around the corner, turns into the gas station lot, pulls up next to me. I hop into the car. He's still so handsome it brings tears to my eyes just to sit next to him. Everything's all right. It's old stuff, what happened, and we've moved on. We're cool.

At the one exquisitely-timed moment when he's stopped at the red light and I'm right there on the sidewalk, I encounter someone whose warm touch I've missed, a soul I never meant to hurt, and become friends with him again.

This is why synchronicity is my atheist substitute for faith, God for the godless.

So You Wanna Have a Gay Orgy?

You're in the dead zone, that stretch of time somewhere between 2AM and dawn, when normal lovers of every configuration, from standard issue to unimagined, are

enjoying the sweaty fulfillment of eagerly-anticipated dates made early the previous evening, or even, in cases of terminal normality, entire days in advance.

You, on the other hand, threw out *normal* decades ago, along with those toe rubbers your mom bought for you during the great blizzard of '91; monogamy; and the office job that interfered with your superior alternative of sitting at home, poor, staring into space while smoking.

That's why you never have any idea what's happening until it happens. This is what you call "spontaneity".

And when you think about it, as you now do for the first time, you've always assumed that spontaneity would free you up to choose one of the unlimited, or at least several, equally delightful options waiting for you, like an enticing selection of donut holes at Tim Horton.

Right now the only choices are tedium (staying where you are) or defeat (leaving). You're naked and sitting on the edge of some random dude's bed in some random condo somewhere between Maitland and Homewood, watching porn with a bunch of other naked dudes who, just like you, were hoping to show up, score some drugs from random dude, and then sneak out before random dude caught on.

Random dude is currently unavailable. Random dude is in the bathroom, scrubbing the floor tiles with a toothbrush. He's been there for an hour.

Someone breaks the awkward silence. "Gee, I sure wish we could be doing that!" he says, indicating the porn on the screen.

Everyone laughs politely, he sure does have a point, but no one makes any kind of move.

What does Miss Manners say about starting the orgy without the host? It seems impolite, but then again, you wouldn't want the orgy to get cold! Ann Landers and Dear Abby are non-committal. Is the answer a kind of esoteric knowledge, like which fork to use for the fish, and always refusing a second helping of the soup? Or should it be obvious, like not tying your napkin around your neck like a bib or drinking the contents of the finger bowl?

This is when you get the idea: You could do this *so much better*. Right? Your very own great, big, sleazy gay orgy. It needn't even involve canapés or stuffed olives.

All you need to do is a bit of—and here you give an involuntary shudder, you may even experience a wave of nausea, so deeply upsetting to you is the idea—*planning*.

Nonetheless, over the next few days and weeks, once you've accepted the need for planning and can just about tolerate the accompanying dry heaves, this idea becomes an obsession—

—until, one fateful night, every greedy puff on the glass pipe is urging you, like a Pilgrim foisting a small-pox infected blanket on a wary native, to throw a great, big, sleazy-to-the-max, partied-up gay orgy, so you can finally shout to whoever's got their windows open, "Hand me those fishnet tights, Lana Del Ray—I've arrived!"

PRE-GAY ORGY PLANNING

This is where I come in, and I should probably first qualify myself.

Naturally, a great, big, messy, body-fluid-stained gay orgy is not something to be taken on lightly.

I mean, up in Fenelon Falls you might settle for a box of Triscuits, some onion dip in a pull-tab can and spin-the-bottle with whoever turns up from Bell Canada, but dude, you're in Toronto, now.

No running down the aisles and follow the arrows, OK?

It's a Buddhist thing. This is my first qualification. I am Gay Orgy Buddha. Follow the protocols I give you, because when you try to do things exactly the same way as everybody else, you reveal your unique, true self.

Which is just another way of saying that your incompetence at following the protocols sticks out like an endlessly entertaining sore thumb, but at least it's YOUR incompetence.

So, take heart, little klutzky!

Second qualification, I am well known on the Toronto scene as the guy who spent forty-eight hours, naked and high, in a bathhouse, alternately wandering the corridors and lying on the little cot in my room in my signature position, the "Joan Collins" (knees behind my ears making me more attractive to men, or that's the theory).

And during that forty-eight hours I was not so much as glanced at by another person. Yes, that's right: I failed to have sex in a bathhouse. And that got me a-thinkin', as Barack Obama surely must have said at some point.

Bottom line, I know where you're coming from. You've had it with togetherness at the breakfast table, eating broiled grapefruit with the broiled-grapefruit spoons, arguing about which Freedom Convoy trucker is totally hot; Justin's beard?—Yes or No?; and whether Alberta, to be honest, even exists.

I get it. You're tired of that weird intimacy of dinners for two, making eye contact over the pork tenderloin – I mean, what's that icky, breathing-down-your-neck boondoggle?—and knowing someone's name—as if!—before you excuse yourself, head to the men's room and blow the busboy on the baby changing tray.

When you get back to your table, your dinner date, "oojamacallit," is upset.

Upset? Whoa! Don't smother me, Princess Cling-Wrap!

FUN AND GAMES

Anyone can throw a party, hand his guests a garbage bag for their clothes, then lie face down, in a coma. You're better than that.

Devise some games that will give your evening structure and your guests something to bond over instead of just bending over.

Try these fun, ball-stretching icebreaker party games on for size!

Let's play: "Opera Diva"!

Paper your tiny, junior one-bedroom apartment with life-size photos of Maria Callas. Then, while everyone stands around naked, griping about how long it took them to get there on the TTC, pelt them with radishes.

First round: Everyone hunts for an ugly, eligible Greek billionaire, nails one, bores him, gets whiny, blows all their high notes at La Scala, then gets jilted for someone who's not so totally high maintenance 24/7. Give it a rest, Screecharella! Prize is a good night's sleep sometime way in the future.

Second round: Everyone stands around naked, eating radishes and griping about how long it took them to get to the Four Seasons Centre on the Queen streetcar because of all the work on the tracks. It's, like, they deliberately do it on weekends just to annoy people!

"Vissi d'Arte" naked karaoke: Players have to sing the entire aria from "Tosca", then jump off your balcony onto a mattress while screaming Tosca's immortal dying words: "Fuck you, Scarpia! Last one before God's a rotten egg!"

First one to hit the mattress and not bounce up again gets the blue ribbon. While you're at it, might as well just stay on the mattress.

Time-saving tip: There's no need to warn the neighbours in advance as they're pretty much beyond caring at this point.

Quick Between-Game Breather: Everyone stands around naked, griping about how long it took them to get there from Burlington on the stupid GO Train. And you'll never fucking believe this but—a Chinese person sat right next to them! Why are they so goddamn pushy?

Let's play: "Naked QAnon"!

Complete the final word in this sentence: "A world-wide cabal of pedophile Democrats and liberal Hollywood elites are destroying my beautiful, freedom-loving c_unt_ _."

"Save the Children" Nostalgia Time: We celebrate the murky-lurky origins of QAnon! Toss a coin to see who has to sing "Come to the Florida Sunshine Tree" as professional homophobe Anita Bryant, then re-enact getting fired by the Citrus Marketing Board after all the gay bar no-orange-juice "protests" of outrage.

Extra points for explaining why alcoholic gay men believe that not drinking Screwdrivers for a week is like a suffragette throwing herself under a horse.

Finish with a Satanic Ritual involving a trafficked baby, followed by a leisurely grooming supervised by Baphomet, Hillary, or, honestly, whoever's available.

As a special reward for being such good sports, participants are offered either a shot of "L'Oréal Infernal Rejuvenation Serum with Adrenochrome", or "How about you lie down for a nice little nap on the vivisection trolley?"

Hard to decide, right? LOL!

CHOOSING YOUR GUESTS

You can't have just anyone come into your home only to find their bare feet sticking to the floor you haven't washed in five years. You've got standards!

And whether they like impaling their taints with needles, snorting horse tranquillizer, or just crave the odd snack of steaming-hot excrement, there's one thing you must must *must* remember: NO FAT PEOPLE! Or OLD PEOPLE. Like Millennials!

Are you kidding me? You didn't get yourself all buffed up just to let a bunch of fat Millennials touch your astonishing nine inches (when shot at the right angle), then trash the place.

Instead, be sure to invite:

The Only Bottom in The Room

"Little Miss Bossy Butt". Don't try to steal his limelight, detach any of the body parts currently suctioned to his mouth, or squeeze yourself onto even a corner of his Lululemon yoga mat.

You're hoping for something like NAFTA, but for your junk. Forget it! It'll be like, you're a bunch of Canadian cheddar and he's Trump slapping you with import duties.

You might as well just let him be the star, which rank he clearly deserves simply by having the gall to assert his dominance—while everyone else stands around griping about how the ticket collector at Davisville Station was asleep in the booth again, so they just took the train without paying. Fucking TTC!

The Person Slumped, Weeping, in the Corner

This guest adds a piquant dry-down to the proceedings. He is the pinch of smoked Spanish paprika, the finely-minced lemon balm, the chiffonade of Thai basil, garnishing the roiling, soupy, sweaty, man-meaty cassoulet of the main course; in other words, that throuple arguing in the bedroom, or anyone still breathing on the mattress underneath your balcony after the paramedics leave.

Why is he slumped, weeping, in the corner? It's possible he just spotted his ex enjoying himself with—actually, just "enjoying himself".

He could be tripping out on one too many gummi bears, or he might have failed to, as it were, cram the sad clown of his flaccid tool into the clown car of the new guy in town.

(New guy—? Seriously? If these guests were ground beef from

Loblaw's, they'd all be stickered "50% OFF! ENJOY TONIGHT!")

Our long-suffering host—event planner, Mollie Maid, and High Priest of the Cum Rag—will set him right. He'll spot Person Slumped from across the room and, with a vocal projection that would do Merman proud, belt out: "We think we found your Prince Albert. And you'll never guess—it was inside Albert!"

Can't Hold Their Street Drugs

Blessèd Judy, Mother of Liza! These influencers are very very busy locating the secret cameras hidden in the walls, the computer monitor, and the soft furnishings.

They are frantic as they discover new hackings of their phones they don't know how to use, mysterious transactions in their empty bank accounts, and pictures they've never seen before taken in the bedrooms they've never slept in.

Look! Patrick is standing naked on your West Elm wing back chair, exposing himself, like a dowager Sugar Plum Fairy harrowing the ballroom of ingenues who would usurp her crown, to a entire class of fledgling ballerinas in the rehearsal hall across the street!

Look! Jimmy is cutting his favorite recipe—Boeuf bourguignon, of course!—out of your priceless first edition of Julia Child's Mastering the Art of French Cooking, Volume 1!

And there's Evan, painting over the camera lenses of your iPhone 12 with a black Sharpie, the better to foil any beam of taboo porn that might be, right this second, snaking into Gmail, addressing itself to his boss, his mother, his fiancé, Roger, and the news desk at The National Post, and pressing SEND!

Better leave town, boys! What a bummer, to have all their sketchy paranoid secrets finally uncovered by an alien army of invisible cyber-criminals who were just bored enough to find them even remotely interesting.

The Talker

It sure was open-minded of your Uncle Phil to agree to come to your super pervy gay sex orgy. He's so cool!

He's rooted to a spot in the rapidly-emptying centre of the room, flaunting his 70's man bush, sipping cranberry cocktail, smoking Black Russians, and talking very loudly about Justin's ankle bracelet, his decades-long struggle with constipation, and his evening class in concrete furniture design.

Also, can you believe he waited *sixteen minutes* for a Leaside bus, then three came at once! What, do they travel in packs for safety?

The Gigglers

What is it about the tinkle of campy, barely suppressed giggles that grates fingernails down the blackboard of your dark journey?

Lee and Billy are all breathless gossip, tart assessments and dog-whistle-pitched chortles that bring to mind a Teletubbies convention being chaired by Alvin the Chipmunk.

Not if, but when, they get asked to leave, they'll just cross the street and haunt Spa Excess with their glittering repartee; haunt it the way the soft plink of falling tentworms haunts your citronella-scented picnic spot on Cherry Beach.

Please note: when Billy finds something amusing, he actually *says the words* "tee-hee!"

The Only Top Who Could Make It, and He's Really Just Versatile When Forced by Circumstance

First of all, even if his profile states, "Brutal Top"—he's a bottom. *We're all bottoms, Murgatroyd McGraw.* We're gay for Pete's sake!

Even so, his profile insisted "no total bottoms!", which, as he's a Brutal Top who's really a bottom, seems a little finger-pointy. He gets away with this because, truly, he's a gay unicorn, the elusive shape-shifter known as the "versatile", which is to say, a bottomy-top or a toppy kind of bottom, depending on your needs.

Sure, he'll come to your gay orgy, but before he does, he needs to carve out some territory so you know how lucky you are.

He also casts doubt on the authenticity of your photo, your choice to use substances, and is adamant: if you use words like "mangina" you are *persona non grata* before you even had a chance to be *grata*.

Look at him go! With a build like Thomas the Tank Engine and the stamina of the Energizer Bunny, this guy's gonna be selling subscriptions! If we're lucky, he might even take off his sunglasses while he services the room like a prize bull let loose in a feedlot.

But it's iffy: after all, his colleagues at the World Bank, Goldman Sachs, Parliament Hill, and all the other places he's never worked might recognize him!

Still, we're grateful he took time out of his busy schedule staring at his messaging app for a word from the two guys he hasn't blocked, and using the FlexMaster chest expander that cost him two box tops back in

'73, to be God's gift to faggotry.

Well, flush out my hole with a saline douche! Thanks for the memories, Helena Hungwell!

The S&M Queens

Surely even the slowest heteronormative hunk of alpha male knows by now that this is Toronto shorthand for "Stand and Model."

SNACKS AND CRUDITÉS

Conversation

Conversation at your hot gay orgy must be limited to sex talk only! This really is no time to be bantering about the climate change hoax, blaming George Soros for your failures, or tossing out statistics about gaseous nebulae.

You should need no more than the following vocabulary—which, incidentally, can be repurposed for a multitude of different occasions, from solemn (you get married) to silly (you get married in a church, with groomsmen in sweet-pea chiffon):

- Fuck
- Fuck yeah
- Holy fuck
- Oh yeah, unhunh, you love it
- There Ya Go!

Let's deploy our corpus in a hypothetical scenario: John sees Timothy and decides he's ready for a glazing of hot jizz like a pan of brownies fresh from the oven is ready for a drizzle of chocolate ganache.

John sidles up to Timothy, intending to ask him if he enjoyed the Moncrieff version of Proust or the Moncrieff-Kilmartin retranslation, then remembers it's a big gay orgy:

John: FUCK....
Timothy: Oh yeah...
J: Unhunh!
T: Fuck Yeah! You love it!
J: Holy Fuck! Yeah!
T: Unhunh there ya go!
J: Oh, FUCK YEAH! Unhunh!

You can see that what you dismissed as a limited vocab can actually hold its nuanced own in the poetry stakes against, say, the King James Bible, any day of the week.

Verbal our socks off, Oscar and Wilde!

Bowls of peanuts: a cautionary tale

Some snacks are ill-advised. You scarf a handful of honey-roasted peanuts to keep up your strength, then dive onto someone's dick like a hungry piranha, only to surface and see... Yep.

That's why Tommy the Toothbrush recommends flossing after every meal! There's nothing for it but to do a quick hand-off to the next guy in line.

Bonus tip: Your taste buds may shout "pralines!" but resist the urge to bite down.

Pizza

Slime on a slab tempts you to a greasy time-out after demonstrating reverse-cowgirl. The boiling hot Mozzarella slides off the slick of tomato sauce right onto the balls of the guy who groped the pizza delivery boy, and who is now unconscious in the front hallway, from what you interpret as a good dose of GHB.

After you've addressed the first-degree burns, it's fair to consider him your prey!

But in fact the pizza delivery boy decked him unconscious, and is right now calling the sexual assault squad at 51 Division.

Fun while it lasts is the name of the game!

Condoms

Unless you're referring to one half of a legendary Broadway musical partnership whose first name is "Betty"—*Huh?*

Wet wipes

These come in handy for those icky moments, like when you're covered with J-Lube, that elastic, stringy gloop used for veterinary scenes like inseminating a cow.

And they call *us* kinky!

This is when you notice that the host just used a wet-wipe to tackle the J-Lube, but the wet-wipe dissolved.

What's in J-Lube, seriously? And why do nine out of ten cows prefer it to all other brands?

BACKGROUND AMBIANCE

It is essential, at this your first, and probably last, out-of-this-world gay orgy, to have background porn videos. This helps people remember that this isn't just any old party.

This party has had *planning* alternating with the dry heaves.

This isn't just a gathering where some random guys ("your friends") get naked, and stand around not having sex while bitching about how long it took them to get to work on the Scarborough Light Rail because of all the immigrants. Not the whole night, anyway!

This is a gathering that's all about everyone else getting it on, while you repair to the bathroom and scrub the floor tiles with a toothbrush until 51 Division arrives.

You, our gracious host, will appoint someone to choose the porn from the vast selection available online, because, delegate; also, you're way too busy scooping up big, stretchy, mucous-y strands of J-Lube after someone spilled the half-gallon container all over your vintage cherrywood RCA Victor entertainment console.

The delegated pornmeister overthinks. He wonders if it would be hot to watch straight porn for a change—and just to clarify, no, it wouldn't—but, too late: he just clicked somewhere random on StraightOrgyTube dot com, and is now regaling the three remaining guests, currently coming to blows about who stole whose stash, with *"Trashed big-tittie'd Latina ho's desperate for cash gonna shave their beaver at the CN Tower".*

You, gracious host, enveloped in mucus, start shrieking, *"Why are you subjecting us to this?!",* prompting the terrified pornmeister to click somewhere random on ClassicEuroTwinks dot com.

The final dregs of the party—you and the pornmeister—are immediately bathed in the nostalgic orangey glow of old videotape, and hypnotized by the synthesized THROB of a soundtrack which stands in for "music" in the same way that a faded photocopy of a hamburger satisfies the desire for an actual hamburger.

Man, could you use a big, juicy hamburger not covered with J-Lube right now! Just before the door slams, you hear:

"Choose your own fucking porn!"

...

It's blissful, being by yourself again, isn't it? Go on, have a little happy-cry. You deserve it.

You're sticking to the floor, the place reeks, and later today, around three PM, while waiting for your almond-milk pumpkin-spice latte at Jet Fuel, you'll discover that used condom on your head, but still.

It didn't go too badly, really, considering. Right now you're mesmerized by the hot gay shenanigans onscreen, because this porn has a plot, and here's when you get The Idea: you could do this *so much better*. Right? You stare, fascinated and repelled, drowning in the orange glow as...

> *The Boy Scout troop of EuroTwinks—hand-picked by LuLu LaRoche, porn director extraordinaire!—has arrived at the quaint Bavarian mountain lodge that looks like a giant cuckoo clock, and by an almost inconceivable act of serendipity every last Boy Scout has forgotten his wallet! The solution is obvious: they must offer themselves, each and every one, as gay-pervy, hot-orgy, sex slaves—*

—but before you can start taking notes, your instinct for survival—god knows it's rarely off the mark—tells you that you should really offer a couple of slices of cold pizza to

those officers from 51 Division who are standing in your hallway.

Apps in Development

I was exploring "WhyDon'tchaDoodly", a new app that suggests counterintuitive, humiliating ways to fill up your stupid, empty life, when it occurred to me that developing a few apps of my own might be in order.

It's only a legend, by the way, that I was the inspiration for the IT specialist's maxim, "the problem is between the chair and the keyboard."

What does that even mean? The only thing between the chair and keyboard is me. *Random!*

I've always been an "ideas man," which has saved me a lot of the grief which I would have suffered if I'd actually taken any of my ideas and coaxed them that one step further into reality.

Reality? Who needs that kind of downward vibe, squelch-your-hopes-and-dreams boondoggle? I like the purity of ideas, unsullied by tawdry concepts such as realization or iterations.

I did get interested at one point in "agile development," which is basically taking your idea and getting a bunch of nerds to build a concept version, then releasing it to the unwitting public, that's you, when it's not even remotely ready so we can get free quality assurance testing.

This goes well with "agile attention spans" so that by the time we've ironed out all the bugs, our target audience is already bored with our product and have moved on to something else, like iPhone 35, which folds into a piece of origami, charges with a cord that hasn't been invented yet, and reinstates the headphone jack.

That is, IF you're invited to buy it! It's pretty friggin' exclusive! LOL!

This app development thing is really like standard business stuff. You gotta have a vision and a mission, so like : "I see this company running a small banana republic in cahoots with the CIA in five years," could be your vision, and the mission would be "sell a whole shitload of something people don't really want" but don't fret about that because that's where my marketing genius comes in, boo-boo.

So the app bit is like, the same deal as finding your "niche." You try and find a void in the market, something that causes burning, itching and flaking, i.e. pain, and then you make up something that heals that pain, and then that's what your business will be.

This is like a "widget". And don't worry if you don't know what that means. It doesn't matter if you couldn't tell a widget from a big pile of spaghettini with clams, widgets are now your new life—which you already hate!—and for which you gave up your corporate middle management job, with healthcare and pension.

Take a moment and pat yourself on the back, or anywhere you can reach, frankly, and contemplate how far you've come. There's no doubt about it: this, my wannabe self-made, crying-cause-you're-happy billionaire, is a business decision made of win!

Now, moving forward, you focus relentlessly on that niche. You don't try to be everything to everybody. Heavens to Betsy, no!

So for example, some people are in pain when they are not popular. Invent something, no matter how ludicrous, that could boost their popularity and they will flock to that product the way white cops flock to a Black ten-year-old with a suspicious-looking My Little Pony knapsack.

Thinking of two approaches, one is a sex widget and the other is a money widget.

Because I am a marketing guru, I'm going to use a startling, off-the-wall anecdote that will nonetheless give you in-depth understanding of the problem, viz., the sex approach.

Just this afternoon I heard some pigeons—or "New Brunswick chickens" as I like to call them—coo cooing and wattle wattling and whorr whorring like the entire female cast of "Depraved Family Fun dot com" on my balcony and I ran to investigate.

Well, no less than three pigeons were having group sex in the corner of my balcony, the same corner where they gave birth last year to a congenitally deformed baby pigeon that was, freakishly, bigger than the parents.

I nurtured that six-toed, Dodo-feathered gimp pigeon until I couldn't take the stress anymore and just shoveled it off the balcony under cover of night. Let the downstairs people take care of it for a while!

But the salient point here is: Even pigeons are hanging out without you, having group sex in broad daylight, and you can't even score on GrindScroff! Even with those pics from '85, which you still get away with because, irony of ironies, no one actually meets you to experience the terminal door shock that would arise from the in-flesh reckoning.

And, eureka! Here comes my inspiration, directly from those hi-rise hobo hawks: For the sex approach, you will design a "penis extending glove" that fits over guys' small, barely visible penises and, like, voila!

As long as they don't take their pants off for the rest of their lives, they are instantly more popular with those modern-type women who directly control their own sex lives and are into guys with large, or even just normal sized dicks.

Face it, they're probably thrilled you *have* a dick! Which kind of tells you that, with a bit more research, you could have determined that a penis extender was not really a viable idea because no one needs it, not that being unnecessary is really a drawback, generally. I mean, who *needs* a half-gallon yogurt incubator with more settings than an ICU intubation pump? Exactly.

So, anyway, ignoring that SNAFU, major bump in popularity there. And I've got the perfect name for it: Dickly! I can see the packaging artwork like it was already in my hands!

Or maybe, whaddaya think, Cockify. Is Cockify better, does it resonate, differentiate, is it synergistic, does it give you the look and feel, the brand? All righty, then!

This is all just off the top of my marketing-guru head, you realize. Right? Pay attention, you've already wasted the first half of your life, before you met me, so it would behoove you to pick up a tip or two.

The only possible glitch is, how would you let your target babe know about your new-found fake hung-nification, beyond just you and your lawyer taking her to a food court at the Eaton Centre and announcing it while she's got a mouthful of chop suey? Right? Good job one of us is on the ball!

I see a raised hand. What's that? A sandwich board with a big hole in it at dick level? That is an awesome idea! Then also this would be synergistic with gay men, who are all about the big dicks, it's all they think and talk and dream about. Very good!

Because you could have a trillion bucks in Bitcoin, look like Ryan Gosling and have the cure for COVID-19 in a jar in your three-car garage but without a big dick? Get over here to the end of the line-up that starts with Gomer Pyle, ya big goof.

Gay men are The Big Dick Meisters, that's for sure. In fact if you sneak up on any random gay man, you'll find he's muttering to himself constantly and if you get close enough—but not too close, because AIDS, right?—you'll hear what he's actually saying is : *"big dicks, big dicks...!"*

So now your sex widget is a gay penis extender with "optional" portable glory hole. Agile! Adapt!

Except you know, and I know, that a gay man would not consider a gloryhole optional once you've casually mentioned it's available. Without a glory hole, and most important of all, the wall the glory hole is in, they would have to see the guy's face!

Ewwww! What sort of sicko needs that kind of weirdly intimate connection on a routine blow 'n go? Seriously? LOL!

So, gather round, gay demographic, don't forget the knee pads, or maybe one of those throw cushions you got from Wayfair which are on special because they use them as packing material for transporting children to their white slavery delivery points. On close inspection, some of them are, shall we say, not in the most pristine condition. The throw cushions, I mean.

I'm pumped, I dunno about you! So that's how the sex approach might work in determining what it is you're going to sell. Remember though, it's never what you actually sell that you're actually selling. Jesus Murphy, did you miss the remedial classes?

You're selling hopes and dreams and relief from pain. And some people are in pain because no one loves them, and others because, no Rolex. It's all down to the human condition.

Wow, that got deep!

The financial approach is more straightforward, i.e., if you have more money more people will love you, plus you can pay for all the sex you want. Crack whores have to feed their kids, after all!

Gay guys need a little brown bottle of that room freshener, and definitely some new piercings in unusual places, because they can still ride a bike in relative comfort. But whoever is paying homage on the other side of the wall, look, it's a pair of gender-agnostic lips on someone's little buddy, and that's their hope, dream and relief from pain. We've solved the problem that you made up!

Give yourself a nice, big pat somewhere you've never thought of patting yourself before. Why? Because You Deserve It. Does that feel good or what?

So, we've covered your vision, and probably your mission statement, too. Think of all the money you saved not going to the Rotman School of Management! You can invest that dosh in something useful for your 'ho, like a hand-blown crack pipe from Sunshine Paraphernalia. It will look *so meta* when she yanks down her panties on Gerrard Street and screams

"Where's my baby daddy!" while pulling used condoms out of her up-do.

Anyway, here are three of the apps that I've devised and am tendering for development.

SUBMERGEDLY™

This app for Influenzas—or is it "Influencers"? I always get them mixed up—monitors South Pacific islands for water levels rising due to global warming.

Choose any random South Sea Island, and when water levels are peaking, fly in on your private jet, stay at the Ooga Booga Inn, where the hand-sewn bamboo sheets caress your lithe young body and the fish is so fresh on your plate it winks at you as you take the first delectable bite.

Eat good food, fuck the natives, and fly out again, after giving a 10-star review on YELP. Post to Instagram, then watch the wannabes wet their Victoria's Secret undergarments when they find the island is now inaccessible because, being submerged, it doesn't exist anymore! Right?

Beauty!

MY DOG DIED-IFY™

Owe money to friends? Owe anything to anybody? Don't perspire all over the miniscule annoyances!

This app will generate iron-clad excuses as to why they're fucking unreasonable to remind you over and over. Settings for "Pushover" (What do you expect? They kicked me out of rehab!) to "OnToYou" (My five-year-old daughter, who I just found out is NOT MINE, was diagnosed with ADHD! I've got more important shit, dude!).

See them squirm with the cognitive dissonance of angry plus sad, until they break down and say, "OK, OK. Give it to me in product."

Win-win with both wins for you! *Gnarly!*

ANON-SEX-GRIND-SCROFF RANDOMIZER™

Here's a familiar scene: You, tearing your hair out every Friday night after you've got wasted on Molly and are trying to line up, helloooo, some anonymous casual sex on GrindScroff. And let's face it, you're popular, dude!

Hashtag *Quel ennui* **So Boring!**

Problem is, all this time you've been thinking there was a right choice. Random!! Hashtag Loser! *Hashtag Sad!*

Just fire up Anon-Sex-Grind-Scroff Randomizer™ and let it do the heavy lifting of having no standards! Anon-Sex-Grind-Scroff Randomizer™ arranges up to ten "dates" for your evening, then blows off nine of them with a fake address, leaving lucky number ten headin' your way!

Now you can relax, take some more Molly and lie face down on the living room floor, primed for the time of your life with—who cares, right? You're so fucked up, even solo masturbation would count as anonymous sex.

Premium version includes insurance so you can replace your stolen smartphone, laptop and Amex card, and an AirBNB account so you can move restlessly from flat to flat all over Europe after they post those nude pics of you passed out on your living-room floor to LinkedIn!

Hashtag Totally Worth It!

SO I'VE GIFTED YOU MY ideas. No skin off my nose if you just go back to bed and pull the Cheetos bags on top of you. I'm heading for one blissful week, possibly less, to the Ooga Booga Inn,

where the linen sheets and the hungry natives await!

Pandemonium

CoronaZombies

There ain't no one in this whole wide world more outraged than a white American who has been told they can't do something they want to do, or that they must do something they don't want to do. Got that?

This is especially irksome if the must-do or can't-do has been mandated in order to help other people, maybe even society as a whole.
Other people? Society as a whole? Are you *nuts*?
That's *communism!*
I will attempt to explain. The rather freakazoid people shown in the illustration are in Columbus, Ohio, where I think they are storming a legislature because they have been told to wear masks. Honestly, I've forgotten the exact details, but I'm fairly confident they are not just super-excited shoppers pumped up for the Black Friday door-buster at Walmart.
 It will go something like this: Being told to wear a mask is government overreach and a slippery slope. Instead of complying, they'll organize a giant freedom protest, even a full-bore mini-revolution, with historical costumes, openly-carried firearms, placards, an army tank (a bitch to rent, but, seriously, you gotta have an army tank) as well as, who knows, a ring-toss booth, Shetland pony rides and Miss Industrial Waste Ohio waving like indulgent royalty from her float.
One thing's for certain, though: because they're renegades for the day, and don't want to be identified, they will all be wearing masks.
Just—not the masks they were told to wear...
Then there are the people who can't go to their vacation homes. They are the affluent white people of Michigan, whose governor, Gretchen Whitmer, a Democrat, has enacted just about the most rigorous stay-at-

home orders in the US.

She's had to, because apparently Michigan generally and Detroit specifically have extremely high rates of infection, the brunt of this borne by—and I only hope you are standing well away from your vitrine filled with Lalique crystal, lest your fainting from surprise causes you to slam into it—the Black people of Michigan.

African Americans, many of them being the people who have the jobs that keep society moving during a lethal pandemic, the fast-food workers, the health care workers, the grocery store staff, the front liners in essential businesses, have, of course, got it covered about who is going to get that fuzzy end of the coronavirus lollipop.

But the white people, the angry outraged spluttering CoronaZombies, have grabbed their rifles, their bazookas, their automatics and their semi's that the Founding Fathers explicitly recommended— *"... the right of the people to keep and bear Bazookas, shall not be infringed;"* it's right there, in fluent goose quill—and they are mad as hell and not takin' it anymore in front of wherever Gretchen hangs out, and they are chanting "Lock her up!"

(Or, save labour costs and do it yourself! On October 8th, 2020, the FBI announced the arrests of thirteen men who had plotted to *kidnap* that scoldy Gretchen Whitmer and—well, what do you do with a kidnapped governor? We would have been entering, as the phrase goes, "uncharted territory".)

Gretchen Whitmer is called "that Michigan woman" by Trump, the Adolescent-in-Chief, who never met a broad unwilling to toss him her panties while pole-dancing that he could relate to. And it must be said: For Gretchen to be in power as a woman seems well-meaning, if a bit careless. But to be a woman in power and a Democrat is just asking for trouble.

"Lock her up" is not only misogynist but problematic in another way. You see, I have this theory that it shows maturity — remember maturity? Yeah, neither do I—when someone in their teens, or twenties, or even beyond, stops rebelling against parental controls and realizes that some of the advice is actually helpful and sensible.

One day, sick of the emotional effort of being contrary, and deciding that kicking and screaming while pounding your fists and heels on the floor looks a tad undignified, you have a *satori*.

The clouds part to reveal a chorus of angels and you hear them singing that the advice you found so hateful is not just offered so your parents can annoy you with a demeaning reminder that you're a helpless, wet-behind-the-ears, financially dependent walking fetus who wouldn't know to come inside when it's raining and who can't figure out how to press the "ON" button on the microwave.

It's meant to save you the heartache of repeating the same mistakes until your forehead is flatter than Saskatchewan and you've lost all that time. And, to your amazement, because you're now mature, you just go ahead and follow the advice, because now that you're a grown-up you no longer worry so much about what other people think.

You don't have to prove how cool you are, because now, without even noticing your own coolness, you actually are. You don't have to "fit in" any more. Other people can fit in with you, instead.

You've earned it. You've discovered that, although there are seventy-eight buttons on the microwave, one of them for "popcorn" which unfailingly burns popcorn, so that everyone from Orville Redenbacher to Thomas Keller advises, "For the love of god, whatever you do, DON'T use the 'popcorn' button," all you actually need is three buttons: the one for "Beverage," a second button to choose one minute, four minutes or ten minutes, and "ON."

Microwave popcorn, pizza pocket or your twelve-course tasting menu for the George Brown College Culinary Arts Diploma, this is how it works.

But not for the CoronaZombies. They've learned and earned nothing. These guys, and of course it's mostly guys, regress to an embryonic state of helplessness the second they encounter a woman in charge. She instantly morphs from brainless sex object to psycho-mommy, so, stuck in eternal resentful, thwarted adolescence, they automatically rebel.

Their sense of adult, independent manhood is so tenuous, so fragile, that to follow a woman's advice, even the advice that will save them from catching and/or spreading a potentially fatal disease, is to them tantamount to sitting once again in that highchair while she goes, *"And here comes the airplane into the hangar ooogie boogie mumsy wumsy puddin' pie!"* with that spoonful of Gerber carrots.

So they take out their dicks—oh, fine, excuse me for living, guns and cars—and shove their masculinity in our faces. It's all such a tedious, predictable shit show.

I left the apartment to shop for groceries during the past couple of days. I wore my mask. If it saves even one person from infection, why would I not do this simple thing? I do-si-do'ed around the few people I encountered on the sidewalk, and I stood in line, with six feet in front of me and the next person leaving six feet behind me, to enter the grocery store.

Everyone I encountered was wearing a mask.

It was a sunny day, with Spring being all coy about putting on her make-up and peeking around the corner in nothing but a towel.

The day felt calm and there was a big world happening, bigger, at least in that moment, than anyone's problems. There was no one complaining. There were no guns or crazy demos.

That's because Canadians still retain the idea of the social contract. We still understand that there are times when the good of society has to prevail over individual autonomy. Because we have benefits like universal healthcare and subsidised day care, we understand that our elected government works on our behalf. Government isn't an evil entity snatching away our freedom. It's us, working collectively to achieve what we could never accomplish on our own.

As always we have our watered down, hearts-not-in-it, bargain basement versions of the American neediest cases. We have Derek Sloan, an actual member of the Conservative Party of Canada, standing in a freshly-plowed field questioning whether our Chief Public Health Officer, Theresa Tam, "is working for us or for the Chinese," a defiantly racist comment that is universally scorned—

—except by the erstwhile party leader, the gutless Andrew Scheer, who blushes and giggles like a trainee geisha when he's asked if he will condemn the remarks.

Scheer demurs. He waffles. He prevaricates. He breaks out in more nervous dimples than a newborn baby's butt having its first diaper change by Dad. He does everything it's possible to do with words except answer the question or condemn the remarks.

Once again, a woman in power is targeted by whiny, insecure, immature males who just don't know how to deal with her, and who are tacitly given the seal of approval by their wimp leader who's scared that conservative voters won't play with him at recess if he condemns racism and misogyny.

(Derek Sloan also darkly hints that Dr Tam is transgender, and no one has the heart to tell him that, even if she were, being transgender is neither a scandalous secret nor even remotely relevant to her competence at her job. Try to keep up, Derek.)

We then have another guy, who I sense will not be appearing on Mastermind any time soon, noting that the number of Covid-19 cases is nowhere near what was predicted, so he questions whether all this freedom-squashing sheltering in place was necessary.

Dear Stupid Person: The reason the number of cases is lower than predicted is that *we sheltered in place and it worked.* Just exactly how flat does my forehead have to get?

I DO RATHER LIKE THAT THERE'S a Democratic Governor of Michigan called "Gretchen." This is really the first time I've heard that name in real life, the only other instance being as the protagonist in a famous song by Schubert, *"Gretchen am Spinnrade"* or "Gretchen at the spinning wheel," which he wrote just a few days after he was born (child prodigy).

Unfortunately, no sooner had he scraped the grape-jelly-like afterbirth residue off his velvet smoking jacket than he lost the friggin' manuscript in an Uber. Jeezus, dude! No way are you getting that iPhone!

"Das ist *sooooo* wie mir!" was his anguished comment, as the little show-off Schnozzler scrambled to write the whole thing out again from memory. He just happened to be competing with his friend Felix Mendelssohn who had himself just lost the entire manuscript of his incidental music to "A Midsummer Night's Dream" in a London cab a week before.

"Alvays I am immer making ze big *vergessenses* when my Fanny is distracting me," Mendelssohn added, gazing at his firm, really quite toothsome bubble-behind in a huge, Baroque gilt-framed mirror. But of course, he was referring his Schwester, errr, sister, Fanny.

"Fanny," as you know is the diminutive of— What *is* Fanny the diminutive of? Seriously. Let's reverse engineer this.

So "Peggy" is a diminutive of "Margaret." So then, by analogy... Take the "f" of "Fanny" and change it to two letters previous in the alphabet in the non-dim version. So, "D." Then, change the "a" to "e" and then the "g" in "Peggy" represents the doubling of the third consonant, so "n."

Ladies and gents, the mystery is solved. Felix Mendelssohn's sister's actual name was: Dennis Mendelssohn.

I know that Dennis isn't really a Jewish girl's name, but don't forget the horrible anti-Semitism in 19th-century (not to mention 20th- and 21st-century, also this afternoon) Germany. They obviously called their only daughter "Dennis" to give her a big social advantage, which is extra fortunate because, if you look up any pictures of her, Dennis, that is, you'll see she is *keine Ölgemälde*, not even an oil-painting-by-numbers by your six-year-old.

But getting back to Gretchen and her spinning wheel. This song is a setting of a scene from Faust, which is easy to guess because Germans have two pieces of literature: "Faust" and "Steppenwolf" and it's a toss-up on any given day which one they prefer. I don't recall anyone called Gretchen in Steppenwolf, do you? Well, there you go, Faust it is.

Goethe wrote Faust; he's kind of like the German Shakespeare, but more efficient. Germans are all about efficiency. Why have Shakespeare and Christopher Marlowe both sweating buckets getting all those plays ready for the Globe when you can have an all-in-one?

Goethe is the laptop where the screen comes off and turns into a tablet, of German literature. You could probably read Kindle books and make phone calls on a Goethe as well, knowing the Germans.

However, Goethe's most famous achievement is writing the slogan for Audi, "Vorsprung durch Technik" which means "We'd spring some work on you, but technically there isn't any."

HERE'S THE DEAL: THAT STUDY THAT you spent fifteen minutes reading, even though you maxed-out your scientific career in grade nine, the study that "proves" that the risk of vaccination is much higher than they're letting on, proves that the study is faulty, nothing more and nothing less. That's because it "proves" something that, taking the majority of scientific studies into account, cannot be true.

That's right. The fact that it's an outlier counts against it, not for it. It's not the brave face of a renegade scientist revealing secrets of the Deep State. It's the shameful, engineered result of someone with an agenda or the embarrassing outcome of someone who is incompetent at the basic design of a peer-reviewed study.

I may seem rather touchy on the subject. This is because I was the target of a Twitter pile-on (or is it peon? I always get them mixed up) for daring to suggest that the public need not be privy to the esoteric conversations of scientists, seeing as the public is barely competent at remembering their Twitter password, let alone interpreting arcane data.

I was quoted at by angry Twits who'd dredged up info on vaccine "dangers", and called a nasty snob by more angry Twits who wanted to defend the right of ignoramus publicus to make damn fools of themselves.

But seriously. A little knowledge is a very, very dangerous thing, probably worse than no knowledge at all. I wouldn't be a snob for suggesting that most people wouldn't be able to open the hood of their car and point out the carburetor, let alone fix it. I certainly couldn't, could you?

Can we accept that there is specialty knowledge in the world, and specialists in that knowledge, and that scientific knowledge, peer-reviewed, tested and re-tested, and always contingent on new knowledge being revealed, is some of the most, if not THE most, reliable knowledge that exists?

We rely, as Jaron Lanier famously pointed out, on an exquisitely beautiful, all-encompassing web of trust in this world.

Every time we step into an elevator, or enter a building, or cross a bridge, or stick a Pop-Tart in the toaster, we are handing over oodles of trust that the makers of these things employed their specialist knowledge competently, and that we will be whisked to the 49th floor, gaze up at the Sistine Chapel ceiling, end up on the other side of the river, or be transported to Pop-Tart heaven without incident. A thousand-thousand times a day we rely on this web of trust.

But I could no more engineer a bridge, calculate its load-bearing capacity or lay its foundations than I could flap my arms and fly to the moon.

And I'm forgetting airplanes! How very much we rely on the attentiveness of airline mechanics and engineers. To those of you who think checking your emails for correct use of the Oxford comma counts as "being OCD", I am not ashamed to admit I'd like airline mechanics to be certified obsessive-compulsive before taking one of those flying coffins which we're assured are safer to slip into than our bathtubs.

Well, I assure you I count zero times for the occasions on which I have slipped into my bathtub, been depressurized, then sucked into my living room, frozen solid and wearing only one shoe and a pair of cheap earphones.

Given all of these everyday examples of underlying trust, why then do we insist that science and the scientific method, which demand a lifetime of intellectual commitment to truth and verifiable evidence, are football scrums for the masses? These are the same people who don't get that Dr. Fauci, who should have his own Netflix series, a Nobel and maybe an Oscar for his heroism in funding AIDS research, among his many achievements, was simply reporting new knowledge as it happened, and is not a sneaky conspirator pulling the wool over our eyes.

This isn't snobbery. It's heuristics. It's a chance for our brains to say, "OK, I'm taking the short-cut on this one. He's a scientist who agrees with a thousand other scientists, I'm gonna trust what he says."

I just received my first dose of the vaccine. Competently administered at a community centre one block from my home, with almost no waiting in line, no muss or fuss. (The fact that I waited since April to receive this, even though I followed all the instructions for reserving a time online, is a mark against our incompetent provincial leaders, not the scientists who informed them.)

And I can't count the people who asked, "Which one are you going to get? Make sure it's not the—!"

Holy Mary and the Magdalene too! How would I possibly assess "which vaccine" I should ask for? They're all fine, dears! When did you garner your PhD in virology? In between sleeping in the park and shoplifting dinner at Loblaws?

ITEMS I HAVE BAKED, COOKED, OR BOUGHT, THEN EATEN, BY MYSELF, IN THE PAST MONTH OF PANDEMIC LOCK-DOWN:

Two loaves of no-knead bread; two loaves of whole wheat sandwich bread, six purchased croissants, a box of donuts, a box of Timbits;
    A pack of Twinkies and a pack of those pink cakes with coconut on them (Dolly Partons? Hello, Dollies? something about a dolly, anyway);
    Five batches of chapatis;
    Two mix-in-the-pan cakes from the New York Times online;
    An apple cinnamon cake that serves twelve;
    The bowl of buttercream frosting that was meant for the cake;
    Burgers, French fries and onion rings, with mayonnaise, all homemade;
    Eight boxes of Kraft Dinner;
    Three batches of peanut butter cookies, two batches of blondies, five batches of shortbread;
    A can, Blessèd Judy, Mother of Liza, of Chef Boy-ar-dee ravioli and one of chili (the chili wasn't entirely bad, the less said about the ravioli, which smelled like the hallway in a long-term care facility, the better);
    Countless pouches of microwave popcorn (Beverage; 2; ON;)
    And tonight I'm making Chicken Divan, a casserole of chicken breast and broccoli bathed in a cheese béchamel sauce made with whipping cream.
    Coronavirus has more than one trick up its sleeve to kill me. I see that now.
    Luckily, I smoke cigarettes. Because studies currently underway in France apparently indicate—and I'm not making this up—that nicotine may protect you from infection with Covid-19.

Nicotine.

one day after vaccination and only minor side effects so far!

Semantic Bleaching

"Life on hold sucks!"
read the bus shelter ad.

Talking pandemic
With chummy banality
A conspirator's wink

Life on hold

Customers in the supermarket
Frozen in place
Gripping Yorick-skulls of well-traveled lettuce

Exquisitely poised at the switch from
Succulent to wilting

Cash register drawers
Permanently open

And you with your hand always thrust
Deep in your pocket
Searching for the loonie
With your face burning red

And all the disapproving
Shoppers behind you
Congealed like half-conceived monuments
In ferocious attitudes of impatience

Life on hold

Cyclists lassoed by a
Gravitational lariat as they
Round the corner

From now until who-knows-when
Held like rabbits in the moment-before
The eighteen-wheeler
Bearing down on them

Their lungs blasting fireworks
Forever one prayer like
An acupuncture needle in their
Lizard brains, jiggling and tingling

Life on hold for lovers

Caught just before their mouths
Could touch, their lust
Untranslated, love reduced
To aching balls and
The heart-pin pulled

Stuck in the glue-trap of
Another's eyes, sharing
Garlic breath,

Embrace half in, half out
The storm's soft centre

Set against
The sublime stasis of the
Fountain's jets
Whose water dazzles crystals in mid-arc
Stoney, silent
No fizz of refreshment

Life on hold as

An unmoored sun
Brittle and pale yellow
Scrapes the polar cap

While, galaxies distant,
A little girl
Neither child
Nor grown-up

Seized astonished in her solitude
With an ice-cream cone

Now knows that top-most scoops, all
Pink-turquoise sprinkles and
Chocolatey drizzle, must one day
Totter, slip, splatter on the
Pavement's hot griddle

Little girl on hold
Shorn of innocence
Erased with swift amnesia
Never old enough to say

Fuck it
I never liked chocolatey drizzle
All that much

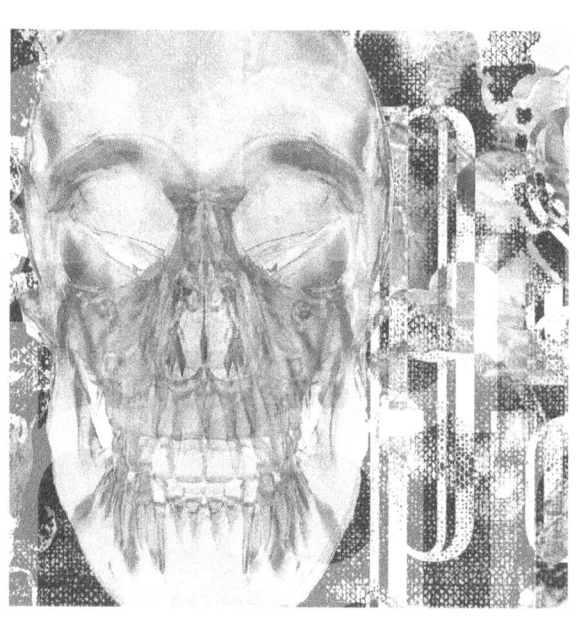

Psychopaths with Translucent Skulls

TODAY, MAY 12TH, 2020—and I'm sorry to be insensitive but, pandemic notwithstanding—today is a gorgeous summer day in Toronto, a day when the natural world, intoxicated, pushes itself to extremes of display.

Heat vibrates over the sidewalks, tulips stand shriveled in their dried-out beds like saints burned at the stake; the sun blazes in a glassy blue sky and the earth explodes with blowsy, funky growth.

Who am I to quibble about the season? No one will understand my misgivings: that it's a hot summer day on May 12th, when it should have been a day of gentler sun and breezes perfumed with lilacs just blossomed; a day animated with robins bobbing-and-listening, bobbing-and-listening, on grass green as unripe limes; a day when you could still smell last night's rain; a day in spring.

That's just the way things are now.

Now we live alone, the way we always wanted to. Didn't we? And there would be no time for social interaction anyway. Our schedules are full. Once every hour, on the hour, Alexa exhorts us to wash our hands for twenty seconds, paying particular attention to the base of the thumb, around the anatomical snuffbox.

We do not touch our faces, our lips, nasal membranes, ears or eyes. Those await the touch of a child or a dog or a friend or lover, in a near future that's held teasingly just out of reach.

Our lives are colored like the dreams of fairy tale princesses:

> As we ache for someone to arrive who will touch our faces, we lie still as cadavers. One pale hand clutches a rose, white for innocence, or red for lust. Every limping hour drags one hundred years through quicksand.
>
> We're disturbed by thunder in the night, a commotion like distant war, and we huddle by the tower's window, hugging our knees, watching as the trees of the forest, stretching to the horizon, bend and whip with the force of the gale, spring up again to their full height as casually as the soft bristles of a brush.

We play solitaire, and for once we really mean it. Queen of Hearts receives Jack of Spades. Done, start over.

What is solemn becomes trivial; what was intimate becomes public ritual. We say goodbye to loved ones at funerals attended in Zoom chat rooms; we say hello to virtual fuck buddies as we masturbate, with astonished abandon, in Zoom chat rooms.

We press our cheeks to the flat screens: "Goodbye, grandma, ashes to ashes and dust to dust..." or "Fuck YEAH!" depending on the circumstances; and the screen burns down to darkness.

Where did everyone go?

We still retain a sense of decorum. We do not masturbate with astonished abandon at funerals as we say goodbye, at least, not yet. But you never know.

I'm not ruling anything out at this point. That's just the way it is right now. *Goodbye, grandma; fuck yeah.*

AND WE ARE BAKING BREAD. Bread! The litmus test for our self-esteem. We are the same bunch of cowed serfs who gave up bread during the Salem witch hunt of the anti-carb craze—*I saw Goody Roddis with the ciabatta!*—we are the consumers who've never bought anything but white sandwich loaves, the lowest of the low. White trash bread.

But now we plan our days around nurturing sourdough starter and perfecting our *autolyse* and oiling the tired joints of the stand mixer. Now we understand baker's formulas and we push the fifty-percent hydration.

We long for the Maillard reaction, but, honestly, any reaction would do.

We look at our loaves that burst, crackling like bonfires, from our home ovens and we pause to admire the reddish-gold hue, the paper-thin crust (of course, because we threw handfuls of ice cubes into the inferno when we opened the oven door, then unveiled the still living, breathing dough in its *banneton*. Taking it by surprise, we fell upon it, wrestled it into submission, pinned it to the baking stone and slammed the oven door shut.

(We watched its first moments in hell through the narrow pane of glass, as it shrieked like a mandrake; watched it grow silent, then stiffen with resignation until, satisfied, we moved on to other tasks.)

Wash your hands, says Alexa.

The dough is now bread. A loaf. This is a miracle. Having admired our success—we live alone now, remember?—we don't wait until the bread has cooled. We want comfort, so we rip open the hot loaves with our bare hands, like predators on the deranged edge of starvation.

We slather the gummy, still-steaming crumb with salted butter and cram it into our mouths until we are choking with comfort. Then we cry, because it wasn't as comforting as we expected; then we rip and slather and cram again, desperate to believe that this next time will click, that satisfaction is a simple function of quantity.

We are a bunch of heartless, grieving, self-absorbed, butter-slicked, overwrought, overweight narcissists, and that was *before* the pandemic. Now we are barely-contained monsters.

We're psychopaths with translucent skulls, ordering submachine guns and anthrax from dark Amazon, in the grip of nightmares in which we boil our pets and rape our loved ones and crash our car into the daycare centre, right through the plate glass, just so we can hear the screams.

But at least we're alive. Aren't we?

I PASSED THE DAY IN THE COMPANY of a homeless friend, while he told me about how Saddam Hussein is staying at the same crowded city shelter on Lake Shore Boulevard. He also recounted how THEY abducted him last year, and, after taking him to Mount Sinai Hospital, implanted microphones in the soles of his feet.

And I have just—*so many questions* about that.

How is Saddam doing, is he manscaping more, and does he have any regrets? Is he OK with the lasagne, does he spend his days sitting on a patch of urban beach, skimming stones? Does he have a WMD with him, as a souvenir, and what flashes through his mind, just before he falls asleep?

What's interesting on the sidewalks that I could be listening to? Are there sensors that direct our feet one way or another? Is it like a traffic system for pedestrians? Does a sneaker sound different from a pair of Oxfords, and how?

Do the ants cry out when they see the shadow descend, or does it just reverberate through the Borg mind, a slight ripple of fear dispersed until it's tolerable, like our fear?

Do these implants have sinister intent, so that you can walk out of your house at three AM, with the streets dead and empty, hop on your bicycle and then be run down by a big rig truck driven by a drunk man, the only other person awake in the city?

That happened to another friend of mine, and he survived. More than survived, you'd never know he'd been run over by a big rig truck driven by a drunk man at three AM. And I wanted to ask him: what is it like, is it like Tolstoy's description of the suicide of Anna Karenina?

> "... she was terror-stricken at what she was doing. "Where am I? What am I doing? What for?" She tried to get up, to drop backwards; but something huge and merciless struck her on the head and rolled her on her back. "Lord, forgive me all!" she said, feeling it impossible to struggle. A peasant muttering something was working at the iron above her. And the light by which she had read the book filled with troubles, falsehoods, sorrow, and evil, flared up more brightly than ever before, lighted up for her all that had been in darkness, flickered, began to grow dim, and was quenched forever."

Tolstoy could imagine being run over by a train, something huge and merciless that strikes you on the head, could imagine the panic and moment of regret the suicide feels in those final moments of clarity, when the bravado has flipped to terror and disbelief, when they want to deny and turn back, but gravity won't loosen its grip.

My friend who escaped just smiles. He's changed, there is something set or sunken in his face, the shock of not being dead, perhaps. I feel that I'm looking at an embalmed version of him.

He's stopped taking drugs. He doesn't live downtown anymore.

I never visited him, or even called him, not even once during his long recovery, but he came to visit me.

IT'S THE END OF OUR SUMMER DAY in May, and I'm sitting on the balcony, having a smoke with my homeless friend. We tried to have sex, but despite our best efforts, he was distracted. I had to stop and ask him.

"What's up, you all right?"

"There's this guy's apartment over on Oak Street, I was there the other day. I looked around and there was my aunt's door, and my cousin's TV and a bunch of flowers I was supposed to get, and I realized, that was really my apartment. Why did they give it to him? It's so fucked up."

It is fucked up, I say. It's fucked up and it's just not right.

We've had a light supper: "chunky soup" from a can, though food described as chunks is not congenial to me, it is harrowing. Still, we ate chunky potato soup with bacon, and I made a salad, grated carrot and apple and raisins and peanuts, very seventies, very Kensington High Street, very *Biba*. He heated up the soup for me, I made the salad for him.

We're smoking our cigarettes and we're just in each other's company, quietly, and I think:

> I'm totally calm. My mind is at rest, there's nothing pressing I need to figure out. Every immediate problem is solved or awaiting a response.
>
> The balcony, facing east, enjoys the benefit of a mild breeze. I've rescued the plants I never planted by watering them and promising I'll plant them tomorrow.
>
> I'm living alone in the apartment, and no one can come here without my invitation. I've received the Canadian government's emergency financial help and I have no worries about money. My rent is paid two months in advance, and for the first time in six years, I'm not in a panic.
>
> Two young men recently told me "you're beautiful," and, what's more, demonstrated that they meant it.
>
> I've learned to play the Opus 126 Bagatelles of Beethoven on the piano, because I revere Beethoven. And I can really play them, it wasn't just an affectation.

This is the most rare and precious thing: a moment of absolute peace and contentment.

And I say to my homeless friend:

Something terrible must be about to happen.

Monday Man Crush: Volodymyr Zelenskyy

Monday Man Crush rears its salacious, gooning head once again, and OMG yes, I know it's not Monday. Are you new here? Did you take your meds? No, seriously, did you?

I'm giving this the spin that it's actually not late for last Monday but early for Boxing Day, which is when you put on those big gloves and punch everybody in the face who didn't buy you the right size anything. Even the bathrobe you ordered from Amazon was tight around the waist.

Monday Man Crush is my asymmetrically (and randomly) produced feature for which I have self-mandated the task of teasing the heck out of unavailable yet luscious straight dudes, who, because I use the veil of the Internet like the Wizard of Oz uses his curtain, are unable to do anything about my gleefully concupiscent disrespect.

I heart Volodymyr so very much, I wrote this entirely in beginner Ukrainian. Mistakes are mine alone.

. . .

VOLODYMYR ZELENSKYY! HOW YOUR NAME ROLLS SWEETLY around abscessed near-toothless cavity of mouth like soothing peeled grape, also putting me in mind of unhoused testicle, but this not for public forum talking.

I cannot helping myself, furry babudshkin!

Valyushya, Valyushya! Ukraine diminutive I just made up! Valushya!

Look at me with grave intensity, you little furry doll with more doll inside, and more doll inside, and yet more doll, you get idea, and tell me what you wanting. Hmm?

A pair of socks I should knitting for you maybe, army green, with national embroidery? To hide hairy knees making you so shy? Traditional white Ukraine shirt for folk dancing? Shirt of romance with pouffy sleeves shall I sew? I am perhaps cooking some tripe, some smoked fish, some kind ethnic pancake and stuffing with kasha?

I love good stuffing! Da!

Speak to me, Valyushya, as I dream you are pinning me to wall in fancy Ukraine Presidential Office, safely underneath giant gilt eagle surveillance camera, and making dancey-dancey with tongue like in Busby Berkeley moving picture.

Volodymyr, you called Putin bastard's bluff and stood in open daring him to kill you! You big sexy hero! You fighting like hungry brown bear of steppes alongside men of Ukraine armed by US, also special weapon: scary old babushkas in headscarves with hot cabbage soup in vats!

Da, is *Chernobyl* of cabbage!

You not leaving town and hiding in bunker like Mikhail Pence before hanging. You saving democracy, you giving Ukraine citizens courage and hope, you giving speeches that shaked and stirred, like very dry martini.

Special tip for you: Just tell vodka that vermouth got taking prisoner of war. Vodka will having make do itself. Da? Da! Ha HA!

You are comedian becomes leader, not like America where leader becomes comedian. But not funny ha-ha like you! Funny peculiar!

Volodymyr Zelenskyy! You without shadow of doubt bravest, noblest, most strongest admirable leader in world today. You are mensch, not "Nazi"! Warrior but cuddly!

You jam of apricots on Davushya cheese pancake! Or who is knowing maybe cherries! Da!

And most of it all, now I am confessing: You man who by holy Saint Wenceslas I swear is one day leaving me ravished in ditch, pants around ankles, maybe bleeding teensy bit, but no worse than after laser wart removal. Davushya is content. Heat is in my very sod!

Now back to glorious war victory! God speed, Valushya!! But not orthodox God!! *God of Ukraine in pouffy romantic shirt!!!*

Side of bed closest to door always available to you. Come soon, when hell of war is behind us and let me inhale man musk of your ripe, stinking, hairy body. Just please not sliding off.

I go now getting sour cream ready, #MondayManCrush of today, maybe of decade—*maybe forever!!*

бу́дьмо!

Night Terrors

Hey Mel. Mel?

Yeah, vhat?

Mel? Is that you? I can't hear too good on this baby intercom thing. What? What was that? Speak up, will ya? Jeezus. Couldn't you just, I dunno. Uber me, like, over to the Hilton? I can't sleep—

Donald. Dahlink. Is four in morning. Is it again terrors of night? You vant I sing again all twenty-nine verses "Polovtsian Lullaby of Steppes"? Please, little dipshitsky, make-up guy is here and—

Jeezus, Mel. Take me off speakerphone. Or babyphone. I have something serious to tell you. And why is your make-up guy… is he a pansy?

Is not normal to know such things. Bruce Make-up Guy are you pansy? Uh-huh, husband vants—No. Is not pansy.

Mostly they're pansies, but then one day one of them turns out NOT to be a pansy, you understand? Hey did I tell you, I'm gonna make them *sing* the morning report to me, you know, and it's gonna be called President Donald's Briefs, they'll go like, "To read the impossible briefs, to sing, la la la la la la—"

Donnsky, Please to be not singing. OK. I'm off speakerphone. You got two minutes. Just a vodka straight up, dahlink—

What was—What are you saying? You want me to Uber you a vodka?

Am talking to Bruce Make-up Guy.

Bruce! There's always a Bruce! Fuckin pansy! I thought I was your Bruce, baby... And why—

Is Wednesday morning four am and you know I must finishing make-up for photo-op. With hedge clippers. Was your idea. Standing in Rose Garden with hedge clippers. Already they call me names. Who is Myra Hindley?

Baby, she's a famous influencer. Myra Hindley Living. Makes delicious apple pie, you never had a better apple pie. Her chickens lay colored eggs. I know her intimately. She adores me, of course.

They call me chicken lady? No. Is not good.

Anyway, I thought you just Photoshopped your face—?

Could you please getting to the—

Mel, listen to me. I've got a sore throat. And a cough. And this weird rash—

You are butt fucking hookers again?

No. Just Democrats!
HaHaHaHaHaHaHaHaHaHaHaHa—

Hahaha! Hahaha high fives, dahlink. High fives! Me too, I am having also temperature—

HaHaHaHaHaHa buttfucking little Fauci, buttfucking little disabled Fauci, little disabled Fauci with Down Syndrome, HaHaHaHaHaHa little, like Hillary Pizza Parlour disabled retards with Down Syndrome—

Donald, is only so much HaHaHa can a girl coping with in one day. Please and thanking—

Buttfucking Hope Hicks! Buttfucking little disabled Hope Hicks. Hey—Donald Trump Buttfucks Hope! How's that for a campaign slogan!

Donald, listen. I am having temperature and thick cough with phlegmas but you, dahlink? No. Is not serious. I am thinking President lungs just line up virus like firing squad in town square, like in old country. Showing always virus who is boss man.

And I had that dream again when, you remember I told you? I was in a cage. A cage! Like an animal—

Horrible, Donny, horrible, so sorry you are having that experience, even though I don't give a fuck, remember?

—an ANIMAL and I was five years old, my parents weren't there and I tried to talk to someone, the maitre d', the director of valet parking, anyone, but then it's fuckin NANCY. Yeah, Crazy Loopy Pelosi herself, and I was like an alien, she pretended she couldn't understand me. Then I'm in Bergdorf Goodman and someone's kicking me, I got my hand over her mouth and she screams and I swear just this, this— shithole Nancy Demtard language came out.

Like crazy bitch grandmother in old country! She should go home, make beet soup. Like this Myra Hindley chicken lady. Stay out of politics. Is men's work.

Listen to me, baby, and I have a temperature! Seriously, what is going on? You think the Dems did this? I'm the greatest, kindest guy in the universe, everyone loves me, and what does the universe do? It breaks—

Breaks your balls, Donny, I know. Tell you what, dahlink. Next time we get off Air Force One and world is watching I'm slapping your face. OK? In front of Press Corps, slapping your face, Donny. You like that?

You don't think it's the rallies? It couldn't be. Nah. They love me, they wouldn't give me viruses and anyway I think once you're immune to the flu and E Coli and—E

Coli? E Boli? Whatever, didn't we cancel that? Monkey Coronaflu? And maybe take a hot shower—virus, you're fired! That's how it works!

Ohhh, that's beautiful, Bruce! Beautiful! Ya, right there baby, don't stop!

Mel. Mel? You still there?

Mmmmmmmflfffafafafaf MMMMMLLLLLALALALAL!!!!!

Mel! Let's just fake it.

Oh, Donny, I'm sorry to be telling you that was not fake. Oooph—! Only with you, baby. Special for you!

Mel, I mean fake the Chinese corona disease and just disappear, can we?

Donny?

Yeah baby? What is it? You want those new shoes, baby? I'm freaking out, Mel, with that E Jean Carroll thing, and they got the tapes of the phone calls to Georgia and Hillary's on the late-night warpath and... Hey, maybe we throw her under the bus again, run a little interference? What did Bill Clinton say, that thing he said that you liked? "Ah never had sexual relations with that woman?" Was that it—

No, I like always when he is saying, "Intern pussy is best pussy."

I love you, Nancy –

Nancy! Vhat the fucking—

Pocahontas—FUCK! I meant, Mel, you, Melania Trumpsky! Promise you won't die on me, baby? If you don't die I'll buy you those shoes, I'll buy you a thousand pairs! I won't know what to do if you die on me, just make it all dis... disapp... disappear....

Donny. Stop crying like, like—pukotnik! Leesten to me. You are so old, you having orange hair on hinge, your dick is like my leetle finger and you are having terrors of the night, always! Are you man or girly-man? I did not marry you for money, but for your being strong!

That's true...

Look vhat I do, I'm not being so old, I am having Bruce Make-Up Guy for terrors of night, I have on always designer gown! And is best of all, I have historical-first First Lady Instagram tits.

Is that a fact? Fantastic, Mel! On Instagram? How—how do I see them, baby? How do I see your tits on Instagram? Or anywhere?

Use keywords "Melania tits." Is working also "Melania MILF big tits." But only Instagram, Donny.

Tell me, Mel. Tell me what to do. I'm trying to cry... Oh god. I want to be sorry, I feel I should be sorry, but—you know something? I don't give a fuck, either. Hey, I don't give a fuck! That is beautiful! Did I get that from you? How does it work, being sorry, is it a feeling or—I don't get it, what's the point?

Point is to be better person. No one is telling me better than what.

I mean, if I do something wrong, I just tell them I didn't do it! There, done! Wrong thing, you're fired! Hey, listen to this: "Buttfuck notorious retard RBG baby killer with Down Syndrome—you're fired!!" HaHaHaHaHaHa—"Buttfuck—"

You know vhat, Donsky? Cry-babsky, pukotnik?

Yeah, doll? Anything. I'll buy you anything, we'll just make it disappear—we could start a charity, a Trump Protection Program! Take the donations and lie low for while. Maybe... some plastic surgery? Can you get that on Obamacare? Did we cancel that yet? Oh god, I love being the fucking President—!

Donny!

Jeezus—what is it, Nancy? Oh FUCK—!!

Pukotnik? Cry-babsky? Uber me that vodka.

Last Liberal Standing

I Have Been Recalcitrant

This is how it works: The title gives a tantalizing glimpse of the theme; the subtitle teases, or elaborates, or sells the title out by explaining it for you. Simple, right? Here's a current example:

Title: "Triggered"
Subtitle: "How the Left Thrives on Hate and Wants to Silence Us."
    A winner, isn't it? And it's his first book, too, the first he's written and possibly even the first he's read.
    So never think it's too late for *you*, Murgatroyd McGraw.
    Donald "Frankenforehead" Trump II, like many people, had a book inside him, but with most people that's where it remains. Donald's book was so deep inside him no ray of sunlight had ever penetrated its fetal cloth covers, and now—Blessèd Judy, Mother of Liza!—he's filled his lungs to capacity, spread his knees, and, grunting and groaning with monumental effort, squatting like an Olympic weight-lifter ready for the clean-and-jerk, squeezed it out.
    Look, here comes the sequel: ker-PLOP!
    Triggered signals that we're a bunch of bored dads stuck watching "The Nutcracker" instead of the game and missing target practice at the old folks' home. And we're about to endure the dance of the leftie snowflakes, that corps de ballet of over-sensitive types who get traumatized when we use good, old-fashioned traditional language, like n****er and faggot and k*ke and cripple, and deploy traditional attitudes like "I don't care what you think you are, I'm not calling you SHE," or "Adam and Eve, not Adam and Elton John!" or "Whites suffer racism, too."

Them SJW's are probably crying like lefty babies as they run off to their safe spaces, eh? Gee, are they *triggered*?

The subtitle with its explanation is supposed to encourage you but its very honesty poses a problem. From just the title, I might have thought *Triggered* was written by a super-sensitive individual who, because of his ability to feel the vibes, spent his days in a virtual torture chamber of empathy.

Except that it's written by one of the Trump Frankenforehead children who was cooked up in a vat of virgin's blood by a Dementor, so I was pretty sure that I had absolutely no interest in the book.

But from having seen the subtitle I *know* I have absolutely no interest in the book (although in fact without even reading it, even before it came ker-plopping out of Don, I had already read it a hundred times).

So, thanks for the heads-up. If you are an angry white supremacist, or an assembly-line Frankenforehead son of Trump, looking to have crossover success and sell more books, take note.

That subtitle is formulaic and the formula goes: Throw out the most obnoxious, outrageously biased statement you can contrive, and present it as your premise (though it is not intended to be a verifiable statement of fact and its offensiveness is its gleeful goal); because as far as you're concerned it's true, and truth in the 21st century is a personalized, bespoke kind of thing.

Old-fashioned truth was dull and inefficient and did not necessarily reflect your beliefs. It was like those eastern bloc Polski Fiats everyone drove in Warsaw in 1979, or Henry Ford's Model T, which he offered in any color you wanted as long as it was black.

Truth was one-size-fits-all. You had to cram yourself into, more often than not, an ill-fitting truth that didn't suit you. And it was someone else's truth, from years, maybe even centuries, ago! Crummy old hand-me-downs!

But now we have petite and plus-size, little white lies and great big whoppers. Now we have truth in all the flavors you would ever want: peppermint bullshit, cherry bullshit, tangerine bullshit and Bullshit Classic.

The Left, so this subtitle says, "thrives" on hate. Important point. Not just likes. Thrives on. Hate is our fuel, our multi-vitamin and our powdered whey protein drink. Hate is our Kryptonite, the fatal substance we must nonetheless ingest to power our hateful lefty energy.

Conservatives stop paying for your mom's cancer medicines and fire your kids' teachers. They fill the parks with the newly unhoused and abandon the mentally ill to a life on the streets and legislate women's bodies, and all of it for love—but progressives? We dare to raise the minimum wage!

Conservatives don't hold back. They stand up for what they value, and what they value is not caring for people but balancing budgets. Your mom will be dead, your unschooled kids dumb as rocks, but the deficit will be zero, the enterprise, free. Criminals will *rot in hell*. You won't have to endure the tragic dress sense or the stench of the unhoused, and your dumb-as-a-rock kids? Naturals as the new generation of conservatives!

Wants to Silence Us. "Us," as in "Us and Them." Donald Junior "knows" your country is being overwhelmed by "illegal" immigrants, your culture and values derided by elites and gays, your wages stolen, taxed to pay for abortions and government programs for criminals and Muslims, your schools overrun by Marxists. Isn't it awesome that the President's son understands and is talking directly to you? Almost like he's your buddy!

Triggered can be purchased on Amazon, and Twitter linked to its dedicated web site that lets you prank-send a copy to prominent liberal politicians and celebrities. He appeared on "The View" and got into a slanging match with the hosts. He appeared at UCLA, but canceled the Q&A after heckling from a hostile student audience. Nearly every quality newspaper on the planet has given it a snippy review which is really publicity. This book is a New York Times bestseller—even though the stats were hugely inflated by bulk sales. So... this silencing by liberals thing ...?

Conservatives troll and shut down every progressive conversation with well-placed shouts of "PC!" "Snowflake!" "Social Justice Warrior!" "White Racist!" and mock anyone who wants to treat more people with more respect, but *they're* silenced ...?

Only in my dreams.

A COUPLE OF YEARS AGO, I WAS INVITED to write a guest article for an Evangelical Christian blog (I've included it in this collection, the last piece in the book.) The owner was a minister, a more than adequate writer and a progressive guy, surprisingly outspoken in his support for social justice.

I knew this because he would say things in his posts like, "Jesus wouldn't have gotten mad at all those refugees from Central America in the caravan. He would have been loving to them, because they're poor and displaced and feeling sad right now. That's the Christian message, yo!"

This is in contrast to his followers, who would respond, "These brown scumbags are just actors and serial killers and drug cartels funded by George Soros, and they're gonna take away our guns and bring in their extended brown families and live offa welfare and steal our jobs! America is under attack! Resist the World Government! White people are dying out!

Build The Wall Now!!"

The blog owner challenged me to provide the authentic voice and viewpoint of a gay man vis-à-vis Evangelical Christianity, which his main audience would probably not otherwise experience, seeing as they all live in white-only gated communities with matching front doors and identical window treatments, and have sharpshooters with assault rifles stationed around the perimeter of the moat who have been instructed to shoot to kill at the very moment they sense waspish humor or catch a whiff of Donna Summer singing "Bad Girls."

I knew that most readers of his blog would shut down if they knew I was a leftie Canadian gay male atheist. I decided I would ease them into my narrative using humor and various other shallow distractions to win them over. I'd mellow them into complacency, and manipulate them with my aw, shucks Canadian diffidence.

Then I'd slap them hard in the face with my true identity as the Socialist Queen of Darkness and drop them down the well.

They would understand in a Damascus flash that gay guys and atheists and Canadians were actual humans with thoughts and feelings just like them, not abstractions cooked up by evil leftists for the sole purpose of vexing their limited brains with the evidence that some people, frankly, just don't give a shit about Jesus, at least, not their version.

"How wrong I've been! This Canadian homosexual atheist liberal has finally convinced me that we're all made in God's image and deserving of respect. I'm gonna call up all the homeless shelters in Des Moines and see if my gay son is still alive, then invite him, a trannie, and maybe even a Democrat, to dinner! Y'all!"

It made sense at the time.

I wrote the best piece I could write, drawing on concepts of Zen Buddhism, poking gentle fun at my Canadian identity, and making a huge effort to come across as a bridge builder who was skeptical but non-threatening, even kind of adorable. I decided the title would be "Pivot Chords," a metaphor from music that is about making a shift from one key—so, viewpoint—to another with finesse.

I wrote and edited and edited some more and wrote some more and submitted. Finally I got the email saying I could check the published post. My title was now the subtitle and a new title, in bold letters at the very top of the page, read:

This Gay, Liberal, Atheist, Canadian's Sermon
on Grace and Compassion
is the Best I've Heard in Awhile

In nearly two years the article has collected just six likes, about thirty-five shares and two comments, from a user base of nearly four thousand readers.

We live in a time when people have to be deceived before they'll drive down the street that houses all those liberals they hate.

They have to be jumped, hooded and thrown in the van before they'll even let you suggest that a bunch of desperate mothers, fathers and children, a bedraggled, tired, poor, huddled mass of wretched refuse from whatever teeming shore isn't just a bunch of actors paid by the Antichrist who've come to overthrow the most powerful nation on earth.

Note I didn't say "greatest."

HOW ARE YOU, BY THE WAY, AT THIS spiffing start to a new decade? I'm here, a scary clown popping out of his scary clown-box, to tell you that making Ukraine's aid money contingent on its digging up dirt on the President's political enemy is wrong, but not impeachable.

Grabbing her by the pussy is not impeachable, it's—I dunno, first base? Are you getting this down? Soliciting charitable donations then using them to buy sex with hookers or self-portraits or election campaigns? Nope. Not impeachable. You wanna know what's impeachable? Hint: Think Bill Clinton.

That's right. *Blowjobs are impeachable.*

As true as that is, it's still not everything. Now we learn this:

Whatever the President of the United States does is OK, as long as he truly believes that his re-election is in the best interests of the nation. The POTUS can do anything he wants, at least, according to Vladimir Putin.

But he didn't get there first. Trump himself told us so. *I can do anything I want.* And, excuse me, bleeding hearts, he would hardly lie about something so important!

Twenty-twenty finds me in the position of a little boy wearing Buster Brown shoes and itchy wool shorts, topped with a crisp white shirt and a pre-tied bow tie, all clashing plaids and male camel toe and sausage thighs, just waiting to be terrorized by the freckle-faced bully, the rapscallion of a boy that everyone likes. *What a little devil he is! He'll go places!*

It's the face plant in the mud puddle, you see, the soiled perfection, that fosters one's appreciation for all the nice new things, gifts (for you would never buy them for yourself) that may well not survive the day intact.

Not to worry. Start from the point of innocence; erase from your mind the script that has you in the final act looking like you walked home in a Category Four hurricane, and put your trust in that pristine pinafore. Meanwhile, allow me to define my salient personality trait: I am recalcitrant—

> recalcitrant \rih-KAL-suh-trunt\ adjective. 1 : obstinately defiant b : not responsive to treatment. c : resistant.

I have been recalcitrant on Twitter towards the People's Party of Canada (PPC), whose guiding light is one of those *au courant* racists, a Québecois who masks his authoritarian lust for *pure laine*[1] behind the pieties of secularism and *patrimonie*[2]—Maxime Bernier.

> Why did Maxime Bernier
> cross the road?
> To get to the other—
>
> Oh my god! THAT CEMENT MIXER JUST
> RAN THE RED LIGHT...!

If populism is the soft cock of Canadian politics, Maxime has his dry, white lips clamped around it so tightly he may pass out from lack of oxygen. *Allez-y !* Go to it! That's the spirit, buddy! You'll never get it up, but it's undeniably entertaining when you try.

The PPC tweets that the housing crisis is the result of immigration (that's non-white immigration) run riot.

(Compare the Toronto version, "the Chinese are buying all the condos," which is approaching the status of a standard friendly greeting on the local streets:

"Hey, Fred! The Chinese are buying all the condos!"

"Fine, thanks, and how's the wife and kids?")

Because no rabbit hole presents itself but that I instantly picture myself burrowing down it, I tweet back that the housing crisis is caused not by immigration but by, oddly enough, a lack of housing, which could be solved by requiring developers to build affordable units in their cheap, flimsy luxury buildings, for example.

They tweet back that I lack imagination, that a trillion immigrants could appear at the borders and progressives like me would still want to

---

1   "Pure wool". The ugly, racist term for the mythical Quebecker whose blood line is untainted by congress in the 17th century with First Nations women.

2   Québec's heritage; this can include religious symbols— if they're Christian.

throw money at the problem.

I tweet back that it's equally [un]likely that white people could breed a trillion offspring and the housing crisis would still exist without a trillion living units, which, [sigh], could easily be built at no expense to the public and entail no tax increases except on units which owners don't actually occupy (a tax which Vancouver and Toronto have already implemented with success).

> What did Maxime Bernier say to the white immigrant?
> "I'm color-blind!"
>
> What did Maxime Bernier say to the non-white immigrant?
> "Housing crisse de Tabernac!"

What is it like, I wonder, being inside Maxime Bernier's head? It ain't the Midway at the Canadian National Exhibition, that's for sure. No one's lining up for the ride, "I hope I pass the height test! The "Bernier" does a full loop the loop and my friend Sandy told me she threw up her pink popcorn twice! It's gonna be *awesome!*"

Bernier burns through Canadian values like a maniac training a flame thrower at a grove of maples. A typical enraged loser and blustering, entitled white male, he projects sour resentment and moral panic at the thought of benefits or income distribution or social justice. He's a card-carrying denizen of the joyless, shadowy, victimized world of put-upon conservatism.

What does Bernier worry about? Not the plight of refugees, our international commitments or corporate taxes. He worries about—yes!— our deficit, even though our financial health, thanks for asking, is absolutely great. (US debt to GDP ratio: 4.6%. Canadian debt to GDP ratio: 0.39%).

He is, or pretends to be, in thrall to the idea that deficits are wrong, even if roads are pock-marked and bridges are falling down, and health care and public transport are so underfunded they barely work.

The modern concept that a federal government issuing its own fiat currency is not bound by budget limitations like a household and can fund anything it chooses, regardless of deficit and using inflation as a guide to deficit limits; the idea that we leave out half the story when we do not balance red in the government's ledger with black in the public ledger, is utterly foreign to him. Pull up your socks, pinch those pennies and crack open the ramen noodles!

Five minutes' research would remind you that Keynesian economics *advocates* government spending when the economy needs stimulus. It's considered a very uncontroversial good thing and it's been standard issue for decades.

Conservatives can build whole fantasy scenarios on a false premise, because people are intellectually lazy.

Well, put the Chevy up on concrete blocks and bang my missus in a trailer, is that a fact?

> **What does Maxime Bernier's breakfast cereal say?**
>
> **"Crap, Wacko Populist"!**

Maxime Bernier throws nasty shade at Greta Thunberg, doomsaying sixteen-year-old climate activist. They make a synergistic pair. He's the title, she's the subtitle. He hates her youth, her daring, her plans to save the future and her being right. She's grumpy, mouthy and, yes, recalcitrant. She gets under his skin.

He's prissy, quasi-intellectual French, his affect tighter than a Parisian's pursed lips; she's the spooky love-child of Anne of Green Gables and Ingmar Bergman. You can tell Bernier's just itching to send her to bed without supper, then drive across town and spank his mistress.

Maxime and Greta! They were made to be a comedy duo, the Laurel and Hardy of the apocalypse, the featured floor show on Planet Titanic.

From slapstick to sleaze: Bernier, promoted to Foreign Affairs Minister in 2007 by Conservative PM Stephen Harper, has to tender his resignation after he leaves a classified dossier lying around his girlfriend's place.

For five months.

The dossier contains top-secret information about Canada's plans in Afghanistan, Iraq and Syria. The *petite amie*, Julie Couillard, cavorts with Hell's Angels and organized crime and people with job descriptions like drug enforcer, and was almost certainly lobbying Bernier on behalf of a realtor, Kevlar, Inc., to procure a lucrative government contract.

On a prurient note, the former model is also extremely well provided for in the boobs department and is not shy about showing us, which obviously cannot have anything to do with her revelation that Bernier is worried people think he's gay.

We find out all of this when she publishes her tell-all memoir, entitled, and stop me if you've heard this one, "My Story." This is a new level of dedication to bringing the federal government into disrepute.

> **Why does Maxime Bernier hate Gay Pride and Dairy Farmers?**
>
> **One's too much homo, the other too little!**

Maxime must lack any sense of irony. He runs for office in the 2019 federal election promising to close down the supply management system, so hated by Trump, that ensures Canadian dairy farmers can get a fair price for their products.

His riding of Beauce, Québec, consists mainly of—dairy farmers. And he loses his seat in Parliament, the only seat the PPC held. This is a new definition of dumb-as-a-rock stupid.

Bernier derides Greta Thunberg as "mentally unstable" and denies the overwhelming evidence about our climate emergency. He takes Greta very seriously. Everyone else understands that we support Greta Thunberg because she's sweet and has no clout because she's just a teenaged girl.

Everyone, even corporations, even governments, supports Greta Thunberg, because she's photogenic and does no harm, especially to the gas-guzzling agenda of big oil. You can pat Greta on the head, say "Isn't she adorable! It's great to see commitment from young people!" and feel fine because she's not a threat to anything or anyone. She has no power.

It's like giving a Girl Scout her knot-tying badge or her "most likeable gal-pal" certificate. She's a protest march by Disney, where the cute kids pack up their signs and go home when daddy thinks that's enough shenanigans for one day. Time for beddy-bye, Little Missy Hooligan!

Greta Thunberg, the most poignant role model imaginable for a doomed generation, is who the media shoves into the spotlight so that there's no room left for coverage of Canada's First Nations people. As I write, they're setting up roadblocks to halt the progress of a pipeline desecrating their sacred land, the land that was never conceded and still belongs to them.

Sacred land? How quaint! Riots about pipelines? Please, I'm eating dinner! Let's see the cute little girl again! She's the future, she's dessert!

We want to consume Greta, because she's a tasty, frothy cream puff of news. The First Nations people are indigestible: ornery, furious, not *nice*. They're not our friends, and they've experienced first-hand how we treat children.

We call out the Mounties. (The Mounties send an internal memo: "Use as much violence as you want." I'm not making this up.)

The protestors cover their faces. They throw rocks. They don't hold out their hands in forgiveness, and we don't pat them on the head. Guns, tear gas. They're dangerous because they insist on their power and their absolute right to be where they are.

> **Why is Maxime Bernier jealous of Greta Thunberg?**
>
> **She travels the world on a yacht, but all his ships sink!**

The PPC accuses me of not wanting a conversation. And they're right. I don't. I want them to line up and bend over so I can shove a People's Party of Canada lawn sign up their wazoos, pointy end first—to approximately the same place where Donald Frankenforehead's book resided— then burn the lot of them at the stake. This seems like such a simple, intuitive demand.

And since the remaining members of the PPC would fit into an old-style minivan, I could take care of it in an afternoon and still finish in time to flash some skin on Chaturbate for a couple of hours. I call my room

> *This Gay, Liberal, Atheist, Canadian's Ass is the Best You've Seen On A Senior Citizen in A While.*

Nothing is wasted when you're a writer. Nothing.

Now, pour the little lady a glass of Chardonnay and get yourself—impeached.

Ottawa Got a Little Out of Control

Hey followers, hangers-on and random stumblers-upon, sorry I've been MIA but it's hard work fending off all the convoy dudes with one hand tied behind my back and a can of Molson in the other.

Yeah, that was all my fault, that freedom-whatsit-trucker convoy snafu in Ottawa. Kind of embarrassing, eh?

On the other hand, yay for me!

It all started as a random Wednesday night hook-up with this dude on GrindScroff—

—and sorry to interrupt myself, but, by the way, have you seen that Pornhub ad that goes, "Want to masturbate, but haven't got a partner?"

WTF? Partner? So you mean to tell me that what I've always assumed was meant to be quality one-on-one time with the baloney pony, blissfully free of online app scrolling and Jell-O shooters, now requires someone to spot me and maybe additional back-up on the benches? Jeezus.

I surely must have missed something in Miss Smedley's Grade Eight sex education class.

I do remember her basic instructions, which were, "To avoid blindness, pray with your dad right before bedtime, then lie very still while he immobilizes your arms above the sheets with the plastic twist-ties." Absolutely no personal revelation there!

Which gives me a clue, probably, why Miss Smedley's lunch was a tuna sandwich double-wrapped in waxed paper inside a plastic bread bag, and secured with a constrictor knot that was so friggin' tight, she had to slash the bag open with a Stanley knife.

Oh, and two apples and a banana.

Anyway, yeah, so this guy Trevor says he's in his truck heading in from Thunder Bay and he's looking for some cab action. So I think, what the heck! After all, you only live once, for eight decades, then get stuck in a medical-grade freezer for twenty thousand years!

Before you know it I'm naked in the back of an eighteen-wheeler and barreling down the 401. Fantasy fulfillment, big time! Once in Ottawa he ran into some dudes, or maybe bros, I get them mixed up, and if there were ten guys, there were twenty haircuts between them. We're talkin' major mullet!

Unfortunately things got a little rowdy, and just between you and me, I thought flashing that camera crew from the CBC then peeing on their Timberland boots was a little "de trop", but basically Trev's "Good People."

(Good People, if you don't know, is the lingo for career criminals or other deadbeats who'll spot you a shard before they disappear with your wallet, then get busted an hour later at Hooker Harvey's trying to pay for a bacon double cheeseburger with your Platinum VISA. Hashtag *sketchy!*)

But it's true. Trev's had a hard life, what with his long days on the road, and overdoing the Fentanyl so he blacks out from time to time when he's driving, which, as a disability, gets him a support cheque with special dietary allowance; and then narrowly avoiding doing time after he was ratted out by—and I quote, excuse the transphobic language—"some chick with a dick."

What a story! Everything but the bloodhounds snapping at his rear end, said Thelma Ritter in every movie!

(But let's nip one thing in the bud right now: Hey Trev! I'll make you a deal: You don't call a pre-op male-to-female transgender woman a "chick with a dick" and I won't call you "a lazy fuck in a weed-stinking truck". Capisce?)

I should have noticed sooner. But when push comes to tear gas, who would have thought jumping into a hot tub naked with a bunch of partied up white trailer trash with a grudge on the gov could lead to such havoc?

What a shit show/*exposition de merde!* Horns honking all night; in-yer-face, overt racism instead of the superior, apologetic Canuck-type racism; Nazis in Canada Goose jackets when they always look much better in black leather; and it's all so obviously Justin's fault, I don't know why they don't extradite him right back to Havana with his mother, La Putana.

Hey! Whaddaya think of this for a meme: *"Convoy Dudes in Hot Tubs Lack Brain-Matter!"* I'm thinking T-shirts, tin camping mugs, and maybe one of those car deodorizer things, very much needed in this particular man-cave of a cab I might add, that you hang from the rear-view mirror along with the big pair of furry dice. You gotta admit, it's original, eh? Shtup me with a socket wrench if I know what it means, though. Seriously.

You know the drill. Pretty soon they invited their buds over, all in these gigantic trucks, and they invited THEIR friends, and on and on and so forth, and one thing led to another—and thank Minerva I was born lacking one of the genes for shame, which certainly came in handy for the "Reverse Cow-Girl" around five PM.

And as for your sad little family restaurant and your essential, stupefyingly boring work at the parliamentary library—*c'mon*. Innocent Canadian fun!

Well, OK, Canadian fun, but that's challenging enough to find as it is. If you don't fancy any of our national leisure activities that involve skidding on an icy surface then snapping off part of a frostbitten limb, you're pretty much stuck with re-reading The Handmaid's Tale, by Margaret Who?, or better yet, watching it.

Does Margaret Who? have a Handmaid's Tale podcast? Because I think she should read it to me in her spare time when she's not busy giving her opinions about transgender people.

Even transgender people tend to learn new things about themselves—for example, that they don't exist, which is obviously going to take you aback when you find out—when experts like Margaret Who? are given a subsidized channel for their alternative, non-fact-based views. Everyone deserves a hearing of their opinions, no matter how obscure they are!

Or just settle for the porn version, what was it again? "Some Handmaid Tail"? "A Tale of Ten Handjobs"? I can't work it out. But at least you won't be alone when you masturbate! Jeezus Stephen Chrysostomus Harper!

God forfend! Anyhoo, a bangin' ol' Ottawa good time was had by all, eh?

BUT APPARENTLY THOSE STIFF NECKS in Parliament, and a bunch of old ladies who couldn't get to Hunt's Blue-Rinse Bakery for their raisin bread, or whatever, all got a whiff of Dave Muggins here having a bit of fun for a change and decided to close the whole thing down. Story of my life! Me versus a world of party-poopers!

Now if Justin could just relax a bit—no, let's get this right. If Justin could just learn to relax whatever muscles are currently clenched, and clench whatever muscles are… you see where I'm going with this?

And when I say clench, I mean clench them tighter than a Quebecker's pouty lips when he catches a whiff of signage in English, or of some radical-Islamic terrorist teacher putting on her hijab and heading out to her job ruining some poor school kids' innocent secularism, you know?

Quebeckers! You gotta admit, they keep you on yer toes! No sooner are they firing hijab wearers for covering their heads than they're mandating covering your face! It's all so obviously what Jesus would have wanted.

Did I say Jesus? Sorry, I meant Maurice Duplessis!

Where was I? Justin. Slacking for clenching, when it's not clenching for slacking. He's basically got everything right—just too slow, too quiet and in reverse!

Never mind: turns out he was gearing up for his own quasi-autocratic, dad's-footsteps, "just watch me" moment.

But first we watched the Ottawa police give Trev's convoy buddies a big yawn and a thumbs-up—police are generally conservative types, politically, right? so understandably, they wanted to cut their trucker bro's some slack—until the chief of police had a quiet, Canadian-style aha! moment about how maybe they should, you know, do something? and then all the policemen looked at each other and said, "I thought YOU were doing something. Was I supposed to do something, too?", which went on for a while, until the chief of police resigned, to be replaced by an actual chief of police.

Meanwhile the mayor of Ottawa, who I think is called something like "Bambi", made a deal with the truckers that they could stay in a moderately inconvenient area if only they would listen to reason and move out of the very inconvenient area.

The truckers then asked for milk and cookies and blankets so they could take their afternoon naps, and the mayor said "Of course!" in his sloppiest, most ingratiating Canadian cocksucker's voice, and then the truckers shouted "Fooled ya!" and stayed right where they were.

The time was ripe! Now Justin could take decisive action to end the illegal occupation, not by telling the police to do it, which would be an unforgivable act of overreach, but by suspending civil rights and habeus corpus and abolishing the rule of law nationwide.

And everyone who was calling JT weak and ineffectual and girly up to this point is now telling him that he's a brutal manly dictator who's thrown democracy under the bus and turned Canada into a police state! It's *always* about Justin.

YOU KNOW WHAT WOULD REALLY TURN voters around? If JT could grow that beard out again. Oh, *yes!*

Honestly? Whenever I see him standing at that news podium, all bed-disheveled and tousle-haired and porn-bearded, like a seventies adult performer ready to prove that dining out can happen down below, I'm thinking, last one in the hot tub's a white-dancing str8 boi! I'll even give you a quarter for a 'tache ride!

That is, *after* I use my tongue to dab up all those loose croissant crumbs that Sophie-Grégoire didn't catch in the first round. He can take the opportunity to deploy the good ol' bottle of Listerine before I thrust my Hansard down his throat.

Ready, little buddy? Swish and spit, swish and spit. There ya go.

Oh, please. Don't tell me a fluid gender-acknowledging cutie like JT hasn't unleashed an anger-dissipating palm or ten on former butt-buddy Gerald Butt's butt. When you reach the zenith of Canadian political life that the office of PM represents, you get an official BFF, and let me tell you, that BFF's butt is to a leader what a pillow is to the rest of us plebs—something to vent on.

You know what it's like. And if you don't, let me tell you what it's like: Very, very pink! Are you kidding me?

Well, then. I couldn't end my sexual shenanigan-themed occupation of our national capital region without putting in my demands, so here goes:

> Hey, bébé! I'm parked here for good until you completely « ditchez la biche et faites le switch, heins?! Calisse de Tabarnak! »
>
> You're not gonna negotiate? Well, then, get a loada THESE emergency measures, cochon! Go on, seize my assets, baby! Double-dare ya!

Uh-huh! You love it! L O friggin' L!

Imaginary PR Voting Outcomes

Justin Trudeau, Canada's newly re-elected Prime Minister, has finally made good on his previous 2015 campaign promise of electoral reform. And about time!

But, hold the phone, we're not *quite* done yet, because—like a wise dad doling out jellybeans to his impatient children—Trudeau realized it wouldn't be advisable to introduce this long-awaited upgrade all at once.

After all, you wouldn't want everyone of voting age to get too excited—we might, I dunno, throw up! Or vote!

Instead, our PM chose to introduce the new system secretly for the time being, by simply continuing with the old first-past-the-post system—which reliably returns the Liberal Party to power—and occasionally emphasizing how much more fair the election outcomes would have been using a new, imaginary proportional representation (PR) model.

Chrystia Freeland, newly-minted Deputy PM, and managing a specially-created portfolio as Minister of Intergovernmental Relations Which Would Already Be Fine if it Weren't for Alberta, announced the long-awaited reforms, which haven't happened and never will, at a press conference just a couple of weeks after the Liberals formed a minority government.

"The Liberals officially won the most seats and a clear mandate to once again give Canadians that comfortable familiarity they crave: A Person Named Trudeau forging ahead doing the opposite of whatever he promised, or just dropping everything like a hot potato and getting mired in some obscure bureaucratic scandal that no one can figure out. Talk about *total* buzz kill!" Freeland explained.

"Today I'm also very pleased to point out that, in a proportional representation model, which we accidentally mentioned once but have no intention of ever switching to, the Conservatives would have formed the government. Yes, that's according to the actual popular vote, and boy, are we ever happy for them!"

She continued, "I know that I speak for Justin Trudeau and all the other members of Cabinet when I extend our sincere congratulations to Andrew Scheer and the Conservatives for their thrilling victory had the election been fair and democratic, except it wasn't. Way to go, Andy!

"As for our official Elections Canada win for the Liberals that wasn't really a win, well—what can I say! Phew! Close one! It is what it is! OK, then!"

New Democratic Party Leader Jagmeet Singh also weighed in on the results.

"Hey! Lookit me! Over here, guys! Lookit— *Hellooooo!?"* he said, waving frantically, while a bunch of MP's murmured, "Who's the weirdo in the pink turban?" "Should we call security?" "Is that the cleaner? He's early!" and other words of encouragement, until it was established that the non-white guy talking was the leader of a fringe-type party that wasn't the Liberals or Conservatives.

Singh continued, "I'm absolutely *over the moon* that, under a system that would actually have made people believe it was worth getting out of bed to participate, we would have doubled our seats to fifty-four instead of losing some of the seats we already had!" he said to roars of delight from his supporters.

"I'm *sooooo* happy for us if the system were an accurate reflection of the wishes of Canadian citizens and not just a frustrating waste of valuable time that you could have spent on Facebook volunteering your personal data and creating free content! Awesome work, team!!"

Former Green Party Leader Elizabeth May, who resigned after the Greens' dismal showing at the polls added, "I'm in shock! Though it didn't actually happen because of our illogical plurality voting system, the thought that we *could have had* twenty-two seats instead of three is just... Well, I'm humbled".

Choking back tears of joy, she added, "These imaginary alternative results have vindicated my firm belief that, even if the candidate were a one-legged armadillo, somebody, somewhere will vote for it, as long as you use the word "green".

"In this fantasy I also don't resign as party leader, instead I'm simply added to the "endangered species" Red List.

"Then I travel back in time to be crowned Prom Queen, my parents can afford dental appointments, and all of Canada is vegan and off drugs 'cold turkey,' no pun intended.

"The Greens: Your Life Will Become Unmanageable," "Just Say No to Global Partying" and "Oh, Yeah, Climate Change, Whatever" were obviously great slogans that totally resonated with voters—in a system that wouldn't make you feel like your vote was just flushed down the toilet, except that's not the system we have."

However, there was one new non-existent result that should give regular Canadian centrist voters pause.

Maxime Bernier's right-wing People's Party of Canada (PPC), which based its nationalist platform on anti-immigrant sentiment, would have made gains in the new, "this is just to rub your nose in it, not-in-our-lifetimes" PR system, from zero seats to six.

Moderates vastly preferred the actual current result, where the PPC and its leader don't exist.

When asked for comment, Bernier replied,

« Ploof! That crazy Thunberg girl is responsible. Socialists! Anti-business climate alarmists! Too much government! Over-spending! Immigrant quotas! Just look at her burqa! *Suis pas gay ! Ça c'est fucké, heins ?* »

Then Mr Bernier and all his supporters climbed into a Volkswagen Beetle and drove into oblivion.

ALBERTA SEEKS ALTERNATIVE TO "ELITE, EAST-RISING SUN THAT DOESN'T REPRESENT OUR VALUES."

THERE IS DISILLUSIONMENT IN ALBERTA post election, as well as the feeling, common to privileged teenagers, that no one cares or understands and that life is meaningless.

Here's why: Alberta for decades has relied heavily on limitless, highly-priced oil and gas sales to fund their provincial programs.

Most recently, Trudeau sucked up to the petulant province by agreeing to move forward with the Keystone XL Pipeline, even though this seemed to undercut his own federally-mandated carbon tax, his commitment to the Paris Accord, his returning all his empties to The Beer Store, and any other green initiatives he might think up on the spur of the moment while setting the trash cans outside Rideau Cottage.

But those ornery Albertans were having none of it. In fact, Alberta has become so angry at perceived slights from Ottawa that separatist sentiment is at an all-time high, with the province threatening to "repatriate" social services and even migrate its Canada Pension Plan to be administered locally.

"Trudeau thinks he can soften us up by giving us just one measly environmentally disastrous and insensitive-to-indigenous-culture oil pipeline so we can continue to prop up the world-wide petroleum vector of waste, greed, global warming and corruption, but we see right through his insincere kow-towing!" said Ginger Spill, Head of Communications for the "Oil & Gas ♥You So Much! Club", an industry-sympathetic think tank.

"Trudeau knows very well that he simply can't continue to fob us off with his Ottawa condescension and half-way measures.

"We want nothing less than total capitulation to our demand that Canada officially renounce carbon reduction efforts, based as they are on the random opinions of a few thousand gas-hating fake scientists. Our soon-to-be-obsolete jobs are at stake, here!"

Ms. Spill continued, "We don't need the rest of Canada! We have oil and gas, which will keep us living high on the hog well into the next couple of years!

"We're thinking oil and gas burgers, oil and gas high schools, oil and gas country & western radio stations, oil and gas internet, and oil and gas traditional marriages!

"You know what else? We're sick of you guys shining that bright light on us every morning! We don't need some elite eastern sunrise, making our eyes hurt and mocking our values, telling us when you think it's OK to get up, when it's appropriate to have a shot of corn mash whiskey, or encouraging the gays to sing "You are the Sunshine of My Life" at their gay weddings!

"Screw your leftie, socialist propaganda about taking our hard-earned money and giving it all way to other people and your green-this and green-that boondoggle!

"We're gonna stick it to *Turdeau* and his band of bureaucratic, job-killing Libs. From now on, every morning, per our schedule, Danielle Smith will stand at the top of the Calgary Tower, pull down her overalls, bend over and spread 'em.

"She can do it ass-east, ass-west, ass-north or ass-south 'cause we're sick of being Missus Nice Gal Co-operative! Whatever comes outta her ass and from wherever is all the sun in the morning we'll ever need!

"Now we just gotta work out how to manage her moon at night..."

Monday Man Crush: Insurrection Shaman Dude

Welcome to another installment of Monday Man Crush, this time two days early, not several months late like you might be thinking.

I seriously have no space in my life for "glass-half-full" types, so please try to be *more* positive, *less* high-maintenance.

This is the recurring feature—and I mean recurring like that asteroid that caused the dinosaur extinction is recurring, i.e. it's definitely going to recur but you might not be around for it—in which I binge out on hunky, luscious, cute straight dudes because I actually literally have nothing better to do. At least I admit it.

This week's slice of hot brisket with red-eye gravy is Capitol Insurrection Shaman Dude Jake Angeli.

Jake is just the sort of low-life trash that I'm drawn to after I've downed a mickey of vodka and set fire to the back of my Banana Republic turtleneck with a coffee table lighter. For one thing, check the body—Shaman dude is slender and a bit furry, an otter, in fact. He's handsome as fuddle-duddle.

And he's a bit of a kinky exhibitionist. He walks around historic seats of government swingin' his flag pole and showing off his credentials and he doesn't give a damn. Stand back, my head may explode!

I pray he has PTSD from his childhood experiences growing up in a trailer park in the Everglades. Without PTSD, it's like, game over in my books when it's a question of possible friend-with-benefits material. I always want to make sure that whoever I'm hangin' with has had at least one worse experience than me hangin' with them, *and then*—in good company with Julie Android in The Sound of Gumption—*I don't feeeeel so baaaad*.

If he doesn't have PTSD, I'll fall back on Plan B, which is not giving a fuck, or Plan C, which is making the experience of me hangin' with him so unforgettably horrible, he'll have PTSD for the *next* superstar blogger. Win-win-win, with all three wins for me!

Let's quickly run through my standard Monday Man Crush Checklist© /*Checklist mancreush de lundi* ©: Wears punky make-up, check. Tattoos, oh yes. Bad childhood compared to the natural offspring of the First Earl Grey, check. Criminal record, are you kidding me?

This little cock-ferret hits all the high notes, aided by that fetching, though rather Wagnerian, antler *chapeau* that's like something Philip Treacy designed for Steak of the Month Club.

But more out of left field than all this—he is *vegan*, for cryin' out loud! Which means, I guess, that the twenty animals draped around his taut, masculine frame just crawled up there and died of old age.

As you can imagine, the food in prison caused him serious gastric distress. I'd love to make him stomach-soothing ginger tea, lie beside him on a rainy afternoon when he's on his meds and massage his belly while we watched my pirated Maria Callas DVDs, or maybe read passages to each other out of "Democracy in America" by Alexis de Tocqueville.

Gay Progressive? I'll have him onboarded in no time.

IN CONCLUSION

Insurrectionists are a threat to public order and the rule of law, totally reprehensible, dumber than concrete, and *where can I get me some??!!*

High fives and a chant of "Hang Mike Pence!" in honor of Jake Angeli, Capitol Insurrection Shaman Dude, for he is your—our!—

#MondayManCrush!

Ministress of Silky Sheen

Canadian Finance Minister, Deputy Prime Minister in a pinch, something to do with Alberta for a couple of days but it didn't work out, Justin Trudeau's Official BFF Next to Sophie-Grégoire,

and Dry-Cleaning Picker-Upper without portfolio Chrystia Freeland delivered her budget speech on April 19, 2021, after performing her customary pre-speech hair-whip, thereby ending the longest period without a Federal budget since Confederation.

Fortunately for Canadians, the budget had been approved in record time by the doddering, 94-year-old descendant of the German dynasty of Saxe-Coburg-Gotha who lives three thousand miles away in a heavily-guarded mausoleum filled with priceless antiquities, and who, for reasons no one can actually remember, is just kind of randomly in charge of everything.

So, like, *Vielen Dank, gnädige Frau!* for every little thing you do.

The popular budget includes funds for Indigenous reparations, subject to haggling, though Freeland made it clear that any frills like clean drinking water will just have to wait until the next election.

Also in the budget was Trudeau's eagerly anticipated "One Litre of Kawartha Lakes Premium Maple Walnut Ice Cream for All Vaccinated Canadians Over Eleven" pandemic benefit, and an optional subscription to FunkyWoolSox-R-Us dot com, which gets him a free month for anyone who signs on using his special QR code.

No word yet, however, on affordable housing, electoral reform, or his plan to lure Jodie Wilson-Raybaud to a hotel in Yellowknife then lock her in the bathroom until she promises to behave.

Funds for environmental initiatives were somewhat reduced as Canada's commitments to the Paris Accord have been delegated to US President Joe Biden, whose canceling of Keystone XL on his first day in office, and recent huge investment in electric cars, caught the Federal Government napping.

We contacted Global Affairs Canada for their insights, or, since no one answered the phone there, any old random shopper at the LCBO.

"Surprised? Gobsmacked is more like it!" said our random shopper, Wendy, as she loaded up her cart with one-litre boxes of Jackson-Triggs Sauvignon blanc.

"This cynical betrayal by our neighbour to the south is completely contrary to the spirit of the Three Amigos Trade Whaddayacallit. I mean, making campaign promises, fair enough, but then actually, like, doing them?

"I'd like to think it's just a rookie mistake," she continued, while shoving a handful of vodka miniatures into her coat pocket, "because otherwise, we'll have to, I dunno. Cave on softwood lumber prices, I guess? Let me get back to you after I... Actually, could you check these out for me? I'm just a little teensy-weensy bit wasted! So what else is new, eh?"

Freeland did have to field some hostile questioning at the press briefing, with one reporter asking, "Does the Liberal Government have a money tree?"

But the Harvard- and Oxford-educated, internationally respected journalist and best-selling author on economic policy, who speaks five languages, is recognized worldwide for her commitment to human rights and democracy, and who, according to close friends of the PM, "makes a killer cup of java and runs out for Timbits for the guys without being asked," chose to deflect rather than engage.

"Can I pick up an anniversary card and some nice flowers for anyone?" she said, adding, quite helpfully, "They have a great selection at Loblaws. Yes, no?

"Anyway, you can catch me in the PMO, I'll be ironing Justin's shirts from eight PM. Toodles!!"

Response to the budget by Canadians has been mixed, with most people ecstatic at the positive, progressive agenda, but quickly sinking into depression as they realize that mostly it will get snarled up in red tape then fizzle out, followed by quiet desperation when they realize that the only real alternative is the Conservatives, and circling back to ecstatic again when they realize they can just keep gritting their teeth and strategic-voting

Liberal, whatever their preferred political affiliation might be.

Jagmeet Singh, leader of the New Democratic Party, however, was vociferous in his criticisms, commenting, "Hey everyone, lookit me! Hey, lookit... Over here, *hellooo*—?" but no one did.

Freeland even managed to keep her cool during an awkward moment when Liberal MP William Amos, supposedly "on holiday," wandered into the House naked and stood directly behind her urinating into his coffee mug.

"Oh, darn," he said, as the Speaker called for order. "I just can't get used to this hybrid thing! Am I supposed to be at home? Sorry! My bad! OK, then!"

"It's disgraceful!" opined one MP from the conservative side. "It's simply disingenuous of Bill Amos to claim he's confused, when he's obviously flaunting his pissing cred."

But a New Democratic Party MP jumped to Amos's defense. "Only a conservative could see a limp, micturating dick and make it partisan—just typical."

Freeland, when asked later how she managed Amos with such aplomb, simply replied, "Seriously? I've seen far more honorable members."

. . .

In other news, US Vice President Kamala Harris, missing since the Inauguration, is still not Black enough.

John Tory's Heart is "Broken"

Working like a Trojan—I wonder, does that mean one of the soldiers from ancient Troy? The celebrated horse? Or the prophylactic? I can never decide—

—pulling together the latest collection of my writing, and even though it's really a simple task of deciding on my best, funniest material, do not for one moment think that I will settle for anything being easy in my life. I demand a *challenge*. Things must be *hard to achieve*.

I could make blinking aerobic.

I cannot leave anything alone: not a box of Kraft Dinner, which I revise with lightly blanched vegetables, white truffle oil and Halal wieners; not my completed blog posts, which I continue to polish like they were grandma's sterling silver turkey baster, the one she kept on the bedside table; not even my epic response to some troll's inflammatory comment on Twitter, which anyway just hits his steel bot-head and slides off, like gobs of brain matter after a trepanning.

I revisit. I revanche. I fiddle, I tinker. I throw in a schooner race, the complete bloodline of Adam and Eve, and Julia Child's recipe for baking croissants at home, and then I think: How can I make this more, you know, *jokey?*

In fact, like an elderly Harry Potter with dementia who got lost on the way home, I live not under but on the staircase, ready to be possessed by its spirit and overthink the snide remark that's forming, right now, in your minds.

I'm still processing slights I received from colleagues in Grade Six that didn't quite register at the time; people who insulted me so long ago, they're actually dead.

Suddenly, while singing a hymn at their memorial service, it hits me between the eyes. I think:"(*Oh, God, our help in ages past...*) Hey, wait a minute. *What* did Danny Milligan say about my hot pants? (*...Our Hope for years to come...*) You know something.... I think he was being ... (*... Our shelter from the stormy blast...*)...sarcastic...! (*... and our Eternal ...*)... WHAT THE — !!?"

Then I return home, ugly-cry into a litre of No-Name Frozen Dessert Substitute until it melts, and drink it through a straw.

JOHN TORY, THE QUITE-RECENTLY FORMER "if you have to have one, it might as well be him" Mayor of Toronto, who filled the rancid, crack smoke-reeking shoes of Rob Ford (late brother to Doug, current Premier of Ontario, because we couldn't manage to take out both of them at once, the technology just wasn't there), like yours truly, has been particularly busy.

Not just busy being the single most boring, least visionary leader in Canada, and not just busy being an old-style conservative.

You know, the kind of conservative where you didn't have to go, "Shall I vote for the Liberals defending human rights and at least *pretending* that they're trying to make my life better? Or for the cranky cons who limit human rights to white, straight males because it's just too goldarn expensive to give rights to all those bleeding hearts, and you gotta balance the budget, except when you don't have to! What good are rights without a balanced budget? Exactly! Or something!"

John Tory comes from the Jurassic line of conservatives who thought human rights were probably a good thing, but could you please pull your socks up? Then, in the manner of my Great Aunt Lula pressing a toonie into my grown-up hands and croaking, "Don't let your mother know!" they'd sign you up for the dole.

He worked as an intern to Margaret Birch, Ontario's first female member of Cabinet, who crafted the "Birch Proposals," a work of malign genius designed to make day-care less user-friendly, more understaffed, and more dangerous for kids.

This is the Conservative way of proving how much they want to "Save (money on programs that help) the Children."

Tory spent a fairly uneventful political career, at one time leading the Progressive Conservatives, a party name whose built-in oxymoron never hit me until fairly recently. The PC's and the Liberals were so similar in policy, one might have imagined they were simply cooked up so we could switch out our vote every other year and not actually go crazy from ennui.

Tory was deemed worthy of the party leadership because he was the most adept at winning easy, traditionally conservative seats by parachuting in last-minute after the incumbent resigned, thus profiting from voters' total confusion.

He has always had deep ties to the business sector, but never sleazier than was obviously unavoidable. Ted Rogers, the media mogul, was a family friend, and, when politics became tiresome, Tory was able to change to a more relaxing hobby of being a radio talk-show host, courtesy of family friend. (Only a Canadian would aspire to be a star on radio, which we think of as "television for the blind.")

He was also on the Board of Metro, a giant supermarket chain, where he —

Hello? *Hellllo?* Oh, do try to stay awake, I promise you it gets a little more interesting. At least, for John Tory.

Elected three times to the post of mayor, Tory was quite popular, as he didn't rock the boat by, for example, making decisions or getting anything of note accomplished. Decisive? The heck!

Making decisions and executing an action plan tend to alienate at least one person. Who needs that kind of confidence-bashing boondoggliness?

He was like a Swanson TV Dinner compared to real dinner: satisfying the basic need without going whole hog in a way that Canadians find tastelessly Over The Top.

Jeezus. Curb your enthusiasm, Cherry Ames, Girl Mountie! We're not revolutionaries at heart, remember? We're loyalists.

An example of one of Tory's not-exactly-groundbreaking "tough on crime" initiatives: Tory teamed up with Premier Ford and arranged things so that Toronto Community Housing Corporation (social housing) would now be able to refuse applications from tenants who had been evicted for "criminal activity" such as drug dealing, assault or property damage.

I was pretty sure that property damage could also fall under a civil heading, but I stand corrected. Selling heroin, knocking over a potted plant; getting snippy with the receptionist or smacking your ex in the face with a two-by-four—it's all equally reprehensible.

This measure was, said an article on Global News, *"... part of a new strategy the province announced earlier this year to help create more housing and combat homelessness."*

And I ask you. Seriously. What better way to combat homelessness than making people homeless?

Reading carefully, I note that the article states, *"evicted for"* not *"convicted of."* I'm wondering, you see, if these are evictions that could be based on perceptions, complaints, landlord harassment or malice.

Oh and wait, that drug-dealing thing. Did you sell marijuana before

October 17th, 2018? Because then you'd be just another low-life. Off to the shelter with ya!

After that date, you would be a Groovy Cutting-Edge Entrepreneur, because suddenly, with another arbitrary wave of the wand that made you a homeless lowlife, you are now, bippity boppity boo, perfectly legal people, and please, sir, this way to your table for two while we valet-park your Mercedes!

Now the Ontario Government sells marijuana, but you went to jail for how many years?

Instead of building new affordable housing, Tory and Ford found it easier to persecute poor people, whose lives are already hanging by a thread, and kick them out onto the streets. "Tough on crime" means we can get all self-righteous about the deserving poor (like us, morally impeccable) and the undeserving poor (hot messes).

SO FAR, DEPRESSINGLY PREDICTABLE. ONE foreshadowing incident from Tory's past haunts me, though. Here it is, as described in Wikipedia, "The Encyclopedia You Write Yerself! ® ":

> *[As a young aspiring politician]* Tory later served as tour director and campaign chairman to then Prime Minister Brian Mulroney, and managed the 1993 federal election campaign of Mulroney's successor, Kim Campbell. In his role as the Progressive Conservative campaign co-manager that year, he authorized two infamous campaign ads that ridiculed Liberal candidate Jean Chretien's face, which is partially paralyzed due to a childhood disease. The ads were greeted with much outcry among the Canadian public. They were withdrawn ten days after their first airings, and the Progressive Conservatives would proceed to be decimated in the federal election.
>
> [https://en.wikipedia.org/wiki/John_Tory]

Got it? A lapse of good taste. An egregious failure of judgment. Something tacky in the woodshed. An ever-so-slight taint of ableism, entitlement, frat-boy immaturity. Hold that thought.

OK, are you ready? After the Toronto Star broke the news and he could no longer hide, John Tory, Mayor of Toronto, confessed on February 10th, 2023, that he'd had an extra-marital affair with a staff member, during the pandemic, and that very day tendered his resignation.

An affair? Oh, of course he did! I forgot: he's a white, straight male in power. DOH! When I remember that, I'm tempted to say, "*An extra-marital affair? You mean, just the one? What noble containment and sacrifice!*"

The Star also revealed that the woman had traveled on several publicly-funded trips with him.

I'm shocked at John Tory, but even more disturbed at the public responses to the affair, and not because people are angry. They're sympathetic, believe it or not:

Stay, John Tory! It was just a little affair, didn't hurt anyone, it was consenting, it's nobody's business, it's a personal matter. It didn't break any laws!

Didn't break any laws? Oh, well done, little soldier! Sheesh. Is that, as Peggy Lee once rasped out from the depths of her oxygen tent, all there is?

The standard to be met is not just right actions, but right appearances. The situation to be avoided is not just actual conflict of interest, but even the perception of it.

Toronto City Council's code of conduct calls on members to "perform their duties and arrange their private affairs in a manner that promotes public confidence and bears close public scrutiny."

Professor Marsha Barber, a media ethics expert who teaches at Toronto's Metropolitan University, had this to say about the Star's investigation:

> "The big question is, was the Star's reporting in the public interest? Yes it was and it certainly met journalistic standards… If you're having an affair with a staffer who reports directly to you, the public needs to know about that. If there's a power imbalance the public needs to know.
>
> "The reason is, when you are elected to public office, you are acting on behalf of your constituents. So, if there is anything questionable, it's in the public interest to know."
>
> [Toronto Star, Friday, February 17, 2023, *"Star coverage of Mayor John Tory met journalistic standards."* https://bityl.co/HIR7]

John Tory's fling with a subordinate would be eyebrow-raising in a private company. It's absolutely taboo for someone in a public role: the mayor of Canada's biggest city, a man who presides over a huge treasure chest of public money, and whose decisions will affect not just us but future generations.

It's NOT a personal matter. It IS a matter of public interest. It is an egregiously unethical failure of judgment. It casts doubt over all of his decisions and actions, it puts the governance of Toronto into disrepute and it fails the low standard we expect of our leaders, that low standard being:

#63-B: DON'T FUCK THE STAFF.

On a normal day, after a good night's sleep and a sustaining breakfast that includes whole grains and a couple of servings of organic fruit so you should stay regular, it definitely would fall within most ladies' or gentlemen's capabilities to not fuck the staff.

Raise your hand if you've been a boss and not fucked the staff. There, you see?

Like, it's not an *insurmountable* barrier to entry for "Mayor." *I think I can I know I can...* Just avoid fucking the staff. All right, cupcake? You're gonna be fine.

But not John Tory. We weren't worth it. Ah, well, you know what they say: You can take the white, straight male out of City Hall. But you can't take his dick out of his subordinate's vagina, not for all the respect in a month of Sundays.

You know what enrages me? That John Tory, in some sweaty recess of his adolescent mind was thinking: "I can get away with this."

I can get away with this is not an existential position that fills me with warm, fuzzy feelings of trust and security.

At his final press conference, Tory said "it broke his heart" to resign. Really?

You betrayed our trust, not to mention the trust of your wife and family, threw all the plans into disarray and forced us to have another election so you could give your penis (apparently *not* broken) some attention and work out your male menopause issues, and we're supposed to feel sorry for YOU?

Spare me.

GOT A NOTE FROM THE COCKROACHES, who I call "William" collectively, because, honestly, they all look pretty much alike.

I know that's desperately chauvinist of me.

The note read:

which translates as:

"Hey, big smelly God-roach. You think you haaaaaave problems?? We've haaaad to move three times in the past 24 hours and we're constantly on red alert on account of yer ongoing chemical waaaaarfare. Totally against Geneva Convention.

"Who's Geneva Convention? One of yer offspring? Anyway.

"Well, guess what, roach-God? Yer chemicals just make us more horrrrrrny, so we have far-out sex and reproduce twice as fast! Last night, Drudella and I had a three-way with a centipede! YOWZA!

"Whatsamatter? You don't believe in interspecies relaaaaaations?

BIGOT!

"Now, if you'll excuse me, I have a new routine to practice with Fifi for "Cirque du Soleil, Édition roach." They've asked her to do her bit with the frilly umbrella and I'm going to swallow a paper clip almost all the way down.

If you think that sounds easy, it's probably cause of yer friend Brad! So long SUCKER!"

Cockroach is a very inflected language. Or maybe I mean "infested," I get them mixed up.

Dyspeptic Digests
& Loopy Listicles

Monthly Mayhem: A News Round-Up

It's a month of Good Things in The People's Republic of Pandemia, which is, like Toronto, a soulless state of mind you can't escape. Our crazed boredom makes us seek out what we previously might have ignored as trivial or bizarre.

FACEBOOK VIDEOS ARE KILLING ME

I AM ADDICTED TO CUTE ANIMALS—which I relentlessly anthropomorphize—interacting in Facebook videos.

Recent examples:

A squirrel smiled while being stroked by its rescuer and I pretended the squirrel was like a grateful human, not a nasty squawking rodent that would chew the guy's arm off if it thought there was a chestnut somewhere in the lining of his sleeve.

A puppy met a kitten and was adorable. Who knew? I think they may have sung something from "Phantom of the Opera".

A kitten met a puppy and did the same in reverse, so like, "I Got You, Babe."

A dog in Shanghai who refused to leave his home, even though his owner died six years ago, was brought to his senses by a new owner who followed the advice of a wise vet.

"Record your voice," he said, "and let him hear the recording while you're not here. Dogs attach to people, not places."

It worked. As the dog followed his new owner out of the courtyard he turned around and paused, wistfully, as though saying a final goodbye to this place of anxiety, grief and torment. Then he fairly leaped into the car.

I have a heart murmur as a direct result of this video. If one day I feel I just can't take it any more and life has no meaning, I'll watch it again and restore my faith in a loving creator. Which won't really help, since at that point my aorta will have exploded.

In contrast, another video compiled scenes of wild animals tearing each other to shreds, but one lady was appalled at the brutish reality of the African savannah and said we should stop watching, or at least enjoying, the crimson horrors of nature.

Someone responded to her with the comment, "People like you are the reason we support partial birth abortions."

This is, I guess, an example of how the Internet enriches our lives and puts us in touch with people so brim full of uncirculated bile, we would gladly walk up fifty flights of stairs to avoid being in the same elevator with them.

MAINSTREAM MEDIA

ELSEWHERE, A MAN HAD A FIGHT WITH his cow (it was not clear who won) and a four-year-old girl took her pet chicken for a walk.

Dr Seuss was "canceled," according to the tut-tutters of the Right, but you know that anything from the Right is a poison pill buried in a spoonful of bullshit to help it go down more easily.

The truth is that the estate of Theodore Geisel simply marked for removal six of his least popular books which contained racist imagery. Horton will still hear a Who, Green Eggs still go with Ham, the Cat in the Hat will still come back, and the Republican party is still considering The Grinch for 2024.

The former Mister Potato Head, that die-hard avatar of identity politics, will henceforth be known simply as "Potato Head" (they, theirs).

The future looks bright, be it as trans ambassador of a more inclusive society, or just served beside a pork loin chop after being mashed with salt, pepper and butter.

Speaking of which, in Canada, homemakers of every conceivable gender and sexual expression rose up in arms about unusually hard butter, the result, it turned out, of feeding cows palm oil.

This is how the pandemic has encouraged us to focus on the important things in life, like our morning toast, and not sweat the small stuff, like the desecration of native land by Keystone XL and homeless families living in tents in the snow.

A study commissioned by the Institute for Propagation of the Obvious showed that the Capitol rioters belong to a class of people who do not process information correctly.

Texas was ravaged by blizzards, and Republicans not only misidentified Governor Greg Abbott as a Democrat, they blamed the extreme weather and the resulting total breakdown of infrastructure on the Green New Deal, which hasn't actually happened yet, and wind turbines, rather than a century of fossil fuel production and dependence, climate change denial and inaction, and privatization.

The class of people who do not process information correctly believed them.

In fact, wind-generated energy provides about seven percent of Texas's power, and the private companies who own the turbines took no precautions to make sure they would work during severe weather conditions, because, well, that would cut into the companies' profits, and require thinking with compassion about people's lives and needs, both of which are illegal in Texas.

The former governor, Rick Perry, comforted Texans by telling them they should just put up with their unheated homes, empty supermarket shelves, and tainted water, because at least they were free from the tyranny of federal regulations; but, inevitably, a few ornery, unpatriotic Americans thumbed their noses at him and froze to death.

Prime Minister of Canada Justin Trudeau and U.S. President Joe Biden had their first bilateral meeting, virtually. They issued a joint statement committing to human rights, equality, financial aid, and strong management of the pandemic. It was like the world was not only normal, but progressing.

I am over the moon and chortling so much I may crush a kidney with sheer joy at how Biden has proved that voting for a "sleepy" centrist is the only way to get your radical socialist agenda implemented; and also revealing that getting old is not a bad decision that we make.

It just happens, youngsters, and we do know more than you after all. There's no moral high ground in bucking the system when the system is all there is to work with.

Trudeau backtracked on his promise of a Canada-wide Pharmacare program, saying it was a provincial responsibility, in order make his backtracked promise on election reform into a matching set.

Facebook had a huge pout when the Australian government tabled a bill that would force it to pay news services for the content that they currently steal. Google fell in line—Google!—but Facebook shut down all

> ## DID YOU KNOW? WELL, I NEVER...!
>
> During his 14-year tenure as governor, Rick Perry restricted access to abortion in Texas, and at one time issued an executive order mandating that Texas girls receive the HPV vaccine, thereby thanking Merck pharmaceutical, who contributed generously to his political campaigns; and proving that conservatives actually love big government as long as its goal is keeping young Texas pussy healthy and ready for access on demand, like Jesus said.
>
> Perry, a social conservative who compares gay people to alcoholics and supports the state execution of intellectually disabled prisoners, has weird flashes of decency and common sense, which are able to sneak through his religious bias when he mistakenly relaxes his anal sphincter; but as soon as he's clenched up again he gets on with the normal Republican business of stripping people of their healthcare and screaming about socialism.

news on Australian Facebook, and in the process denied access to Covid-19 information, a host of other essential government programs, and its own Facebook page.

Trump has rightly been condemned for inciting riots at the Capitol both directly and through disinformation, but Facebook, proving that business is much more efficient than government, has outshone that performance in myriad ways.

That certificate of excellence includes: inciting riots in Asia resulting in minority persecutions and deaths; colluding with Russia in its campaign to destabilize the US and interfere with the 2016 election; illegally providing our private, personal data to Cambridge Analytica for the purpose of performing, without consent, a secret social experiment on us, Facebook's users.

That tiny, well-publicized sample probably represents just the tip of the iceberg that HMS Democracy is foundering on—for what about the breaches of ethics and illegal activities that we haven't discovered?

Is Mark Zuckerberg still at large? When are we going to stop looking at him as a genius entrepreneur, and start seeing him for the nasty, profiteering, psychopathic brat he actually is? The more we're miserable, the more Mark makes and the more powerful he gets.

I used to think that Mark Zuckerberg should be in prison. But I was wrong.

Mark Zuckerberg should be in prison *in a dress.*

Etiquette for a New World Order

We have noted a distressing tendency amongst the young to adopt what we would describe as a "loosey-goosey attitude" regarding the niceties of social intercourse.

Allow us to take your hand—*but never the hand of a lady unless she offers it first, except when a) she is your betrothed or b) the silly cow has wandered onto the racetrack at Ascot under the influence of gin and is in imminent danger of being trampled to death by a horse*—and guide you gently but firmly onto the lavender-scented path to social success!

DINING IN "HIGH SOCIETY"

If after numerous attempts you simply *cannot* get the ketchup to flow out of the bottle at a formal dinner given by the Duke and Duchess of Cambridge, do not despair. We counsel *a cool head* and assure you that one of these clever work-arounds will be just the ticket:

Clever Work-Around 1

Take the ketchup bottle by the neck and, raising it high above your head, smash it with all your might against the sharp edge of the table, all the while coughing to mask any noise.

Insider Tip #1: If the Duchess is blinded by *a flying glass shard*, simply ring up Harrod's and have them black-cab you a selection of sunglasses by Prada or Ray-Ban. This should calm any unnecessary *hysterical crying.*

Insider Tip #2: Creeds' celebrated dry-cleaning service will gladly undertake removal of any vitreous humor from her Vera Wang gown.

Your removal from the *Royal Social Calendar* has been most resourcefully averted!

Clever Work-Around 2

If your neighbor at the table has a multi-tool, distract him by yelling, "My word, old chap, look over there! That delightful young Peeress we were admiring is *dabbing her chests* with the calf's-foot jelly!" and point away from you. As he searches for the young lady, pilfer his multi-tool from his waistcoat pocket and use the glass-cutter to *score around the neck of the bottle* so that it comes cleanly away.

Skillfully deploying the little spoon in the multi-tool, serve yourself *a sufficient portion* of ketchup, wipe the spoon with your cravat, close the multi-tool and replace it in his waistcoat pocket.

This all must be done with *lightning speed.*

Clever Work-Around 3

Excuse yourself for a moment, stuff the bottle under your greatcoat and sprint post-haste to the nearest Academy of the Fine Arts. Immediately upon arrival, enroll in an evening glass-blowing workshop for the *continuing education* of adults. Availing yourself of the facilities, surreptitiously melt off the neck of the bottle.

Race back to the table, explaining, if asked, that the welder's helmet you are wearing is to protect yourself from *allergic reactions to sun spots.*

Note that it is *most essential* that you reach the table well before the molten glass solidifies again.

INTRODUCTIONS

Three ways to easily and quickly remember someone's name

When the person presented to you says, "How do you do, I am Archibald Psmithers, with a silent 'p!'", cry out, "I am most pleased to make your acquaintance, Mister Puh-smithers!"

As you repeat the surname Puh-smithers, punch him hard in the teeth with a *decisive, tightly-clenched fist.*

This will indelibly record his name in your memory, both long- and short-term. OR

Use a mnemonic: A mnemonic, with a silent "m", is a memory aid.

For example, If you should be presented to a Miss Ghorkstein with a silent "g", "hoark" up a big wad of phlegm and expel it discreetly into her Pimm's No. 1 cup.

To stun your new acquaintance with your *exceptional sensitivity* you could add, "Shaken or stirred, Miss GORKstein?" OR

Simply address everyone as "Susan" even though they protest that that is not their name. You must *stoutly resist* these underhand attempts to confuse you and cast aspersions on your *perfect memory*.

PROPER USE OF THE CELLPHONE WHEN IN PUBLIC

It will not do simply to ignore your tradesman or wig stylist, as they ramble on about use of the comma in Jane Austen, by nodding politely, all the while making no attempt to disguise the fact that you are scrolling through the "Family Fun" videos on Pornhub and sorting them by "most viewed" or "length."

Everyone in Barrie and their unmuzzled pit bull can do that! From you, dear reader, we must demand a *higher standard* of social awareness!

The best way to ignore people is to have two cellphones rigged up in a hood constructed of leather straps so that each cellphone's face is in *direct contact* with the eyeball. Such an arrangement will effectively discourage people from talking to you about their *paltry concerns*.

It is likely that you will experience some navigation problems while using the two-cellphone technique. Do not succumb to frustration!

Simply stand on any convenient street corner and shout out, "Excuse me! Is anyone here heading, perchance, to the Saks Fifth Avenue boutique at Hudson's Bay?"

When you receive an answer in the affirmative, press the crotch of your trousers *securely and forcefully* against their backside, maintaining this intimate contact until you have reached your destination.

Do not be overly astonished should the general public regard you as a new Sir Edmund Hillary as a result of your *inventive wayfinding skills!*

If you simply cannot locate your leather hood with straps, make do with one cellphone, but make it the most costly you can buy. Apple daily releases a new iPhone which contractually requires you to throw out your headphones and charging cables and buy new ones. You would be well advised to choose one in beaten rose gold or, if price is no object, marble.

Now, should some *impudent narcissist* beetle up to you and begin to regale you with the Table of Elements, the plot of some episode of "Murder, She Wrote" or a complete, word-by-word re-enactment of a travelogue featuring Joanna Lumley sampling lye-preserved fish in Norway, simply begin *talking over them.*

Should you find yourself at a loss as to subject matter, you could in a pinch refer back to PornHub's Family Fun Category. Employing your most *stentorian voice,* declaim the closed captions for "Leave It In Mom's Beaver" until your *hapless accoster* is so put out, they positively flee your presence!

Drooling will add to the effect and improve your chances of being thought *thoroughly repellent* should your natural manner fall short of the mark.

CASUAL ENTERTAINING AT HOME

When planning a dinner party, be certain to take account of everyone's food likes, dislikes, allergies and mushy-texture problems. Then, to get the conversation going, deliberately serve everyone the wrong dish.

This will provoke *animated comments* and much ribaldry!

When the gentleman who is extremely sensitive to peanuts starts gasping and turning purple as his throat swells, then closes up, exclaim,

> "Oh, bother! If it isn't Miss Anna Phylaxis! And my Epi-pen's at the cottage! No matter! Let me make an incision in your trachea with the butter knife, after which I will insert this *MacDonald's Blizzard straw* so you can continue normal respiration!"

Don't be taken aback if your *razor-sharp quip* sets you up as the "Oscar Wilde" of your special circle!

TREATING THE GENTLE SEX WITH PROPER ESTEEM

If you're out to dinner discussing fishing tackle after a heartfelt reunion with your high-school all-male cribbage club, and a woman at the next table starts breast-feeding her squalling infant, pay no attention. This is simply a normal part of life.

You and *your lusty companions* should respond with empathy. Release your members from the confinement of your trousers, drape them on the chair seats and continue casually sharing your best Stanley Cup stories.

If the woman misinterprets your friendliness and considers this *an affront,* explain that "We thought we'd take out our perfectly natural body parts and waggle them about as well! #GuysMembersToo!" This demonstrates your solidarity with your "sisters."

Suggest to the woman that you are changing your mind and supporting abortion any time up to the one hundredth week.

No particular shock if you are henceforth regarded as a "feminist" because of your show of support!

Don't forget to slip the Maitre d' *a little something!*

BEASTLY VEGETABLES: THE ARTICHOKE

The best way to eat an artichoke is while driving, using a chainsaw. Take each quarter artichoke into your mouth and spit it at any cyclist who happens to be passing. Cyclists are usually poor, so do not often get a chance to sample *"haute" cuisine.*

Be sure to offer your companion in the front passenger seat a sample as well. It is considered *de trop* to completely sever their head with the chainsaw; we recommend the *exercise of discretion* to temper your impeccable power-tool technique.

Swinging your power tool with *too much abandon,* thus inadvertently chain-sawing through the front passenger's mouth, such that the lower jaw is hanging by a thread, is commonly regarded as a "newbie" misstep.

Most experienced artichoke enthusiasts will overlook this, even going so far as to demonstrate correct form for you, thus smoothing over your trifling error and putting you at ease for the long drive ahead. Though not entirely *headless,* one would hope!

LOL, apparently!

A packet of "wet wipes" from the chemist will aid in the absorption of *any heavy bleeding.* A very important consideration if you do not wish to undertake expensive restoration of your *white leather upholstery.*

AT THE DEBUTANTES' BALL

When arriving at the Ball, while still milling about the *porte-cochère,* turn to the footman and confide,

"Give over, Dilmot! I ain't 'arf poncin' to polish me knob with a fresh bit of the ol' shag carpet, know wha' I mean, know wha' I mean? Take these 'ere toe rubbers and present them with all me best wishes to The Lady Georgina Arbuthnot. I hear that slag'll slide down your pole faster than a poofter at a firemen's convention, doo wah, 'ow's yer faver, nudge, nudge?"

The help always appreciate your *condescending attempts* to speak their "lingo" and to demonstrate that you understand how base their morals are.

Dancing the quadrille

As you cross your arms to grasp the hands of the ladies on either side, be sure to "accidentally" brush against any available "bosom."

Should either lady blush, swiftly withdraw your hand, not neglecting to give at least one breast a *strong, manly squeeze* lasting at least ten seconds.

Standing next to you clearly indicates any lady's unspoken request that she be grabbed as rudely and forcefully as possible.

Rest assured that her squeals are *proof of the highest pleasure* rather than indignation!

We hope these suggestions have polished your social graces until they glimmer and *raised the tone* a bit!

Jordan Peterson's Quixotic Quest for Real Manhood

So much has happened since we last spoke! Democracy in the US has mounted its wild stallion and is galloping onto the funeral pyre with an enthusiasm that even Brünnhilde couldn't muster. To yo to HO!

Turns out that, according to the mountains of hard evidence amassed by the January 6th Committee ("witch hunt" in Trump-speak) Donald was In On It From the Beginning, Wanted to Be a Dictator, and generally was A Very Bad Thing.

Well, yank out my fingernails with pliers in the White House basement, who knew?

Also, he threw plates of food at the Oval Office walls, enjoyed screaming I'M THE FUCKING PRESIDENT! and generally gave his staff a squirmy choice: repeat his lies to the American public and hate yourself for a gutless ass-wipe of a sycophant the rest of your natural life; or debunk them and be permanently ostracized, then publicly humiliated at every opportunity. Your leisure time you will spend dealing with the death threats. Fun!

At time of writing, the general consensus is that there's enough hard evidence for any number of civil and criminal trials.

Now, we know that the wheels of justice turn slowly, and that that's a good thing, but honestly, people. When we've been aware since Trump's 2016 presidential campaign that he was a fraudster, a cheat, a compulsive liar, a serial sexual predator ("womanizer" I believe is the old-style term) and a proud, unrepentant racist, and have spent every waking hour since then witnessing him in action, we can be forgiven for wondering just what the connection is between money, power, and justice.

Just kidding! We totally expected that Trump would be well-wadded with protection against any repercussions the rest of us would face for the same activities. Funny, isn't it? It's almost like everyone's dragging their feet because no one wants to be first in line to send the former president to jail or something! Like—they're afraid of him!

At any rate, the soup-to-nuts four-course Trump Trial buffet may be the first indulgence labeled "all you can eat" that we're not ashamed to enjoy. Personally, I'd purge more than once, just to make sure I'd sampled everything!

CIAO, DARLING!

IT WAS ALL TOO MUCH FOR FIRST WIFE Ivana, possibly the one instance of genuine class in the entire clan, but whose ovaries could only hold out for one well-formed infant out of three against the onslaught of Donald's overworked, overpriced Trumpseed. Hence one pretty airhead, Ivanka, but two dumb terminals, the cranially and morally misshapen Donald Junior and Eric, aka the Frankenforeheads.

They say she fell down, but I like to imagine the canny businesswoman and former Olympic ski champion going out with more pizzazz.

In my version she decides she can't stand the shame any more, and invites a photo crew from Vogue over for cocktails. Then, drunk as a skunk on Cosmopolitans, and giving those assembled the promised exclusive scoop, she waits for Anna Wintour to give the signal:

Ready, set—ciao, darling!

Ivana launches herself off the landing, and down, down, down the stairs of her condo she flies, tumbling out the back door like a Sally Ann clothing donation that missed the box, and coming to a stop only because the garbage collectors have neglected to put the recycling bins back where they go.

See which version works for you. Good night, sweet Ivana! We hardly knew ya!

HAIR TODAY, HAIR TOMORROW

MEANWHILE, ACROSS THE POND, Britain's Prime Minister, Boris Johnson, that preposterous, toffee-nosed Hoorah Henry who somehow got to be in charge of something but it was too much like work (and, did you know? a graduate of Slytherin at Hogwarts), took a bad turn a couple weeks ago when his unruly hair set up a press conference and resigned.

"I'm outta here!" explained the tangled blonde mop, as it stood straight up, then flopped to the left all in one piece, like a toupée on a hinge. "There's only so many years you can spend thinking up new ways of making people say *what the fuck, does it owe him money?*, or becoming charged with static electricity with a comb. I need more of a challenge!"

The hair appeared to settle down, then stuck straight out at the sides over Johnson's ears, like an annoyed cat that's just been woken up.

And what did Johnson's hair have to say about Johnson's achievements, such as knowing just which sexual sleazebags to appoint to Cabinet, crafting laughably unbelievable denials then just saying, "OK, bloody hell, I knew, all right? Now naff off!" and partying indoors at 10 Downing Street on the eve of Prince Philip's funeral, egregiously violating lockdown protocols, while Elizabeth, at the funeral, conspicuously following them, sat entirely alone?

Johnson's hair scraped off a bit of dried sick, then spun around in all directions like it was caught in a hurricane. "A little dab'll do ya!" it said, before dropping to the ground in a big, greasy clump.

Speaking of hair, and why speak of anything else, ever, the right-wing intelligentsia in Canada have been upping the pressure on Justin Trudeau, our dictator-if-he-does-that-thing, useless-girly-man-if-he-doesn't-do-that-thing prime minister.

Brian Lilley of the Toronto Sun, a popular tabloid that last year was voted "Best Newspaper to Wipe Your Windows With if you Don't Have a Microfiber Cloth," performed a mind-bending analysis of Trudeau's summer hair cut, comparing it to Jim Carrey's do in "Dumb and Dumber" (and I can't help thinking there was malice in the movie chosen for comparison. Or maybe I just ate a bad lentil for lunch).

This was a newspaper article, you realize. About the prime minister of Canada. Like, an editor chose to print this inanity. You'd almost begin to believe that Brian couldn't really think up anything legitimate to complain about, so he resorted to just being generally negative about the first thing that came to mind.

Justin can't even get his haircut right! Next we might anticipate Justin puts bananas on his oatmeal! or Justin uses vegan leather shoe laces! It's like being swarmed by a bunch of gnats, all this random, jejune conservative carping.

Say anything in a sufficiently aggrieved tone enough times and soon the Whatever Convoy will start its long but noble trek across the continent to reclaim its freedom from the pedophile socialists, and this will make about as much sense as anything else we've heard since we last fired up Chrome.

But back to hair:

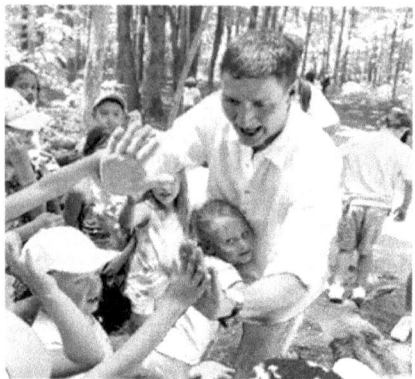 

Brian (right) looks anxious in his photo, but actually that's just the tension from his up-do pulling the skin between his eyes together. Can I be honest? I'm gay, so I get to say this: Brian Lilley just looks like a silly, fat old faggot who dyes his hair. It takes one to know one!

Justin (left) looks like he always does. Comfortable in his own skin and not giving a damn, I suspect, what Brian Lilley thinks.

That little girl hugging him? She's Canada.

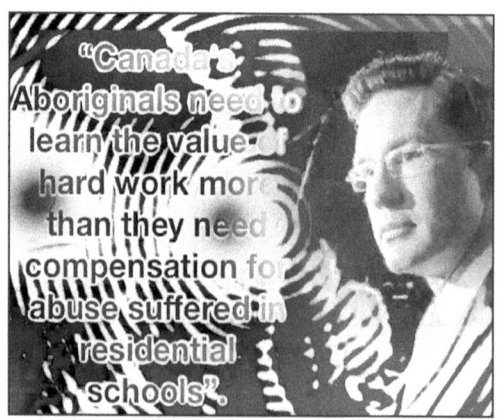

CONVOY PARTY OF CANADA

CONSERVATIVES ARE WASTES OF SKIN pretending to be humans (I like to follow the old rules of composition: start with your thesis).

Turns out that Pierre Poilievre, leader of the Conservative Party of Canada, is a "yikes, are you kidding me?" cesspool of nasty, racist quotes, on everything from First Nations people to grade-school economics.

The theme, as always, is white heterosexual men smacking down any attempt to reduce their privilege and their power. They go low, they go nasty. They don't care. And they're more and more brazen every day, more unapologetic about their goals and the means to those goals.

See the previous page for an example of the sheer poetry of Pierre Poilievre. Seriously: "The value of hard work"!

I'm not sure if Pierre looks like he's done fifteen minutes of "hard work" in his life, but there's nothing like white skin to give you that sense of finger-wagging entitlement. What understanding could he have of what First Nations children endured in the residential system?

But the goal isn't to make sense. The goal is just shut it down. Shut down any potential conversation about widening the circle of economic or social justice beyond white, heterosexual males.

Pied Piper Pierre leads us backwards in time to that sun-drenched Golden Age when men were men, women were baby-factories, charity was a bowl of cold, Calvinist oatmeal and "Injuns" were *more* grateful that we'd saved them from their indolent, heathen lifestyle, *less* awkward about the genocide.

If that weren't enough to put you off Pierre Poilievre, he wears the kind of rimless glasses that South American torturers put on just before they start to dismember you.

Which, if you're queer, female, Black, Native, poor, or any combination of the above, is exactly what he's planning to do.

A PETERSON TOO FAR

HERE'S WHAT WE ALREADY KNOW about Jordan Peterson (whose latest man-crush is none other than Pierre Poilievre!).

We know he's an intellectual lightweight, earnestly serving up lukewarm Camille Paglia (who I actually enjoy when she sticks to cultural insights; her victim-blaming libertarianism, not so much) while making goo-goo eyes at all his young, male mentees. Though he was a professor at the University of Toronto, they seem to have mutually agreed to part company as he pimps himself out in his preferred identity as a self-help guru for incels.

We know he writes silly, unnecessary books in which he makes dadly pronouncements ("Sort yourself out, bucko!") about responsibility, petting stray cats and the necessity of perfecting your life before you can criticize the social order, pontificating with all the sweaty intensity of that Boy Scout leader you always tried to avoid being alone with in the same room.

I know, even before he should open his mouth, god help us, that he'll be on the side of freedom (to give you his truth, which is the only truth that counts, about experiences that others have lived and he has not); that he'll whinge about "political correctness" and mock any attempt to treat the marginalized with respect.

We know he'll talk gravely— "It's a serious problem!"—about "Marxist" university teachers destroying impressionable minds (though I kind of thought that exposure to ideas was the point of university).

Perhaps his big claim to fame is his protracted hissy-fit, back in 2016, when the Canadian government added gender identity to its already-existing human rights legislation (Bill C-16).

Peterson man-bitched up and down the Internet that this would result in people being jailed for using wrong pronouns. This interpretation, does it even need to be said, was completely off the wall. But as we're kickstarting a moral panic, accuracy is the last thing we need.

Jordan Peterson quite simply has, to use a Jungian word he might appreciate, *animus* towards transgender people.

I sense, with my spidey gaydar, that something is alarmingly off in the self-esteem department; that just possibly he's hollowed out with insecurity about not being toxically macho enough to pass muster with his audience.

This is, surely, why his voice, high-pitched, querulous, a perfect sonic profile of the whiny victimhood he would claim to abhor, undermines his stern, uncompromising message about nature's hierarchies.

"Don't hate me, guys," he seems to plead, almost, and sometimes actually, in tears. "Don't shoot the messenger."

I picture him as the quintessential high school nerd, the pimply geek, the least popular dude in any class: despised by the jocks because he's an arrogant loner, uses big words to impress, and knows way too much about the pecking order of lobsters; unable to compensate by taking a cheerleader to Prom because he's so damn creepy, a dessicated male spinster decked out in recherché 1940's fashion.

He's so desperate, in fact, so hungry for those gazes of adulation from the young males in his audience, that he makes me want to lie in a dark room for an hour or two, just to process the pathos.

You see, he's a Gemini. I'm a Virgo with Gemini in the ascendant. I know—and, Minerva, how I wish I didn't—the way he thinks, what he fears, what he cries about. And I say "cries" for a reason: every video of his I've watched has me convinced that Jorpy is a slo-mo train wreck, a sniveling, snot-nosed man-baby, an impotent totem of narcissistic entitlement, simmering with barely-contained outrage and unacknowledged sexual frustration.

Check out any photograph of Jordan Peterson, I challenge you: is there even one instance of a face brimming with joy, erupting in spontaneous laughter or even projecting simple contentment? He has the chronic low affect of the defeated; his two emotions, rage and resentment, he can barely gin up the energy to display (but don't worry, he eventually manages).

(No stranger to defeat myself, I say this as the only gay man in the Golden Horseshoe who can spend twenty-four hours high and naked in a bathhouse and fail to have sex. I admit it, I'm not proud.)

Like me—and out of a possible million quintillion traits we could share, we share maybe two—he is interested in diet and health. But he gets, shall we say, a little stuck. He decides to eat paleo, which is the way we supposedly ate in paleolithic times when we all either starved to death or ended up as the local predator's blue-plate special.

Somehow this is better than everything we've yearned and worked and dropped bombs for, all the dietary knowledge we've gained and improvements we've made, for ten thousand years, that is to say, all human civilization. Just chuck all of that out and eat meat.

Just meat. You see where I'm going with this? I bet you dollars to senna pods Jordan Peterson is so constipated he couldn't pick up a subway token if he dropped one. He's just cement, inside. He'd need a construction-grade demolition drill just to pass a well-formed stool.

He also has had a teensy little benzodiazepine habit, nothing to be ashamed of, I'm sure we all agree? which caused him, in desperation, having exhausted the useless, slow-withdrawal touchy-feely methods of the Ontario healthcare system, to check into a Russian detox clinic.

Yes, Russian! There the manly medics put him into an induced coma for eight days so he could cold-turkey withdraw (it was surely just a bonus that, for those eight glorious days, they wouldn't have to listen to him witter on about Jungian archetypes) and thus come out of withdrawal with his virility—such as it is—intact.

For Jordan Peterson, he'd like everyone to understand, is not some feeble, feminized, namby-pamby liberal with a psychological *addiction*. Holy John Rawls, no! He's a hairy-chested warrior with a *dependency*, a condition that simply occurs, unrelated to any personal choice, and thus free of any possible moral failure, unlike the rest of us psychologically-addicted losers.

What happened, you see—and I hope you're sitting down, lest the shock of what I'm about to tell you causes you to lose your balance, grasp the corner of your Last Supper tapestry and bring the whole shebang crashing down into your Blue Mountain Pottery collection—is that one day, while Jordan was waiting for the bus, a brick-sized Xanax fell from a ledge and hit him on the head! Heavens!

And not wanting to start any rumors or anything, but while he languished in that Russian clinic, did Vladimir Putin come by, reach up inside Jordan with a black, lube-slicked polyurethane glove while making intense eye-contact and relieve him of his constipation? Your total fabrication is as valid as mine.

So far, annoying as hell, admittedly, but in the end this is all good. We're in I-can-handle-this territory. Right? If he'd left it there, we could have coped.

We could have lain in our dark rooms, under our velvet paintings of sad clowns and saucer-eyed waifs, and understood that this baseline of depressingly unoriginal and stupid was all we had to deal with. Half a box of Kleenex, and we're done. He'd be our little developmentally-challenged proto-fascist Chucky-child, with special needs, but still loved, mostly.

But no. He had to notch it up into super-duper-asshole, entitled-white-male freakazoid territory. He did this in what is becoming the time-honored method, namely, getting hysterical and know-it-all-y about—yes!— gender identity.

It's that topic that everyone, from Margaret Who? to J K Rowling to That Black Stand-Up Comic, to almost anyone irrelevant you can name, has an opinion about, with the slight handicap on their credibility that they haven't lived the experience.

Hell, they haven't even taken one second to listen to the people who *have* lived the experience so they might learn about their fellow human beings. Just shut it down!

Thus, Jordan Peterson got himself suspended from Twitter—which, I'm sorry, was exactly what he was looking for—because he just had to wade into the conversation and deadname actor Elliott Page, who had posted a Tweet celebrating PRIDE. Here's our J-Boy:

> *"Remember when pride was a sin? And Ellen Page just had her breasts removed by a criminal physician."*
> – Jordan Peterson, Twitter, June 2022

Pride was a sin! (Now you're a priest? Forgive us, Jordan, for failing to be you!)

So, pour cold water on queer folx celebrating their one month of visibility; disempower a trans person by deadnaming and misgendering them; and vilify a surgeon. How much childishness, bad manners and sanctimonious, sour hate can you pack into two short sentences? When you're as full of shit—literally—as Jordan Peterson, a heck of a lot.

In a follow-up YouTube video, Peterson metaphorically stuck out his tongue at "woke moralists" and declared that "he'd rather die" than take back his words.

Really?

We're still waiting, Professor P. Still waiting.

A Lexicon of Conservative Invective

They say the secret to bricks-and-mortar retail success is location, location, location.

The secret to marketing success—and that includes the conservative marketing of bumper-stickers pretending to be actual thinking—is repetition, repetition, repetition.

Marketing is basically mind manipulation and to this end typically employs the cognitive bias known as the "availability heuristic"—our tendency to take the mental short-cut (heuristic) of reaching for the easiest-remembered, top of mind information.

This is merely annoying when you realize you're buying Coke instead of Pepsi because you start humming *I'd like to teach the world to sing* as soon as you hit the soft-drinks aisle at Loblaws. It's another thing altogether when you see POC in the same aisle and think *"illegal immigrants collecting welfare."*

But, whiter laundry or whiter supremacy, the method is identical: positioning of the messaging as authoritative, then reinforcement of ideas that highjack all standards of logic, common sense and decency to further hidden and not-so-hidden agendas.

Donald Trump, say what you like about him, and if you don't mind, I will, was and remains an evil marketing genius, cooking up hideous Franken-memes in his underground lab of relentlessly re-animated repetitions.

Remember? Never just "Hillary", but "crooked Hillary." Never just "news", but "fake News". "Stolen election". "Enemy of the people." Not once does he deviate or let up.

Repetition, repetition… From Trump's very first speech, fear-mongering about "illegals", "rapists", "gangs"; constant racist stereotyping to such a degree that his base, already simmering with resentment, latched onto this validation of their fears and in poll after poll still consistently over-estimate the number of undocumented immigrants present in the US by twenty percent.

We're all vulnerable, we can all let our guards down. Marketing is the devil to resist. We think we're safe, but the disinformation is all around us.

Worn down by the onslaught of conservative dreck, we start to entertain right-wing tropes, a coffee date at first, just out of curiosity.

Soon the shocking becomes normalized and those sleazy tropes invite you up to their place, plying you with twisted logic as they nibble on your earlobes. Before you know it you're waking up beside them, sick with regret, sobbing, "That Ben Shapiro rant was a gateway podcast!"

Let's be smarter. Let's start pushing back. Let's look through our heads and throw out anything dubious we've been hoarding.

It's like that hideous Christmas sweater with the reindeer Uncle Herb gave you last year. You don't just throw it out because you need the closet space.

You throw it out because one day *you're gonna break down and wear it.*

...

A Lexicon of Conservative Invective

POLITICALLY CORRECT (PC):

The granddaddy of them all

Is it just me, or was "politically correct" at one time the only insult available for dismissing progressive ideas? It certainly seems to have been around forever, like a guest at the Overlook Hotel.

At any rate, "politically correct" began as an in-joke of the left-wing; a term used BY progressives to poke gentle fun at themselves when their attempts at inclusive language became too earnest.

This is the danger of letting conservatives anywhere near language: they're diabolical experts at co-opting progressive tropes in ways that upend or even annihilate their intended meaning, sometimes in a manner that's utterly repugnant (see "my body, my choice" later in this lexicon).

"Politically correct" is a sarcastic, dismissive and trivializing insult directed by, most typically, white, heterosexual conservative males, at all attempts to use inclusive language, and by extension, the people using that language. Being more inclusive involves thinking in a new way, and a tacit assumption that one may have been speaking from that walled-up locus of privilege in a manner that has been less than respectful to other human beings.

To self-reflect and come to the conclusion that one has inadvertently caused harm, and worse, to have to change one's behavior, is, to the current brood of conservatives, an outrageous demand that must be stomped out with storm-trooper boots, burned at the stake, then doused with cold water.

Straight white males *will not* tolerate even one second's interruption of their demanding schedule—having peeled grapes popped in between their dry, white lips, and stockpiling all the cushiest security blankets—especially to think of—hold on—was that the sound of... someone else's... *voice?*

Accurate, but still not everything. Conservatives cannot admit that they are on the wrong side of justice, and thus leap to the conclusion that having to use inclusive language must prove that the *differently abled, the unhoused, the food-insecure, the visually impaired, the people of color, the 2SLGBTQ+* must be a bunch of over-sensitive ninnies who just can't cope with the real world's inevitable sorrows and tribulations (which are actually caused by all the straight, white conservatives, if we're being honest, and I thought I'd give it a try).

Questions that arise include: Even if they *were* a bunch of over-sensitive types, why wouldn't you want to make that better? Are you actually that cruel? Is saying the n-word and other nasty epithets preferable? Do you want to call people "cripples"? "Faggots?" Is that what we're working for, here?

What is at the root of this disdain? Easy. White heterosexual males have held all the power and all the glory since time immemorial by yelling louder than everyone else. Because it's annoying and sometimes fatal when the people who control everything start yelling, we tended to give in just to make them shut the fuck up.

Then we "outsiders" —women, non-straight, non-white people, differently-gendered people, differently-abled, 2SLGBTQ+—started to get tiny table-scraps of equality and freedom and developed a taste for them.

Now straight white guys realize their mistake—but it's too late. The rest of us are reeling drunk with the desire for inclusion and are demanding the equality, justice and dignity that's our due, starting with *talking to and about us using inclusive, respectful language.*

And we can't get enough of it! Because progressives love a big tent, we just can't stop figuring out new ways to talk about our fellow humans with respect.

Here's an example. You all know, I'm sure, of Adobe, the company behind programs such as Photoshop, Illustrator, and the app I used to create this book, InDesign. Now, InDesign uses template pages that save you work and keep your document consistent. These have in the past been called "Master pages". But Adobe, through whatever process of self-examination, apparently realized that the word "master" had ugly connotations. These templates are now called "parent pages."

Are you tearing your hair out and screaming "politically correct"? Really? And did you have enslaved ancestors who were brought to America's shores in chains? I didn't think so.

I find Adobe's thoughtful change nothing less than adorable, because that is how much we have to dig down, become empathetic, and stop dismissing inclusive language just because we haven't shared the experiences of the oppressed and marginalized.

Yeah, it involves thinking of other people, Murgatroyd McGraw. Try not to break a nail, OK?

So "politically correct," a term that was outdated thirty years ago, is a way to shut down conversations that those in power find uncomfortable and threatening by treating inclusive language, and the very attempt at inclusiveness, with disdain. They are trying to position such discussions as beyond the pale by mocking the demands of marginalized groups that they be treated with respect and dignity.

Don't be sucked in. The more oppressed people we include, the more people we'll have to light the matches when we burn down the house.

Inclusiveness, empathy, and respect ≠ "coddling"

"Politically correct" fell out of use in the aftermath of 9/11, but resurged during the later Obama years, with the appearance of Black Lives Matter.

This time, however, rather than professors, it was students under attack, and by self-styled liberals, outraged that their students were being "coddled" by safe spaces, and "acting victimized" by "petty" microaggressions, thus playing into the tired trope that this generation is just a bunch of whiny narcissists unable to cope with the harsh realities of life.

I recently endured, sorry, watched, a discussion on YouTube, from 2019, moderated by Malcolm Gladwell, with Greg Lukianoff and Jonathan Haidt, co-authors of "The Coddling of the American Mind". Here's the clickbait intro:

> "...On college campuses across America, visiting speakers are disinvited, or even shouted down, while professors, students, and administrators are afraid to talk openly, for fear that someone will take offense..."

Oh, *c'mon*, guys! Finding this breathless description just a tad overly dramatic, I listened with skepticism and increasing impatience, but when Haidt declared that *"gays* (and all those coddled students, I assume) *should just learn to suck it up"* I all but hurled the laptop across the room.

Gay people and today's youth are not "coddled". We're also not going to put up with your smug superiority and your disrespect anymore.

The web has made the new generation a little expectant of instant gratification, big deal, and when that's wanting instant gratification for a greener planet and more justice, bring it on.

Today's youth are just not willing to sit down and shut up, despite what their wise elders command. Young women will not put up with the misogynist crap their mothers put up with; LGBTQ2+ demand an end to demeaning treatment as second-class citizens; Black Americans played the game, found the game stacked and unwinnable, and are no longer playing nice to soothe the tender feelings of white oppressors.

And as for my tribe: gay men, in fact, all queer, transgender and gender-non conforming people, are among the least coddled on the planet, because we've lived, and still live, our lives waging constant battle for our dignity and equality, even acknowledgement that we exist.

We throw off our invisibility cloaks so we can get right in the faces of homophobic bigots, then risk mass murder at the disco as we dance our truth, with nothing but love and pixie dust as weapons.

No one in public life these days makes any pretense of protecting us from evil; and *no one will ever stop us.*

So kindly put the lid on the condescending lectures about "sucking it up" and "being coddled."

You know who's *coddled?*

Privileged, heterosexual white men who want to say anything they want and suffer no consequences and listen to no criticisms, then go wringing their hands about it on YouTube so they can sell their inane books about their non-existent problems.

Moving. ON.

WOKE:

POLITICALLY CORRECT FELL ASLEEP as Bambi, and woke up as Godzilla.

Originating as a term used by Black Americans in the early twentieth century, emphasizing the need to be on the look-out for discrimination, "woke" comes already packed with connotations of injustice, white supremacy and anti-Black violence; also of solidarity, struggle and strength in community. Surely it is this etymology that has, to use a right-wing term, "triggered" conservatives.

"Woke" is far more than the sarcastic insult conveyed by "PC". *It indicates that the accuser is experiencing an acute existential threat.*

By focusing on what is being taught in schools, and branding as "woke" any topics, from gender identity to same-sex parenting to critical thinking about racism, that challenge the white conservative Christian narrative, the right has created the perception that exposing students to these ideas is literal child abuse. In other words, *"woke" cannot be argued against.*

CANCEL CULTURE:

THE STRATEGY OF CLAIMING THERE should be no consequences to anything you do or say, regardless of how obnoxious or insensitive it may be, and that anyone who takes offense is just part of a liberal conspiracy.

The best way to deal with this is to point out that everyone's free to say or do pretty much whatever they want, good taste, bad taste or no taste at all, and this includes the people who leave your show, protest outside your lecture hall or comedy club, heckle you, fire you, cancel your contract, or otherwise exercise exactly the same rights as you.

You'll just start another YouTube channel anyway, so what are you moaning about?

Hurrah for ideological silos, long may you stay in yours!

SOCIAL JUSTICE WARRIOR:

ONCE WIDELY USED, THIS TERM has fallen off the map recently, possibly because it's challenging to explain to people why they should feel ashamed of fighting for social justice, and conservatives just don't like to think that hard.

SNOWFLAKE:

AN INFANTILIZING AND (if directed at a male) emasculating term, implying that any kind of push back to being demeaned or bullied proves you're just over-sensitive, not like tough conservatives!

But remember: not only are individual snowflakes unique, perfectly symmetrical miracles of nature, you can get together with lots of other snowflakes to create an awesome blizzard that can blast a conservative's gas-guzzling stretch Hummer into a ditch.

MAINSTREAM MEDIA (MSM):

IN THIS SUBTLE BIT OF SEMANTIC DRIFT, "mainstream" no longer means

> the established media outlets which everyone in the world has come to trust because, on balance, they've not just told the truth but spoken truth to power over decades, sometimes centuries, of dedication to high standards of journalism, all of which is easily verifiable by examining their history.

Through conservative alchemy, "mainstream" is now code for

> the big broadsheet newspapers and long-established media outlets who are just agents of the deep state in the service of shadowy agendas and cannot ever be trusted to tell the truth. In fact, whatever they state to be the truth is the opposite of the truth. That their truth does actually appear to be the truth is simply a measure of their deviousness.

This is opposed to completely trustworthy, rock-solid media such as Fox News (the propaganda arm of the Trump administration); virtual fringe publications like Breitbart which conflate facts with opinions and make no pretense to objectivity; and completely cracker-jack bulletin boards like 8chan promulgating conspiracy theories, racism, and antisemitism, and lacking any kind of transparency or accountability.

I mean, all that being the case, who would trust the mainstream media, right? And sowing distrust, division and confusion is the agenda, so that truth becomes irrelevant and the basis for democracy—an established, shared reality and values that allow the body politic to work together to solve problems—no longer exists. When democracy no longer works, political violence will follow.

NAZI, HE WHO SHOULD NOT BE NAMED, HOLOCAUST DENIAL:

THE GO-TO SLURS FOR CONSERVATIVES who are either tone-deaf to the tastelessness of appropriating the Holocaust for slanging matches and political ammunition, or who are quite aware of the tastelessness and revel in it.

Another example of, invariably, white people taking it for granted that anything, even genocide, is theirs to trivialize and plunder for personal gain.

Are you Jewish? No? Then none of these words should ever issue from your stupid white face.

In fact, let's start thinking of "N**i" as *the other n-word*.

SOCIALISM:

NOT YOUR GRANDAD'S SOCIALISM. Stripped of meaning then redefined by decades of Republican propaganda and fear-mongering, *socialism* no longer refers to the economic system characterized by common ownership of the means of production.

It refers to any kind of benefit bestowed by or administered by government, but with a double-standard: any benefits given to corporations, such as financial incentives or carbon credits or tax cuts, are well-deserved *entitlements*, but any aid given to the poor or disadvantaged is a *handout*.

Capitalism, one of the great laws of the universe—and goldarn that Sir Isaac Newton for neglecting to goose-quill it down in his Moleskin notebook—is so perfect in its outcomes it invariably rewards the hard-working and punishes the lazy, so if you're poor or homeless, it must be your fault.

Because poor people are such a drain on the economy we need to control their rapaciousness by making it so difficult to claim benefits that they eventually give up in frustration.

The hysterical cry of "socialism" is the smack-down for any attempt to discuss universal health care in the US.

Insurance always involves mandatory premiums, that is, pooling money which is then available for use by members of the insured group. People don't tend to complain, "I'm not paying for your carburetor replacement!" So what is the mental barrier to health insurance?

The answer, of course, is race. And the elephant in the room is that no way are white people gonna stand back and see Black people get the same benefits as them.

If people bring up the spectre of "socialism" you could try to explain that the "National Socialists" were no more socialist than the "People's Republic" is a republic of the people, and good luck to you on that one.

SHAMELESS APPROPRIATION:

THE CONSERVATIVE PRACTICE OF APPROPRIATING liberal concepts they've scoffed at previously and using them in a way that reverses their true meaning.

Thus, males who would gladly bomb an abortion clinic, and who profess hatred of feminists, will not hesitate to join an anti-vaxx protest carrying a sign saying, "My body, my choice!"

"Religious freedom" means *"freedom to"* force Christianity into public life whether the public wants it or not. But this doesn't work both ways: there's no *"freedom from"* religion; if you're atheist that's not a legitimate choice, and you must not under any circumstances profess your non-belief within earshot of a Christian. That would hurt their feelings!

"*All Lives Matter!* cries the white establishment, disingenuously implying that Black people want special privileges, when a five-year-old could understand that the message is Black Lives Matter, So Start Acting Like They Do.

PROGRESSIVE STOCKHOLM SYNDROME:

THE CONTRARY TENDENCY WITH SOME progressives to get ornery and argue *against* progressive concepts possibly because they make us uncomfortable or trigger our unexamined biases.

The social scientists who came up with concepts such as microaggressions, critical race theory, white fragility, didn't do so just to get on the news or to annoy you. Their intent, like any scientist, was to find explanations for what actually happens.

"Microaggressions" is not an idea snatched out of the air and then justified post hoc by cherry picking data. It was the name given to a daily experience of disrespect and verbal / physical abuse based on white supremacy / heteronormative assumptions / misogyny, indicated by the data. In other words, the reality and the experience came first; then the label.

Your out-of-hand rejection of any new paradigms that aren't within your lived experience is not a sign that you are a feisty renegade who can tear holes in arguments made by people who have experienced these things.

It's a sign you need to STFU and listen.

SHEEPLE, HERD MENTALITY:

THE LIBERTARIAN CONCEPT THAT ANYONE who takes advice from scientists or defers to authority in any way, even when anyone can see, in real time, that their advice is correct, is a gullible moron.

Taking horse de-wormer, believing that the 2020 Presidential election was stolen, or thinking that Hillary eats babies on her pizza, none of which concepts have a shred of evidence to offer and thus actually do make you a gullible moron, don't make you a Sheeple—because all those millions of gullible morons doing exactly the same as you are proud, independent thinkers.

The best way for you to counter this is to go ahead and be a sheeple, get vaccinated, and not die so you can be on duty in the ICU when the gullible morons are admitted.

They'll appreciate someone with empathy being there to hold their hand.

Monthly Mayhem, Again

Let's take stock. How is the world doing these days?

It's been on fire! Australia just couldn't stop burning, nor could the west coast of Canada and the US, with entire towns wiped out, thousands evacuated, families losing everything, smoke drifting for hundreds of miles.

All part, I guess, of that super well-coordinated, world-wide fake global warming conspiracy. Marjorie Taylor Greene upped even her own crazy factor with her assertion that the fires were caused by "space lasers controlled by the Rothschilds;" an anti-Semitic dog whistle of air-raid siren subtlety.

Imagine: Not only did they let Marjorie Taylor Greene run for office, *people voted for her.*

I just wanted you to let that sink in for a moment.

So who could blame all those billionaires for wanting to take a hard pass? They quickly withdrew a couple days' interest on some of the dollars saved by shifting their money around, keeping their workers lean and hungry, and sucking up tax breaks, built themselves rocket ships and went into orbit.

It was—*touching.* They were so thrilled, like little boys at Christmas, that we could not help being thrilled on their behalf.

We cried for sheer joy as we watched those way-obvious phallic symbols blast off during our unpaid coffee breaks at several of our part-time jobs, until we realized *they were coming back.*

So, to answer my initial question: same as usual, plus our disappointment.

How about hunger? Six hundred and ninety million people go to bed hungry every day; increasing economic prosperity smooths out the rough edges in developed countries, but has virtually no effect in the Third World. The rich get fatter and the poor, hungrier; poor children more malnourished, more stunted.

Jeff Bezos, with the increase in his income for one month, could wipe out world hunger. Does he do it? Pull the other one, it's got a ball and chain on it!

Hunger's been in the news in Toronto, with our food banks reporting record numbers of the newly food-insecure as a result of the pandemic. In fact, food bank use has more than doubled; there are more new customers than regulars.

"Who could have predicted this!" gasped CityNews.

How about anyone on ODSP (disability support) or OW ("Ontario Works," Orwell-speak for welfare) with a calculator? With ODSP at around $1,400 max for a single person, which includes allowance for non-existent housing, and OW for a couple with one child at around $1,991 a month for basic needs and accommodation, it doesn't take a Nobel laureate to crunch the numbers.

According to my calculations, let's see, carry the one, add a decimal point… OK, got it—You're screwed.

How can we still be waging war on the poor, in Canada, in 2021?

Doug Ford, Ontario's conservative Premier, and scion, ever since we managed to kill off Rob, of the most brazenly corrupt dynasty of low-lifes in Canadian politics, gutted social services and education funding the minute he was elected.

Why? *Because that's what conservatives do.*

What solution has any conservative ever proposed to the problems of homelessness? Child poverty? Unemployment? Inequity? Name me one.

You can't, because they don't believe it's their job to find solutions to social or economic problems, even though we elected them to serve the public good—all politicians, liberal or conservative, are supposed to be serving the public good, by default.

This doesn't matter to conservatives any more. If you're poor, you're lazy or a loser. A welfare queen or the last rat in the race. Either way, they're preparing for the cull.

Instead, not believing either in government or the public good, they simply take the power and govern for their own benefit, turning a term of office into their personal four-year business networking event, with public resources and free admin support, lubricated by entitlement and powered by sleaze.

Ford's policies are directly responsible for the grind and misery of hunger, homelessness, child poverty, and desperation, during a pandemic without end, and with winter approaching, in Canada's biggest, richest city. So I reckon Doug Ford "could have predicted" all of this.

He just doesn't fucking care.

ONTO—FREEDOM. THE WORLD VEERS dangerously to the right, a big, luscious, melting democracy cake that we all left out in the rain, check; how about women's reproductive rights?

Texas passed a law restricting women's right to choose, but by means of private citizens bringing an action against anyone having, or helping someone procure, an abortion. This means the law can't be challenged, because... it's not a law enforced by a state prosecutor. It's a law that doesn't exist as a law... Are you hyperventilating yet?

We are in the mindset of the former East Germany, with neighbours denouncing neighbours. Regular Joe citizen brings an action against a woman getting an abortion, even out of state; anyone helping her by, for example, being the doctor, advising her, or Ubering her there can also be targeted.

The incentive? A ten thousand dollar *bounty*. The Supreme Court of Trump washed their hands, but Handmaid Barrett remarked, helpfully, "...c'mon, girls, you can always stick your little gift from God in a wicker basket and leave them on the steps of the local police station!," adding, as she lay on her back and hiked up her robes, "Now, if ya'll excuse me, we got a megachurch to fill!"

Texas is all about the sanctity of life and the will of God. If your kid is gunned down at school, who knows? Maybe they would have turned out gay! Thus, a lone psychotic man with a gun can decide the fate of someone's child. The state, or a neighbour, can decide a woman's fate if her pregnancy develops complications. *Everyone decides the mother's fate and the child's fate except the mother.* Did I get that right?

Moving along! How's "cancel culture," specifically, the canceling of Margaret Atwood? (Or, in Doug Ford-speak, "Margaret who?") Let's double down on Margaret Atwood, shall we?

Bless her for that elderly person's slip-up about transgenders. Such harm Margaret Atwood has caused, I don't know why we don't just go back to Rob Ford's original plan: tear her down and replace her with a casino.

Margaret Atwood was a feminist when it really meant something, back in the times of Gloria Steinem and Ms Magazine, when it was radical even to question the status quo, when feminists were mocked by the mainstream media, derided as "bra-burners" and "women's libbers," and "lezzies"; *these girls need to get laid!"*

Margaret was the avant-garde, on the front lines and blazing trails. Margaret saw the future and it's no one's fault but yours and mine if we crash and burn while virtue-signaling our superiority and shunning her for her viral outbreak of foot-in-mouth disease.

Let's hear instead what I suspect she has given voice to—the disorientation of many women of an older generation struggling to interpret and understand complex issues of sexuality and gender identity which are suddenly central to the public discourse. It's as though a two-ton truck loaded with explosives just crashed into High Tea at the King Eddie.

I venture to say the most willing allies among us, myself included, are struggling, a little, because, apart from my absolute insistence that trans persons and all gender-non-conforming people are, first and foremost, *people* with the same rights as anyone, deserving to be heard and believed, there are thorny problems that need working out. OK? Can we have some empathy, here? Can we focus, please? Ya, I didn't think so.

If, after considering Margaret Atwood in the context of her lifelong dedication to both feminism and her art, her eminent intelligence, and her sly, subversive good humor, you can call her the enemy, there may be no hope for us.

If she needs an ally to take her aside and have that conversation, point out her misstep, be that ally. Teach, don't screech. Because if we continue like this, there'll be no one left to help *you* when you make an ass of yourself, an event which I sense may be just around the corner.

Coming, as it does, to all of us at some point.

MARGARET MAY BE FEELING A LITTLE LIKE the lady in Golden, British Columbia, who was awakened one night this past October by something crashing through the ceiling of her bedroom and burying itself between her pillows.

It was *a two-kilogram meteorite,* the size of a small cabbage. The lady, Ruth Hamilton, said she was in shock, but "grateful to be alive." She's hanging on to the space rock as a souvenir. And rumor has it she's taken to sleeping in the basement.

{I just made up that bit about sleeping in the basement because it feels true. OK? That's my journalistic promise to you: I will always own up to my total fabrications. Or, usually. It depends how much work is involved.

Moving along:

According to Peter Brown, Canada Research Chair in planetary small bodies: "The chances of experiencing a meteorite big enough to penetrate a roof and hit a bed are about one in 100 billion per year."

So sleep easy!

Unless you're poor in Ontario or an elderly literary icon who said something goofy about transgenders. Uh-oh! No sleepy-time for you!

Oh, yes, Earth. How's Earth? Ontario car drivers, who we apparently elected when you conservatives scratched an "X" next to Doug Ford, are salivating at the prospects of a new billions of dollars highway, through the Green Belt, that only they, Ford, and a handful of property developers want, and that will save them thirty minutes on their drive from Mac's Milk to Toronto General Hospital with their sign screaming, "Stop Medical Tyranny!"

Check.

Which reminds me: How's the pandemic? Well, you see—it's *complicated*.

It's waning unless it's waxing. The numbers are up when they're not down and more people are getting vaccinated except they aren't.

The anti-vaxx brigade, restless, bored, and sublime in their stupidity—and I do mean "sublime" in its true sense of filling those who experience it with awe and terror—have switched from ingesting a veterinary-grade dewormer called Ivermectin, just the very thing for someone who's concerned they're putting, you know, poison in their body, to Borax.

Borax—so someone said on Facebook or Twitter, or maybe they just scrawled it in magic marker in a local toilet stall, but someone authoritative anyway—Borax will magically (of course!) flush the vaccine from your body.

So, get vaccinated, rush home, enjoy a sparkling yet caustic Borax on the Rox afterward, and hey, presto! You'll still be thick as a brick between two short planks, definitely have zero cockroaches in your panties, and, in a few rare, lucky cases, you might just keel over, be rescued by our already stretched to the limits healthcare system, and finally see the light about vaccines!

I'm not gonna wish you dead. The politicians who bungled the messaging, were caught unprepared, and cared only for "the economy", not the people who looked to them for guidance—that's different. And that's as far as I'm going with that one.

Well, everything's ship shape, it seems. Just another Monday in Toronto, the city without a soul, on this frail, sick globe of luminous blue, which, Facebook assures me, is flatter than Eric Trump's Frankenforehead.

Facing reality is one of my main tasks of a Monday, after a self-indulgent weekend spent rinsing out my corona mask, opening cans of tuna, and lying in bed with my tears dribbling backwards into my earholes. So glad to get my state-of-the-world survey completed, and damned if I don't already regret the time wasted on sad, serious boondoggles like:

Should we keep recycling now that the CBC did some investigative journalism—the old-fashioned kind where you scrummage around in a trash can and dig up some facts that no one at the Toronto Sun knew what to do with—and as a result have revealed that virtually none of those plastics we've been recycling for twenty years actually got recycled?

It was all a big lie! Seriously! We just sent it all to—now, no fair peeking!—that's right: Asia! Which is the new, polite word for "mostly China."

And guess what Asia did?

They dumped it in the ocean, then blamed China, or, if you're China, everyone else!

The fun, as the man said, never stops! Oh, my ribs!

But that's OK. Now, when they haul a giant tuna on to the deck of a ship off the coast of Japan, it's already covered in Saran Wrap, inside some disposable Tupperware. Handy!

OK, READY FOR THE BIG GUNS? HOW ARE we doing with regard to... *racism?*

Well, you know. It's—*super complicated.*

In Canada, we pride our selves on our ever-so-specially not-American historical being on the right side of so many things. Racism included.

Now, it's true we had enslaved people up here. No doubt at all. But we did benefit from a rather enlightened King of England, who outlawed slavery by decree throughout his empire. Neat, eh? We became a safe haven for slaves who had escaped their "owners" and traveled north, via the Underground Railroad.

Throughout the ensuing centuries and decades, through Detroit race riots in 1968 and more riots after the savage beating of Rodney King in 1992 and more riots still after the televised murder of George Floyd in 2020, we shook our heads and tutted our tuts, and glowed with pride as we stuck the jockey figurines in our front lawns and never, until really quite recently, saw, let alone got used to, a Black friend crossing our doorstep or a Black teacher teaching us or a Black physician administering medical care.

Now, Black waiters at the Royal Canadian Yacht Club—that's different. We always had those. It just felt, you know. Right. And super handy, because there's hardly any Black Jews!

We never stop tut-tutting as we clutch our pearls and look southward. How—*tasteless*, somehow!

And our sensible gun laws, and a Constitution that dates from the 1980's instead of the 1700's, helps, in that we don't expect guns as a right, and thus did not get into the habit of reaching for our automatic weapons every time we encountered a Black ten-year-old holding a great, big Oh, Henry! bar that's easily mistaken for a handgun.

Freed from the tiresome tasks of keeping unruly POC in their place, at least, overtly, and with an admirable restraint born of our Loyalist sympathies, we could focus our attention on the systematic cultural genocide of our Indigenous people.

Here are some quotes from our first Prime Minister, Sir John A. MacDonald, giving his strategic direction:

> "I have reason to believe that the agents as a whole ... are doing all they can, by refusing food until the Indians are on the verge of starvation, to reduce the expense."

> "When the school is on the reserve, the child lives with his parents who are savages; he is surrounded by savages... He is simply a savage who can read and write."

> "The third clause provides that celebrating the "Potlatch" is a misdemeanour. This Indian festival is debauchery of the worst kind, and the departmental officers and all clergymen unite in affirming that it is absolutely necessary to put this practice down."

> ".....we have been pampering and coaxing the Indians; that we must take a new course, we must vindicate the position of the white man, we must teach the Indians what law is; we must not pauperise them, as they say we have been doing."

> "I have not hesitated to tell this House, again and again, that we could not always hope to maintain peace with the Indians; that the savage was still a savage, and that until he ceased to be savage, we were always in danger of a collision, in danger of war, in danger of an outbreak."

> "The executions of the Indians ought to convince the Red Man that the White Man governs."

Well. That's—pretty clear.

The recent discovery of mass graves of Indigenous children who died, nameless and forgotten, while in the Residential School system—designed to "civilize" these "savage" children by effectively abducting them as necessary, separating siblings, and making them available for the occasional diddling-followed-by-torture by the horny-but-celibate followers of Christ who executed their mandate, and then some—has sent shockwaves, lasting entire minutes, through the collective hearts of white Canadians.

But, let's be reasonable. We know it was bad, but that was then, and this is now. Enough is enough. Right?

We lowered the National Flag of Canada on Parliament Hill. The problem is that the First Nations of Canada will tell us, not we, them, when those flags can go full mast again.

White people are *beside themselves*. We desperately want to be in control of the narrative, but we can't take control without, well, looking like the controlling racists and imperialists we are.

We want to commit the genocide, then decide how much grief is enough, how long it's appropriate to mourn for a mother or father, sibling or child. We want, as usual, everything.

The leader of the Conservative Party of Canada, Erin O'Toole, best expressed this view when he said, on October 4th, that he was tired of "continued hand-wringing" over the history of Residential schools.

The collective grief of an entire people reduced to "hand-wringing" is what we want. But this is one thing we can't have. Because all we managed to break were bodies.

Canadians who want the flags raised again are the worst people in the world right now. And Erin O'Toole, with that flippant remark, whether calculated or just unfiltered, is the worst of the worst.

AND, NOW, TO WRAP, LET'S turn our attention to—Paris Hilton's wedding!

Paris got shackled over the past few days to a man with a Pink Panther last name ("I'm Inspector Clouseau and I am come to eenspect your Reum!") who makes his vast amounts of money doing something either unbelievable or unthinkable with vast amounts of other people's money.

PopSugar thought she looked like she'd "stepped right out of a fairy tale" in her purpose-built, hand-embroidered Oscar de la Renta gown, a lot of the fairy tale, admittedly, consisting of the gown being white.

But she did look radiant. And I'm glad for her, I tell you.

Dear Paris Hilton:

Thanks for proving once again that having mountains of cash, which you earned by waking up and blinking, works miracles around making your every fairy-tale come true. I wish both of you joy as you begin your journey together.

And may the IRS tax that friggin' dress right off your back.

Skipping Rhymes of Gen Z

I've been undercover in my sailor suit and adorable Hudson's Bay dress shorts—available in Québec only in polyester, due to the current shortage of "pure laine—"

—reminiscing about "The Friendly Giant" and "Razzle Dazzle" with unsuspecting school-age Gen Zed-ers as they go about their daily activities. No one had heard of either of these shows, then I realized they were CBC kids' programming from the sixties. Talk about blowing my own cover!

Luckily it was over the kids' heads, and the teachers just figured it was part of the new PornHub sex education curriculum which is apparently running riot in schools these days.

In my day, you had minimal sex education at school. Mostly it was your parents or self-study. At least, that's how I eventually found out about dingleberries and bleedywunquets—Encyclopedia Britannica; or, wait was it— Jerry's dad who ran the numbers out of his garage? Hmmm...

But, seriously. Looking authentic while trading *prosciutto di Parma* and Dijon mustard sliders on artisanal *focaccia* at lunch break, or fake-crying when it was time for yet another "milk and cookies power-nap," stretched my humorous-blogger incognito reporting skills, and my already gossamer-thin patience, to the limit and beyond.

However, I did net the following cultural gold: Non-traditional skipping rhymes, who knew, and I have to say these kids are the future, always assuming we have one.

And it's off I go for another "Ankle-Biter" portion of chicken nuggets and French fries at Pickle Barrel or I'll start to get cranky around four o'clock, which is typically when my ADHD kicks in.

. . .

"HERE IN TORONTO"

In case you're thinking of visiting The Big Smoke, here's an Insider Tip: We have a unique way of greeting each other on the street. Memorize this, and you'll sound like you were born here:

Fred: "OMG, hey, the Chinese are buying all the condos!"

Jim: "Fine, thanks, Fred—and how's the wife and kids?"

Here in Toronto
Housing is a bitch

"Hordes from China,
Stinking rich!"

White Torontonians
Cry, "What cheek!
"How many condos
Bought *this* week?"

One condo
Two condos

Three condos
Four?

Mandarin on
A red front door

Five condos
Six condos

Seven condos
Eight?

Let us natives
Speculate!

Cut down trees
And pave the lawn
For practising
Tai Chi at dawn!

What's wrong with
Buying condos, please?

Hordes from China are—
All Chinese!

(— *From the archives of the Canadian National Railway*)

"JUSTIN SCANDALS, COUNT HOW MANY"

Justin scandals
Count how many!

ONE for blackface
(How embarrassing!)

TWO for a journalist's
Sexual harassing

THREE for India
Shoe toes curly
Wearin' a sari
Lookin' all girly

Justin scandals
Count how many

FOUR for Jody
Attorney G
He broke her balls
Over SNC

FIVE for comrade
Castro, Fidel
He eulogized
So we gave him hell

SIX is the pipeline
We don't like
Tell Alberta to take a hike

"Feminist! Snowflake!
"Drama teacher!
"Manliness is not a feature!"

Seven, Eight, Nine
WE charity guys
Employed his family
(Big surprise!)

Interns waved
Goodbye to summer
And so it went
From dumb to dumber

A worthy cause had
Met its doom

Cause Justin
Couldn't leave the room.

"IF THE CPC* WERE AT THE TOP"

The Conservative Party of Canada. They used to be called the "Progressive Conservatives." This became an oxymoron in the 1980's, and just plain old moron around 2016.

If the CPC
Were at the top

How many abortions
Would they stop?

One a day
Two a day
Three four five?
Keep those embryos alive!

Rusty coat hanger
Dish soap mild
Jump off a table
And lose that child!

If the CPC
Could have its way
They'd lock you up
If you were gay!

They pretend
They're just political
(Actually —they're quite Levitical)

Six friends of Dorothy
AIDS you're dead
Sodom and Gomorrah
In a marriage bed!

Save seven kids
From drag queen readings
Send in Proud Boys
For the beatings!

Eight, nine, ten
Subservient wives
Can't hold their tongues to
Save their lives

And Canada
Our fine endeavour

Soon undone by
Pierre Poilièvre.

"MAXIME BERNIER ISN'T GAY"

He really isn't, you know. He's just scared people *think* he is! Anyway, one thing's for sure: He's "leader" of the People's Party of Canada.

And what could possibly be totally whack-job about a political party with "people" in its name?

Maxime Bernier isn't gay
He just likes to be *au fait*

Maxime Bernier's
Heterosexual!

Why so camp?
It's just contextual!

"Be my beard, Ms. Julie, sweet!
Populists should be discreet!

"Beard me, Julie, just this one time
(You've got bikers for a fun time)

"Beard me twice, I'm such a charmer!
(When you're not a dairy farmer)

"Beard me three times
Beard me four—

*"Top-Secret files
On your bedroom floor!!*

"Beard me five six seven eight nine—
Tabarnak!! I must resign!!"

Maxime Bernier isn't gay
Julie says: *" 'E's not 'zat way'!"*

(Julie doesn't care,
'Cause, gay or straight,

She's really only
Screwing for the
Real estate!)

So You Wanna Be—Somebody?

It has come to my attention that a huge proportion of the adult population is dissatisfied with the crappy, inadequate personalities they were born with, and desperately seek to, as it were, upgrade their software to something with more pizza.

(Or is that "pizzazz", I get them mixed up.)

Anyway, if you, dear reader, are indeed one of these restless specimens who forgot to be specific enough, you've come to the right place. Here's your second—or third, or twelfth, or hundredth, if *you're* not counting, *I am* sure as crabapples not counting—chance to make good at your dream, for I've cobbled together a few examples of alternative personalities, somebodies, in fact, who, whatever you might say about them, would never be described as inadequate.

What they're adequate *for* is a different kettle of horses.

You know, and can I just say, seriously. I'm known for my uncushioned honesty, my hit-em-in-the-face frankies, which I typically deploy as soon as the person I'm being honest about has left the room. But I care enough to say this right to everyone's face: stop being such a people pleaser! I mean it!

Learn to be assertive, for pete's sake! Let so-called climate change know that you're not going to put up with its lies! If someone asks you why you gained so much weight, call them a pedophile! If you resent that someone's smarter than you, threaten them with jail! Get my drift?

I'm pumped, I dunno about you!

So, to gain insight, possibly your first, into how you might actually fare as one of those somebodies you wish you'd become, just review the multiple-choice-type questionnaires below, and answer honestly. But remember: Only one of the answers in each case will qualify you.

Just don't get your hopes up. Or is that down?

I get that mixed up, too.

So You Wanna Be—?

SO YOU WANNA BE PIERRE POILIEVRE?

When I wake up, the first thought in my mind is

1. How lucky I am to have a fresh new day
2. God bless my family
3. What's for breakfast
4. I wonder what Trudeau fucked up during the night

If I find I have some spare time, I arrange

1. An appointment with my barber
2. Some flowers
3. A date night with the missus
4. A freedom convoy

My preferred form of address is

1. Mr Poilievre.
2. Just "Pete," I don't stand on ceremony
3. He, him, his
4. Twenty-four Sussex Drive

I like to stay fit by

1. Running
2. Weight-lifting
3. Calisthenics
4. Throwing rocks at a rival's campaign bus

I knew I wanted to be a politician

1. When I got angry about poverty
2. When I read a life of Churchill
3. When Lester Pearson got the Nobel Prize
4. The day I made my entire kindergarten class cry

SO YOU WANNA BE MARJORIE TAYLOR GREENE?

Ideally, the words that best qualify "job" for me are

1. Challenging
2. Well-paid
3. Creative
4. Right-Wing Nut

The most valuable skill for kids to learn at school is

1. Getting along with others
2. Science and Math
3. Writing a coherent essay
4. Sheltering from snipers under a desk

On a hot summer's day, there's nothing so refreshing as

1. A glass of lemonade
2. A dip in the pool
3. Sitting beside the air conditioner
4. A nice chilled bowl of Gazpacho police

My favorite kind of humor involves

1. Witty dialog
2. A pie fight
3. Raunchy language
4. Paul Pelosi getting bashed with a hammer

When I'm feeling restless and bored I like to

1. Focus on my work
2. Read a new book
3. Arrange lunch with friends
4. Divide the Republic

SO YOU WANNA BE ALICE WALKER?

I find it really annoying when

1. It's rainy and cold
2. There's no cream for my coffee
3. I forget my keys
4. Oprah calls so much I have to block her number

Over the years, I've had the good fortune to

1. Become famous
2. Mentor talented young writers
3. Travel the world
4. Divorce a Jew

When I'm feeling out of sorts, I cheer myself up by

1. Counting my blessings
2. Writing in my journal
3. Marveling at nature
4. Telling vulnerable strangers they don't exist

My favorite meal is

1. Italian
2. Vegetarian
3. Home-cooked
4. A ritual offering to our lizard overlords

It's shocking to think that

1. I haven't taken a day off for a while
2. Wars still happen
3. The kids are all grown up
4. People would actually fight to wear high heels for less pay

SO YOU WANNA BE JORDAN PETERSON?

When I was a child, my parents taught me always to

1. Brush my teeth regularly
2. Say my prayers at night
3. Do my homework on time
4. Ask someone's name, then roll my eyes and call them whatever the fuck I want

My candid opinion of the Russian Federation is

1. A failing kleptocracy
2. A fount of priceless literature and music
3. An oppressed people ruled by an autocrat
4. Best detox in a medically-induced coma EVER

I love the paleo diet because

1. It's so simple to follow
2. It's scientifically proven
3. I keep effortlessly slim
4. I only have to take one dump a year, while the family's out shopping

When I need to chill, I like to

1. Take the dog for a long walk
2. Watch a thriller on Netflix
3. Have a cold beer at the pub
4. Practise looking ghoulish under a spotlight

Of all my contributions to the field of psychology, I think the most valuable will turn out to be

1. Exposing the left-wing bias in universities
2. Teaching disaffected youth to be responsible
3. Getting my Jungian masterpiece published
4. Losing my licence

Angelic Visions

When William Blake was a young lad, he saw trees filled with angels radiating light. I mean to say, more than once. Regularly. When he was a bit older, his brother, Robert, often dropped in to give useful advice about William's magnificent celestial art and his mysterious visionary poetry, which was a nifty trick because Robert was dead at the time.

When I was a young lad, the only object I saw radiating light was our clapped-out black and white TV with the twisty rabbit ears. Every so often it would go on the fritz, chirping and buzzing with static, or get stuck with the picture distorted and partly off the screen like a crumpled, discarded photograph rescued from a wastebasket.

And instead of angels in trees I saw Lucille Ball getting pies in the face, or submerged in vats of green dye, or smothered with honey during some sadistic game show because she'd thought she knew the answers in advance, that she'd beat the system.

We all knew that was cheating. *Why was Lucy Ricardo cheating—?* That was setting a terrible example, which is probably why she had to get stuck behind the new wallpaper or set fire to her nose or wrestle in a vat of wine grapes. She had to be punished for cheating, for trying to be famous. Why couldn't she just be satisfied with being a housewife? *Silly woman.*

You take yer angels as you find them. I used to cry when Lucy was the hapless victim of yet another crude piece of slapstick, because I had too much empathy for a little boy, the result of bringing up my mom. I spent my childhood tuning into the signals that preceded her mood swings; I had learned to ignore the fundamental note and focus on the overtones: the portents of nervous collapse or imminent rage. I was like an adept who had trained himself to hear the grass grow.

And I cried for Lucy as though she were a dear friend. I cried over such avoidable humiliation, that she should suffer this way, week after week. I thought it was cruel to subject Lucy to these indignities, not funny at all, and the proof that she felt the same was that she always wailed in this theatrical, not very convincing way. *WAAAAAAAAHHHHHH!*

Vivian Vance would go through the motions of comforting her, which was no comfort, simply the job description for "sidekick." There was no one to comfort me, because my mother, the only person left once my sisters had slipped the surly bonds of home, and with my father traveling during the week, was lying in bed, indulging in her own private version of *WAAAAAAAAHHHHH*.

I feel like a douchebag complaining that there was no one to comfort me. I sound so needy, and honestly, I didn't think twice about it at the time, because I didn't know there was anything else. I figured, I guess, that raising your mom was just what happened.

I brought up my mom well. She turned out to be a really polite, reasonably well-behaved mom, a real credit to me. It was hard work, though, requiring mastery of so many routines: comforting her when she didn't get the right presents at Christmas; calming her down when she muttered that my oldest sister had secretly won the lottery, or screamed with outrage that my ten-year-old nephew had stolen her emerald and diamond ring; scolding her, my face burning scarlet with confusion and shame, when she entertained the boys wearing her baby doll pajamas.

She'd have a drink in one hand, and her bare feet would be tucked up underneath her in the armchair. Sometimes I would notice that she'd painted her toenails. Coral was the color, very on trend; a reddish orange that hinted at exotic experiences yet mostly conveyed safety and cheery good taste, like the accent color in a fast-food franchise.

She was a little bird sitting on its nest, hatching things...

The boys! The boys! First comes the blood, then the boys!

Carrie's mom. Right? She was even scarier than my mom; one good *thwack* in the face with the Basic English Bible, *Eve was weak, say it, woman!* and you knew who was boss. You could blissfully fall to pieces and let someone else be the grown-up for a couple of hours.

And is that movie quotable or what? *They're not called dirtypillows Mama. They're called breasts, and every woman has them.* That's freakin' *magic*.

If it's two AM and you don't feel quite up to lip-synching Judy at

Carnegie Hall, just *dirtypillow* twice around the *chaise longue* and you're good to go. Pull your own hair really hard if you think you've got off too easily.

You can then drift away to fag dreamland knowing you've kept up your end of the bargain for one more day. Kept the faith. Laughter and beauty and sex! A brisk dirtypillow, flailing your arms vigorously—in case there's any aerobic benefits—in between emptying the ashtrays and sipping the dregs of all the unfinished cocktails. Surprisingly satisfying, even economical, and you don't have to take all that speed.

It's war time, for Pete's sake. We have to pull together.

I THOUGHT, WHAT WITH THE WORLD coming to an end, and democracy folding up like a card table after an altogether too brief poker evening, I needed to revisit and revise Blake's Proverbs of Hell, hear them crackle with sardonic wisdom.

Though inspired by Blake's, my proverbs, as you'll see, are less nourishing, less for-the-ages. They are, how can I put this, jokey. Flippant.

If you gave them to Moses on stone tablets, I'm not one hundred percent sure he wouldn't crack them over your head.

Blake was the prophet of Albion, avatar of Romanticism, mourning for humanity's lost innocence. He danced ecstatically in the last pure rays of sunshine humankind would ever know, while London slowly suffocated under its new mantle of industrial smog.

All so I could sit here in 2022 eating ramen noodles with oyster sauce, drinking low-cal soda, waiting for The Great Reset.

. . .

Proverbs of Post-Truth Heaven and Hell

Life is a comedy to those who think, a tragedy to those who feel,

and a gay drama queen's chance to flounce off during Thanksgiving dinner. ◆ Toss him in the toilet who drives the honeywagon of hate. ◆ Public transport is good for the environment, but men over twelve on skateboards should be herded to the edge of a cliff, then water-cannoned. ◆ Men are finally learning to express an emotion besides rage; unfortunately, that emotion is humiliation. ◆ Conspiracy theorists are as prophets whose empty skulls make foolishness more resonant. ◆ O Hamas! O Israel! who will first drop bombs of righteousness? Who will weep for your enemy's children? ◆ War is built with stones of certainty on the bones of innocence; peace more resembles a macramé plant holder. ◆ Modern Monetary Theory brooks no deficits, but the taxes remain a rough nest for tender fannies. ◆ Bernie Madoff was a shanda for the goyim; Peter Thiel is a shanda for the gayim. ◆ Fentanyl addicts are white and get treatment programs; Crack addicts are Black and get prison, Food addicts are Rubenesque and wear full-body condoms. ◆ One in five racists is white, also the other four. ◆ "I want something to trickle down on me," said no person, ever.

◆ *Republican Rep Taylor Greene runs*
After kids who've escaped having seen guns
Blast off classmates' heads;
In QAnon beds
She bears down and gives birth to machine guns. ◆

When you pardon someone for pot possession after their twenty years behind bars, pray include the card that says, "Just kidding! You shoulda seen the look on your face! Priceless! LOL!" ◆ *Capitalism is God's plan for punishing the lazy and the shiftless, but they just keep playing golf.* ◆ Red sky at night, sailors' delight; red sky at morning, sailors take warning; red sky in the afternoon, you overstayed at the bathhouse—it's actually night. Also, you're a sailor. ◆ *The more homophobic the comment, the more they covet your junk, and the more theirs looks like the curled little finger of Maggie Smith sipping tea in "Downton Abbey."* ◆ American Democracy was established by men of the Enlightenment who loved freedom, hated tyranny, and who we refer to with reverence as the Founding Cocksucker Asshole Slaveholders. ◆ *Pierre Poilievre is to Stephen Harper as Trump is to Pol Pot: an underachiever.* ◆ How shall India wield the plough, O Vandana Shiva, thou sacred cow? ◆ *Mary had a little lamb, Little Miss Muffet sat on a tuffet, but Kyrsten Sinema prefers something in silicone that you can just throw in the dishwasher.* ◆ Quantum physics is a mind-boggling construct, but nothing beats Alex Jones complaining about being silenced to a million subscribers. ◆ *You realized your boyfriend was gay when he ordered dessert; his repurposing the whipped cream as lube to ravish the sommelier was a bit "de trop".* ◆ Note to men: Your buddy was in error who thought the hash tag #MeToo indicates that "the chick is feeling left out." ◆ *Any gay man knows how to please women better than any straight man, starting with the words, "Killer ensemble, girlfriend!"* ◆ The cub becomes a lion, the lamb a sheep, the fawn a deer, Elon Musk—Elon Musk. ◆ *The nine most terrifying words in the English language are, "I'm Ron DeSantis and Republicans now control your vagina."*

◆ Science is certain grief: To fashion vaccines for a virus, but none for disbelief. ◆

Men at war make late abortions. ◆ *Jesus loves you, but Christians are just after your retirement savings.* ◆ *Allah is the one God, the Sublime Truth, the Almighty and Powerful, yet betimes The Very Soul of Manly Butthurt.* ◆ Hindus worship bizarre, vengeful animal beings; but, verily, who amongst us would dare call a Trump voter Hindu? ◆ *Jeffrey Epstein was an evildoer; yet who at sixteen does not long to groom a billionaire?* ◆ Transgender persons are the most discerning: for not one has become a straight white male. ◆ *When Boebert's son dialled 911, what drag queen reading had begun?* ◆ God, every second, watches everyone's genitals; yet children with cancer dare to wonder if He could do better than a plush toy. ◆ *However thrilling to watch billionaires fly away in spaceships, how much greater the let-down to watch them return.* ◆ Conservatives like their government small enough to drown in a bathtub,

which is exactly how one likes conservatives.

Unhinged States Of America

Refugees Are Delicious...!

I'm experiencing an iconic Canadian moment. Specifically, I'm eating some chicken wings that flew up to Roxham Road, in northern New York State, at the Canadian border, to claim refugee status—but were refused asylum, then referred to me.

These delicate situations don't just work themselves out, right? They take intense international, cross-border diplomacy. After meeting with Joe Biden during his whirlwind visit to Ottawa (I hid behind a potted palm in the Prime Minister's Office and jumped him on the way to the genderless bathroom) I've agreed to receive fifteen thousand of these tasty liberty-loving morsels, all of whom are fleeing the transphobic craptardery down south.

After they got the news that they were given special appetizer status, the wings—and a couple of drumsticks who tagged along for the hell of it—crowded around me, crying with gratitude, throwing themselves onto a blazing metal container fire to crisp themselves up and slathering themselves with Buffalo Hot Sauce. Make no mistake, fellow Canadians: Refugees are freakin' *delicious!*

Alas, I cannot avoid turning my permanently rabbit-holed attention to the looney bin crammed to overflowing with three hundred million crack-smoking inmates that is the Unhinged States of America. And let's be honest: from Make America Great Again to My Ass Got Arrested has felt like a *sloooooooow* transition.

Many of us have been worried that the arraignment of Donald Trump, The Great Mouth Breather, was proof that the Rich White Guy Justice System had broken down, for a license to perpetrate daily criminal acts upon the splayed-out body politic with impunity is one of the many perks top-tier politicians enjoy.

But I was gratified to note that at least Trump is not being held in custody during the leisurely wait for his next court appearance — in December. This means I'll be spared the usual cynicism about jail time being "like a staycation at the country club." Please!

I'm constantly having to remind the more punitive-leaning public that prison is never a "five-star hotel" and that, despite the 300-count bed linens, fine wines and comfort girls that the most privileged prisoners without question enjoy, the point of prison is that you can't say, at 5pm, "All righty, then, see you soon! It's been real!"

The perks are not the point. The actual punishment is that *your freedom has been taken away*. Got that? Remember "freedom"? An extra pack of Twizzlers from the privately-run tuck shop does not take the edge off.

So. Eight months of freedom. It's almost like they have some crazy idea that he's innocent until proven guilty! And lord knows, it's not like he's a danger to the rule of law or world democracy or women's rights or something!

This will give him plenty of time to run for President, whip up his base, mimeograph and distribute some new copies of the Capitol floor plan, have those fake Electoral College members lined up, and, like a latter-day Jackie Gleason in a just-discovered episode of "The Honeymooners" written in a time warp, shake his fist at the next MAGA rally and cry, "*Straight to the moon, America!*"

This set of thirty-four counts of cooking the books (matter of fact) in order to cover up a conspiracy to influence an election (still-to-be-proven matter of law) was not, alas, the sexy Perry Mason moment we'd hoped for.

In fact it is downright geeky, starring as it does that nice girl gone bad, the shy, unassuming Miss Demeanor, she of the good intentions and sensible shoes, who spends way too many hours per day staring bleary-eyed at her calculator.

To be fair, you have to remember how impossible it would have been to put together a case for any of the other offenses in the mere seven years of lawlessness so far:

- the twenty-plus sexual assaults reported by the victims,
- the attempt to interfere with the election results in Georgia, with nothing to go on but a recording of the phone call in which Trump loudly and clearly requests another eleven thousand votes;

- The January 6th, 2021 Insurrection (I assume it now deserves its own capital letters), for which we have a mere airplane hangar full of evidence detailing a vast pre-planning effort by Republicans, supported by the official state media, Fox News, consisting of

- around five trillion texts and emails from key right wing conspiracy theorists and white supremacists in which they explicitly state their intent to overturn the election results

- plus texts sent by Fox News hosts to their colleagues, revealing that they knew very well they were peddling disinformation, and in some cases stating their disdain for Trump

- all documented by the January 6th Committee in front of the entire world and glued into a lovely Victorian-style lace-and-ribbons-decorated scrapbook called "I Heart My Insurrection Take-Down!" that Nancy Pelosi created on Craftsy

- also video of Trump's pre-riot speech in which he unequivocally exhorts his audience to, you know. Stage an insurrection.

Not forgetting:
Trump's theft of hundreds of top-secret documents which he scattered around his Florida compound—in the garage, the bedrooms, the hallways, alleyways and byways, by the swimming pool—anywhere he might decide to take a dump and need something to read.

The evidence for that is so flimsy I'm almost embarrassed to mention it: *Trump confessing he took them,* in an interview, and his lawyers stating that they'd *one-hundred percent definitely returned every last one of them*, when, you know. They hadn't.

These are cases which would clearly require the genius of Newton and the wisdom of Solomon allied with the sleuthing acumen of Sherlock Holmes in order to prove *mens rea*, the guilty mind, and *actus reus*, the criminal act itself.

So it's perfectly understandable why the New York DA chose instead to stage a frat-party hazing of thirty-four charges on one defendant, so we could watch sweet, unassuming Miss Demeanor, duly grabbed by the pussy, magically transmorph into sex-crazed porn star Felony Trumpington and maybe even take over the Lancôme spokesperson role when Isabella Rossellini's done with it.

I dunno about you. I'm just so relieved that, after close to a decade of impending authoritarianism, Alvin Bragg chose the not-at-all-certain-to-win option![1]

America generally continues to implement its master plan: turning the former shining city on a hill into a banana Republican split, topped with illiberal helpings of nut jobs, such as Marjorie Taylor Greene, "The Pedophiliator", and hard fruit like Lauren-the-Moron Boebert. Boebert's pet projects include working to ensure every restaurant in the US will encourage open carrying of firearms, advocating for a return to Christian theocracy, and rambling on about public urination on C-Span, no doubt inspired by her husband's conviction for lewd exposure in a bowling alley.

Sarah Huckabee Sanders, Governor of Arkansas, that lodestar of forward-thinking business friendliness, is doing her part by signing into law what I'm imagining is called the "Kindergarteners Relief Act", which will allow eager entrepreneurial children, currently forced to eat vegetables, go to bed early and indulge in no more than two alcoholic beverages per evening ("big government") to work twelve hours a day, then relax in a smoke-filled back room eating hamburger sliders before the bell rings for their morning shift. Citizens of Arkansas: Kiss your sooty chimneys goodbye!

Another nostalgic throwback was the failure of Silicon Valley Bank, which tanked due to recklessly putting all its investment eggs in the basket of tech startups and simultaneously investing in long-term bonds which relied on low interest rates to remain viable. Because interest rates would never go up!

Interest rates went up, bond values went down. Nervous depositors scrambled to withdraw their money, only momentarily interrupting the Silicon Valley executives awarding themselves one final golden handshake.

If only there had been legislation to ensure banks had sufficient liquidity to cover their deposits and oversight to make sure they diversified, mitigating risk! Sigh!

Oh, wait — there was. The Dodd-Frank Act, consumer protection enacted to ensure 2008 wouldn't happen again. And where was Dodd-Frank? In a back alley, bleeding from a thorough gutting administered by The Great Mouth Breather.

But that's not the only reason SVB was reckless. They also knew

---

1 But Jack Smith's indictment for the confidential documents case and Fani Willis's indictment for the criminal conspiracy to subvert the Georgia election results seem rock solid and hard to beat. Prosecutors at that level would not bring a case without copious evidence and a reasonable prospect of success.

that they wouldn't, couldn't be allowed to fail, and that the government, suddenly looking awfully like those socialist governments they've been warning us about, would come to the rescue, in effect, nationalizing them. There was nothing to discourage any bank from going for short-term mega profits by leveraging their clients' vulnerable assets.

The bail-out decision, a guarantee of $175 billion federal funding to cover customers' deposits, took about five seconds to implement. This easily beat the timeline of two years and counting during which the Biden administration agonized about whether it should forgive the crushing burden of student debt, which it then decided it was maybe going to do, but on the other hand, maybe it wasn't.

Student debt's a tough one. Right? Just you tone it down, Mister J Biden Rockefeller! What, you think the government has a money tree or something?

Finally, Biden came through, and the celebrations lasted at least for the rest of the day before the Supreme Court decided that, unlike big-ticket investors and banks, who are Too Big To Fail, college and university students are Too Small To Worry About.

They achieved this by allowing a case to go forward in which the complainant, the State of Missouri, brought an action even though it suffered no injury by the cancellation of student debt; in legal terms, it had no standing. In her blistering dissent, Justice Elena Kagan pointed out that the court was deciding policy issues when it should not even have heard the case.

Joe Biden, more progressive than Obama, the most effective US President in living memory, should get his own Broadway musical and a soothing chamomile facial every morning just for waking up and getting dressed.

Ron DeSantis, Supreme Head Honcho of Florida, has more important tasks to attend to than bailing out woke students. He's currently enjoying a super-majority, and, to celebrate, he's reinventing Stalinist-style leadership by enacting punitive legislation targeting anyone who disagrees with him.

So far, he has ensured that K-12 education doesn't mention critical race theory, which anyway it never did, personally vetted every math and history textbook to ensure there's no mention of Black oppression or the gender-non-conforming, and still found time to nationalize a Disney theme park and a public university by firing their Boards and replacing them with groveling Republican toadies.[2] His message is clear: The Republic of Gilead is open for business!

---

2 Are toadies always groveling? Is it like "strident feminists"? For that matter, what *is* a toady? Too late now!

We all thought Margaret Atwood's "The Handmaid's Tale" was a piece of scary but implausible dystopian speculative fiction, but apparently she's a visitor from another time-space continuum warning us fifty years in advance with factual reporting. And did we listen? Does the Pope wear Spandex?

Incidentally, when readers can't tell if you're stating facts or being satirical, it normally means your satire isn't crazy enough. How then to divulge that the new American history standard in Florida schools has been rewritten to assert that slavery *"helped Black people learn important job-related skills..."*?

I'd love to jump out of my clown car and honk my horn right now, but that claim, that concept, is one hundred percent, cross my heart, slated for the new history books in Florida.

Slavery was like job training. Right? Talk about obvious, staring-us-in-the-face advantages that we just totally discounted in our typical woke, judge-y way. Lighten *up*, Selma Sadface!

Seriously, I bet you're glad you were delusional about slavery, you know, thinking it was morally repugnant and a crime against humanity, when in reality it was probably how Aunt Jemima launched her pancake business!

Like Kickstarter, with lynchings.

BUT THAT DESANTIS, EH? IS HE THE No-Fun Zone or what? He's like Trump, but without the sparkling wit and cuddly relatability that keeps Trump adorable, even as he stands behind MAGAphiles at the polls and rubs his tiny erection against their thighs.

Ron is the absolute incarnation of a Soviet-era thug who, unable to appreciate the clashy chords of the avant-garde, storms out of the Mariinsky Theatre to write an Op-Ed in Pravda putting everyone on notice that this cultural abomination is not going to happen on his watch.

Then come the arrests. Then come the executions.

And nationwide, in a stirring display of democracy in action, mobs of concerned parents—in a country where kids are routinely murdered at school, or, if they manage to survive, are traumatized permanently by mentally deranged owners of assault rifles they obtained without a background check—are screaming "Protect our children!" outside devastating scenes of feather boa and sequin carnage at Drag Queen Library Readings.

AS USUAL, CANADA, SMUG AND SUPERIOR down to its frostbitten toes, achieves harsh, unjust outcomes via less convoluted means.

For example, the US gets all high and mighty about immigration, with Republican governors busing or flying refugees from Texas to Martha's Vineyard to make a point (some might call this kidnapping, or human trafficking, but, hey. They're just refugees, right? The outside of the greeting card they include says: "Funny brown-looking people!" and on the inside: "You deal with them and see how *you* like it!")

Their reasoning? One public appearance in that community without a twill maxi-dress from Nordstrom or a Tommy Bahamas dad-shirt and some espadrilles and you'll be scuttling back to Guatemala to very possibly die of shame, I guess. That'll teach 'em! To be... refugees...

There is no reasoning.

Up here, we do things differently. We pare down the drama. You're Fellini, we're Mike Leigh. We're dreary kitchen sink slice-of-life, swilling Laker tall-boys in a grey wasteland of concrete social housing; you're life in the fast lane, driving a Ferrari, on acid, wearing a Chucky mask and waving an unregistered assault weapon, with music by John Williams. Taste the freedom!

We Canucks, hapless do-gooders, simply forget to provide shelter space for our refugees—who we invited, by the way, so they could rattle around our empty millions of square hectares—drive them up to a shelter in downtown Toronto ("Entertainment District") that's already full, because, you know, no money for poor people, then go, "Oopsies! Trick or Treat! Fooled ya! Just wait here for a moment while we sort this out!"

Then we drive away and don't come back.

The refugees, puzzled, but happy to be in a place where they might not die in the civil war or the floods or because some pumped up mercenary decides they're a drug addict, curl up on the sidewalk and sleep, which obviously is like, five-star luxury to them already. Then Justin says, "I guess there's not enough money and space and stuff! How did we forget to factor that in? Gee, willikers! OK, then!"

Toronto Mayor Olivia Chow (progressive) and Ontario Premier Doug Ford (reprehensible), mortal enemies politically, and infuriated, but for different reasons (Olivia: poor refugees! Doug: more refugees!) make a joint statement urging Ottawa to step up to the plate with funding. Their temporary détente evokes awe, like a Facebook video of an interspecies animal friendship. Finally, local residents step up to the plate without funding and take the refugees into their homes.

It's all very well for ordinary Canadians to give and give. But what if it wasn't their turn? What if they're giving when someone else should be giving?

As Jordan Peterson would say, now that they've taken the padlock off his mouth: " What do you mean by *plate*, what do you mean by *step*, what do you mean by *up*, what do you mean by *the*?"

AS SPECTACULAR AS THIS ALL IS, IT'S STILL not everything. We have our pork barrel politics, too!

Premier of Ontario Doug Ford, scion of the country's most shamelessly corrupt political dynasty, promises to leave Toronto's fragile, encircling Green Belt alone, then doesn't leave the Green Belt alone.

Instead, using the transparently false justification that he's "building affordable housing," he parcels out a nice, big chunk of it to his developer friends, anticipating billions in profits (for his developer friends, not Ontario) post-development, and guaranteed future campaign contributions for himself.

This neatly solves the housing crisis currently experienced by wealthy Ontarians short of a down payment for a six-bedroom monster home on a couple of acres of prime golf course.

The Auditor General of Ontario looks into the workings of the Green Belt parceling and issues a critical report. It turns out the process

- was rushed, secretive and driven by politics
- favored two developers who, after intense lobbying, received ninety-two percent of the land identified as available for development, thereby instantly increasing the value of this land by an estimated $8.3 billion

and that the civil servants tasked with the parceling

- ignored the thousands of angry comments received after they solicited public feedback
- insisted that Greenbelt lands were necessary to build affordable housing, when there was no shortage of already available land.
- as necessary and without consultation rewrote the rules governing how available land would be identified to the benefit of the developer landowners.

The public response to the Auditor General's report?

"Of course, corruption, it's Doug Ford! Duh! But I was surprised by the $8.3 billion—I was thinking maybe $8.2!"

HOW ABOUT TAKING A LITTLE BREAK and finding out how they're screwing up things at the south end? Toronto so wants / doesn't want a beautiful waterfront for the ages.

But here's the thing: if Ford doesn't care about food bank use being up sixty percent since he took power, if he doesn't care about defending the citizens of Ottawa during the convoy invasion—the report on the use of the Emergencies Act (1988) during that crisis singles him out in a testicle-withering rebuke for dereliction of duty, no doubt because he didn't want to alienate his suburban, city- and liberal-hating base—if he doesn't care about suffering people, why would he care about a few acres of park?

I'm talking about Ford's plans to privatize the beloved but decrepit Ontario Place site, with its iconic architecture and carefully-planned and accessible lakeside landscaping, by razing it and replacing it with a huge private spa.

The plans for the spa indicate a gigantic, thirteen-storey structure that is ludicrously out of scale in its context, makes the public land inaccessible and requires an underground parking lot that would necessitate removal of eight hundred mature trees and infill to Lake Ontario approximately equivalent in land mass to the Principality of Monaco, but with little of its charm.

All of this for a luxury facility that turns its back to the waterfront and which is targeted at a wealthy clientele. And when the spa fails as a business…? This may not happen for a while, thanks to a cushion of *$650 million of public money.*

If you're staring blankly at the page, it may be that you're a conservative politician who just read the word "public" but haven't yet rung for the intern to bring you the Concise Oxford Dictionary and a jigger of Crown Royal for your caramel latte.

I get it. The word has been erased from your vocabulary. Conservative politicians, like all politicians, are supposedly in power to work for the public good, but that brings us to the Conservative Paradox: Conservatives run in elections so you can vote for them, but they don't actually believe that government should have the power to remedy social ills, nor are they interested in doing so.

They just want to defund and eliminate programs. Because this agenda takes about the first week, they're then at a loss for what to do for the rest of their four-year term. Inevitably, they just treat it like their own private business networking event with a bit of evil mad social scientist experimentation thrown in for the rainy days.

They starve social programs until they no longer work, then tell the frustrated constituents: See? Public healthcare / public transit / welfare / has failed! then set about privatizing everything while telling poor people to just work harder.

The Ford government has been using Minister's Zoning Orders (MZOs) to force through development. An MZO is meant to be used in situations of extraordinary urgency. It overrides local planning authority to approve development without expert analysis, public input, or any chance of appeal.

The Ford government has issued more MZOs than any other provincial government in the past thirty years.

Doug Ford loves bypassing "petty" rules. It makes him feel like a maverick, the gun-totin' sheriff of the one-hoss town, and as a bonus, lets him piss off all us Toronto "elites," who, having cashed in our season tickets to the opera, can currently be found lining up outside our elite homeless shelters and food banks.

His favorite thing is ignoring expert advice about touchy-feely issues like the effects of development on the environment, or wage demands by teachers and nurses. MZOs, the Notwithstanding Clause: forget the sign that says "Emergency Use Only". He'll do exactly what he wants, regardless of broken promises, detriment to the public good, or conflict of interest. His slogan is "For the People"; but it really should be "For the People Called Doug Ford."

No, forget public consultations. Far kinder to just go ahead with the parceling, then off to the next meeting to decide what benefits to take away from those useless old people ("seniors"). Shall we axe dental care? Seniors in Ontario can no longer afford food, so good call on the no-teeth thing, Doug!

SPEAKING OF UNAFFORDABLE FOOD, Canada's main purveyor of that expensive luxury item, mega grocer Galen Weston, understands that Canadians, except for him, are concerned about haves and have-nots.

After he explained, or, some would say, lied, that his margins are the same, and that he's not gouging vulnerable Canadians for obscene profits after all — record obscene profits, that is — we realized that deciding whether to pay rent or feed our families is just the way it is.

Billionaires are struggling, too, despite Galen's three million-dollar raise in the past year. It's expensive being an unlanced boil on the butt of society!

And it was simply not possible to be happy with the same obscene profits like from before the pandemic; a pandemic is a once-in-a-lifetime business opportunity to play smoke and mirrors with supply chain issues that makes your previous strategy—colluding with every other grocery chain to artificially elevate the cost of bread Canada-wide, until you're caught—seem inelegant in comparison.

I see from my balcony that the food bank crowd is a football scrum today. I better line up before Galen Weston convinces them to join his latest price-fixing cartel.

Food banks are just unfair competition, and he's got No Shame.

HUNGRY AND POOR? YOU SHOULD STEAL FOOD. JESUS WOULD WANT YOU TO.

THIS PAST SUMMER MARKED THE FIRST occasion when I shoplifted. It so happened that in the rosy sunset of my life I found myself in a dark grocery aisle, before the Wall of Cheese and the Ace Bakery concession, and lo! I was sore afraid.

I had no food in the house and I wasn't yet up to speed on the fact that there was a food bank twice a week in the church across the street from me. So I decided to steal from the local temple of food, Loblaws.

If you'd like to recreate my adventure, here are the steps. I take no responsibility if you get caught and it's your choice to do this. So take your lawyer off speed-dial, Sally Mae.

Bonus if you're a senior and can plausibly present yourself as a recent denizen of the local Sunset Lodge who has just ripped out her morphine stent and is wandering in an advanced state of dementia, confused and in imminent danger of soiling her underwear. I can't absolutely guarantee that will help but it might give you a shot.

- Go to a Loblaws location or any local version of foodie paradise near you. I went to the flagship store on Carlton Street at Church (the one with the Wall of Cheese that a friend of mine thought was fake).
- Get there shortly after the store opens, if you're lucky, 7 or 7:30 AM. There will probably be no security on the front door at this time. If there is, you may want to rethink your timing.
- Pick up a small shopping basket and get yourself into leisurely shopping mode.

- If you're really hungry, swing by the prepared foods, which at the Carlton store are on display right by the front entrance. Help yourself to two or three items. I picked up a roast beef sandwich and a clamshell container of chicken tenders (cooked!), coleslaw and potato salad.
- As you walk around the store, indulge in the roast beef sandwich, like I did.
- Don't pick up more than you can easily carry in one hand.
- When you've casually pretend-shopped enough, proceed to the front entrance, check for security and wait for some people coming in / going out.
- Drop the shopping basket and walk out with your food. Be purposeful, not guilty looking.
- Enjoy! Or do your elderly dementia patient routine, if you're caught.
- You could also go to the self-serve checkout, pretend to scan the items, then leave.

Good luck! I think we should organize a mass senior citizen shoplifting event. I think I have some bell bottom jeans and a paisley shirt tucked away somewhere ...

STEAL FOOD!

Putting the "Stick" in "Lipstick Lesbian"

Princess Kyrsten and her Gollum-faced jester, Joe Manchin III (you mean there's two more of him? Yikes!) once again took a great, big, gleeful dump

on Joe Biden's progressive agenda, to my mind far more proof than necessary that there's got to be money behind this madness.

They "supported" voting rights legislation, but went all fake-*verklempt* at the very thought of axing the filibuster rules because, to quote the Troll of Coal, you're the "United States of America, not the divided States of America." (As Seth Myers mischievously reminded us, Manchin is *literally* from a divided state, West Virginia.)

The voting rights bill, revised, by the way, to suit Manchin, combined elements of the two original bills, the first of which seeks to make voting easier for everyone—not just liberals!—and the second restoring parts of the landmark Voting Rights Act weakened by Supreme Court rulings.

Sinema, who kits up like a high-end stenographer out of the Sears catalogue to telegraph solidarity with her respectable, middle-class constituents, then has a few too many white wine coolers (I don't know that for sure, it could be vodka stingers), and goes all Game of Thrones Barbie, complete with batwing sleeves and décolletage, to flash some boob and signal she'll be a good sport at the political frat house, sold us the same line of malarkey about not creating more divisiveness, *the cancer that is threatening the nation.*

Apparently the best way to counter divisiveness is to watch from the sidelines, pretending to be helpless as Republicans gut voting rights, and by preserving arcane, but apparently more important than voting rights, Senate traditions, in the end shoring up the Republicans' unrelenting divisiveness.

Is this the second or third time that Manchin has played the Dems for fools, holding out for endless negotiations and legislative changes, only to say "no" again? He's like that bossy bottom at the S&M party who insists on three hours of being tied up in intricate, Japanese rope bondage, then uses the safe word the second you're done and ready to put the alligator clamps on his nipples. Annoying!

As for Sinema, what can I say? She's mastered the dark art of being *"loud or lewd or lah-dee-dah-dee, everything to everybody"*—and *yes*, Sondheim gave me *permission*—and the key is that shifty-slidey word "bisexual".

I used to think "bisexual" was always an authentic self-description, defending the concept to uppity, short-sighted fellow fags who'd simper, "they're gay but won't say!" And I still would... I think. Yet more and more, and not only on account of Sinema, I'm realizing it's also used disingenuously as a cop-out by closeted queers seeking to pass—a kind of "having their cock and eating her out, too".

I wish that had turned out better, but at least I tried.

Bisexual equals *straight* in the average straight mind, accustomed as most people are to thinking of straight as normal, the default; gay as an aberration, or at best just a "nice to have;" so that in the context of "bisexual", man-on-man sex becomes simply a kind of rainy day activity to keep restless willies occupied when there's no pussy in the immediate vicinity.

And let us not forget: straights' brains are currently so under siege from the transgender wars that they initiated, they can barely cope with remembering "blue is for boys, pink is for girls" as it is.

Bisexual becomes a handy, performative label for the ambitious, like Sinema, a full-bore narcissist whose tawdry exhibitionism and exasperating illogic guarantees her a roomful of negative attention (when you live or die on attention, it doesn't much matter if it's high-quality). She'd run you over with a hybrid Prius if she thought it would get her on the evening news or stymie a Democrat.

Because she's also a "bisexual" Democrat, at heart really a conservative, but unable to resist partying with a pipeful of progressivism, then waking up in a ditch, panties around her ankles and swearing off the stuff for another day.

Sinema has always insisted she's not beholden to partisan loyalties, making her in effect an independent. Which begs the question: Why advertise yourself as a Democrat? (And why do Democrats fall for it?)

Sexual orientation, political orientation: in both ways she swings both ways. She's an opportunist, a shape-shifter; the lipstick lesbian to a "t". As a time-share queer, she profits from the edgy vibe, while really living in that respectable space of conformity. Her bisexuality is just something quirky, like her costume changes that keep you guessing; a meaningless label that gives trendy straights who'd like a little "open-minded" on their resume the cachet of being tolerant.

And Democrat is just another identity to slip on or off as convenient, giving Republicans a little frisson, like 1970's suburban housewives throwing their keys into a hat—they'll try anything once, even justice, just to remind themselves why they're not into it.

Progressives never learn, and we never will. The very qualities that make us progressive—acceptance, kindness, the messiness of working together, a big, welcoming tent, a willingness to believe others' truths and think the best of their intentions—work against the qualities we'd need to win against the ruthless, the unprincipled and the powerful.

Never trust a dyke without a toolbelt. And never trust a Democrat who won't go to the wall for democracy.

SPEAKING OF WOMEN WHO DISAPPOINT ON an absolute equal par with men: How about Andrea Howarth, erstwhile leader of Ontario's New Democratic Party? Yeah, me neither.

I was listening to her speech in the Ontario Legislature, which was posted on Facebook, the modern equivalent of throwing someone to the lions.

It was *excruciating*.

I really want to support the NDP and Andrea Horwath. And I hate to be unkind, but I can't listen to her.

(What am I saying? I don't hate to be unkind—it's what I live for. Yes, I'm shallow and heartless but you made me this way.)

She's so inarticulate, I get panicky wondering if she's going to be able to finish her thought.

I keep thinking she's having a stroke. And then she grinds to ….a…. h..a..l….t. And then she chooses a weird word that's not quite right…

I find I'm mouthing the words along with her, then when she stops, I stop too, with my mouth open, making the high-pitched encouraging noises you make when you're doing "here comes the airplane into the hangar" for babyboo with a spoonful of Gerber asparagus.

"Ah…ah….AH…. THERE we go! *Whoza whooza widdle NDP shnickums!*"

It's worse because she's a woman, so of course the fate of all womankind is depending on her every utterance.

We all know the drill by now. If a woman is forceful, she'll be "strident" or "a virago". If she's gentle and kind, she'll be a "snowflake" or "dizzy" or have "no guts," but if she has guts then she's a "bitch." If she's emotional, she's "hysterical," if she takes our criticism to heart and reins in her emotions, she becomes "cold." (Just ask Hillary.)

Her very cuticles will be examined, her achievements minimized, her sex life, if any, dredged up, at which point the whole shebang might just grind to a halt (what's the definition of a slut? A woman with the morals of a man).

Every blunder she's ever made will be put on top of the Great Big Pile of Female Blunders that kicks off with Eve, a put-up job if I ever saw one, and crashes upwards through history in slow-motion like a giant display at William Ashley Fine China that had the table kicked out from under it.

How can we fix Andrea? Maybe they just need to work a little more on her machine learning features. Maybe she just needs some sleep! Maybe she needs an oil change! Maybe—

Andrea Howarth—I don't doubt your sincerity. And I look forward to that great day, which I'm sure is just around the corner,

when you pass the Turing test.

> " never trust a **DYKE** without a TOOL BELT "

The Emotional Blackmail of Bernie's Babes

Sander-nista babes are hot for Bernie. They LOVE Bernie! They love his angry, shouty old-man speeches about the economy, his absurdly over-ambitious election platform, his inability to compromise, and (or so I like to fantasize), underpinning it all like a couple of size ten granola bars, his well-worn Birkenstocks.

Sander-nista babes love Bernie's windswept coif which, so legend has it, was last neatly combed for three days back around 1964, about the time he was marching for civil rights in the Deep South.

(Because what could Black people possibly have more need of than yet another condescending liberal white male lending his expertise so they don't fuck it all up?)

Sander-nista babes find it adorable that he's able to sleep so peacefully for all those decades in such a stressful environment as the Senate, and just shake their little heads with an indulgent sigh that says, "Oh, that Bernie! Isn't he incorrigible!" every time he gets stuck in his chair and has to be pried off with a serving utensil and some WD-40.

Being on his team makes every day into a cherished childhood visit to Gramps, with the Senate standing in for the Sunset Lodge: Palliative care with filibusters.

He'd be perfect in one of those saucy British comedies: Sanders as Bernard, Lord Buttpinch, living out his useless final days in his ancestral home at Slapfanny-on-the-Minge; the wealthy, safely-neutered toff in a bath chair who, though presenting no sexual risk, still manages to be inappropriate as he gooses a behind or leers at a "nice rack." Sander-nista babes are the indulgent nurses, fairly busting out of their unbuttoned uniform tops as they spoon rice pudding and Pepto-Bismol into his mouth and smack away his wandering hands.

But let's be frank. Sander-nista babes aren't all dewy eyes and tenderness. This is, after all, a cohort of millennials (and some Gen Z's). Millennials are impatient for change, they want it now, now, NOW! They are confrontational as a result; they are intolerant of compromise or even other points of view.

And millennials' idealism and urgency come pre-packaged with healthy doses of cynicism and rage at what they're inheriting in terms of moribund systems and collateral damage. As idealistic as they are, Sander-nista babes have no illusions.

(Well, except thinking Sanders could ever be elected President of the United States in his lifetime or ours, and believing he'll necessarily wake up the next time he falls asleep. But only those two illusions! Honest!)

They know, in private, that Bernie has always been a teensy bit unelectable, which unfortunately just makes them more insistent, in public, that the DNC is engaged in a vast conspiracy to interfere with the electoral process, play dirty and generally be a bunch of selfish, possibly borderline senile, boomers.

Politics is one area where a hard-line, no-compromise stance is particularly unproductive and often repugnant—witness the impeachment fiasco, where a hard-line Senate undid weeks of hearings, made a mockery of justice, and set up the perception of Democrats as vindictive liars.

Which makes Sander-nistas' hard line on policies, their impatience and their distressing penchant for nasty ad hominem attacks on other candidates all the more regrettable, as Sanders' policies are just the ticket for financial and social change and long overdue.

The problem comes in selling them to an American electorate scared gormless by the socialist bogeyman, and whose minds have been rolled back to pre-Depression expectations—a kind of collective gaslighting in which two generations' worth of social democracy has been expunged through the power of one cleverly deployed word.

Incidentally, have you ever thought that, considering Sanders is an old, white male, his being unelectable is actually quite an impressive achievement, albeit a perverse one?

It's like the triple-ripple-loop-the-loop-with-a-backward-flip-and-a-knickerbocker-twist of tournament ice-dancing, performed to "Bolero" by two heterosexuals; or getting hit by lightning in your bathtub, twice.

Under normal circumstances, you will recall, any human with a penis is electable. I mean, that's Trump's only qualification for the job, so apparently penis-having is top of the must-haves.

AS I WRITE, IN DARKEST 2019, IT'S the consensus that Bernie is toast, even though he's stubborn as a dead mule and there's months to go. Don't think it's a sure thing that Bernie will throw in the towel, though. He delivered Trump four years ago, out of sheer spite, and there's no guarantee he won't again come November.

Bernie *will have* Americans eat that spinach that they keep spitting in his face. He *will be* right. Forget Pete Buttigieg "never going away;" it's Bernie who'll still be here sixty years from now, held together with electrical tape and wrapped in ice-filled, double-layered freezer bags, still as insistent, prickly and unadorable as today.

Bernie has learned nothing about persuasion, for he has resolutely refused to understand that there is no word that arouses more terror and confusion in the average American lizard brain than the word *socialism.*

If I came to America with scientific proof that socialism would cure newborn babies of cancer in an hour, they'd scream, "Throw those babies over a cliff then grind them into sausage before we'll let the scourge of socialism through our garden gates!"

If Jesus came to America and said He was in favor of universal health care, showed them projections proving how much better off everyone would be and how much money they'd save, they'd hold Him down, pound the nails through His hands and feet, spit in His face and taunt Him with, "Behold, the King of the Jews, funded by George Soros and the Deep State! Nice try, Commie!!"

Journalist Chris Ladd, way back in 2017, saw the light—and the irony. Writing in Forbes magazine, he pointed out that white Americans who have good corporate or government jobs...

> "...live in a socialist welfare state more generous, cushioned and expensive to the public than any in Europe...
>
> "...taxpayers fund our retirement saving, health insurance, primary, secondary, and advanced education, daycare, commuter costs, and even our mortgages at a staggering public cost... Socialism for white people is all-enveloping, benevolent, invisible, and insulated by the nasty, deceptive notion that we have earned our benefits by our own hand."
>
> —Chris Ladd, Forbes.com, March 13, 2017

What is the "staggering public cost" of government subsidies of white socialism?

Companies can deduct the cost of their employees' health insurance, and employees don't have to declare that benefit as income. In 2017, that was four hundred billion dollars annually of federal and state funds to insurers.

Mortgage interest? Up to a million dollars deductible. Seventy billion a year (roughly the cost of the food stamp program).[1]

This all came to pass when Truman's plan for universal health care was rejected in 1945. Instead, nine years later, Congress approved a plan *controlled by employers* and publicly funded through tax breaks, giving corporations a nice stick for beating unions. Because of worker demographics at that time, benefits thus accrued to white families via their male breadwinners.

Americans think socialism means peasants starving during Soviet famines, or dissidents dying in gulags. How does that compare, I wonder, with low-income families and their children starving in the midst of plenty in inner cities, and Black men dying in privately-run, for-profit prisons?

Whether your de facto rulers are corporations and capitalist oligarchs in the land of the free, or self-confessed dictators of fungible proles, the results are remarkably similar. The one percent is the one percent, plain or fancy versions notwithstanding.

And there goes Bernie again, calling himself a socialist, unable to hold off with the perfect for the sake of the desperately needed, to relax the hard line a little, or to come down to planet earth with the rest of us and choose the language and narrative that would reassure nervous voters.

Unable, in other words, to play the political game of deal-making to take steps towards a future goal ("being a corporate lackey" as the Sandernista babes would say).

His insistence on revolutionary rhetoric, his Wall Street hard line, all of this suggests he loves to shock the bourgeoisie at least as much as he wants systemic change.

He's the Grand Mogul of the left, and gives every indication that he finds campaigning to be beneath him. He might prefer a coronation to an election, which is why it's like watching Meryl Streep being forced to audition for the high school play.

You have to admire, almost, his pig-headed self-righteousness and his Mount Everest of ego upon which progressive policies which would save lives falter and die half-way to the summit.

What a strange bird: A socialist claiming to work for the public good but thinking only of his profile on the currency and the arc of history that

---

1   stats via Forbes.com

tends towards justice for his never-ending campaign.

How like a man...?

Still, you gotta hand it to him: Sanders has forever changed the political discourse in the US—from "I will never vote for a socialist" to "I will never vote for a socialist, especially Bernie Sanders."

SANDER-NISTA BABES GET THE UNELECTABLE bit. That's why they upped the emotional blackmail quotient, and maybe they're right.

Maybe "Vote Bernie or the Bunny Dies" will actually add a few more boomers or Black voters to the roster.

After all, starving kids are a dime a dozen, not to mention a strain on the nerves; but cute bunnies lower your blood pressure and don't grow up and start demanding things.

No compromise! It's not progressive, it seems, until Wall Street, the wealthy, the middle-class, small business owners, social conservatives, older and independent voters are all scared away.

Then, once the body politic is so spooked by "socialism" that even Trump seems like the better deal, the Sander-nista babes and Bernie chumps decide it's just way too much trouble to actually open their front doors, walk down the street, be part of "the corrupt system"—and vote for him.

HERE IS THE PROOF THAT Bernie's unelectable, and that his nomination would have been—or, who the hell knows, will be—a tragedy:

Russia has openly admitted that they have been actively working for Bernie's nomination. And Trump has been salivating at the thought of Bernie as the Democratic choice.

The autocratic President of the Russian Federation and the wannabe-autocratic President of the United States, working together for a common cause... In another place, another time, with a different cast, this sort of détente could have been a million kinds of warm and fuzzy,

but in reality—not the sort of reconciliation, partnership or goal one had in mind, is it?

Skipping Rhymes of Gen Z Redux

Here I am, still undercover at the Acme Prep School, disguising myself with chocolate milk mustaches, playing with Dinky Toys at recess and praying the Grade Ones to Eights don't notice.

The things I do for my blog! If I have to choke down one more packet of "Snackums" at lunch I may hurl.

I think I've got it pretty much under control, but I do have to squelch a tendency I have to answer the arithmetic questions too quickly. One more incident of my knowing the sum of 2 + 2 and I'm going to raise suspicion.

One precocious kid, named Becky, of course, is having none of it.

"What you were doing driving that car after school?" she said to me the other morning after we'd both awakened from our "Futons and Oreos" nap break. Becky has that annoying, smarty-pants-girl way of making you *hear* the italics. She lifted one quizzical eyebrow.

"Nine-year-olds *aren't* allowed to drive like you said. I checked with my dad. And you seem to have reached puberty *quite* early." She just stood there, hands on hips, looking, I swear to god, like she was a miniature Elizabeth Warren, and I was the Wall Street CEO.

I was all in a cold sweat, but luckily the bell rang for the start of classes. Becky flounced back to her desk, ready to overthink, colour her map well within the lines and stick her hand way, way up so she could show off her smarty-pants-girl knowledge whenever Miss Sidor asked a question.

I'm outta here. Knowing when the party's over is half the battle, after all. I have plenty of material.

By the way, in view of my dedication to ethnographic field work, I kind of consider myself the Béla Bartók of skipping rhymes—just minus the primitive wax cylinder recordings.

Also minus the stout Bulgarian women fermenting goat's milk and regaling us with toothless smiles as they sing incomprehensible ditties, about goat's milk, in the Lydian mode.

I'M A MEMBER OF THE LAST GENERATION to have a meaningful label—"Boomer," meaning that we talk loudly and over everyone else. This minor tic provokes complaining from the more sensitive types, to which I reply, "If anyone had anything interesting to say, maybe we wouldn't have to. Pass the apple-cinnamon-scented candle? Thanks! And Flower Power!"

Just as the children's rhyme *"Ringa ringa rosy, a pocket full of posies"* transformed the unspeakable horrors of the bubonic plague into a delightful tea-time frolic for the wizened, hairy, toothless little adults that passed for kids in the fourteenth century, I've been uncovering skipping rhymes that serve to help this era's fragile, hot-house crop of little sprouts process current events and make Aspartame-coated sense of them.

I'm sharing this latest batch with you with just the one condition. If Gen Z will please agree, once you've made sense of them, to, ummm, tell the rest of us?

Never forget how good I am to you.

...

"VOTING RIGHTS ARE NOW ABOLISHED"

{Traditional, early 21st century. "Voting" was some kind of group ritual, I believe. This must be the G-rated version.}

Voting rights are now abolished
No more wondering who's in charge

With democracy demolished
We are all Madame Defarge

Bernie's prospects weren't too ducky,
Just his waking up felt lucky

(Votes suppressed count one, two, three
For gerrymandered POC)

Socialism people doubted
So, to make his point—HE SHOUTED

Wouldn't vote, those fans of Bernie,
"Down the street's too long a journey!"

"After all, it's not a sin
to cast your vote for—sleeping in!"

Voting rights are now abolished
No more wondering who's in charge

Ballots lost, just four, five, six
No evidence of dirty tricks

While Repubs hoping for a boner
Fund recounts in Arizoner

Hours in line count seven and eight
For extra laughs, he'll change the date

Stupidity remains systemic
While he bungles a pandemic

With democracy demolished
We are all Madame Defarge

No more Hillary and her email
Kamala is, still, a female

Nine, ten, eleven what does she lack?
The requisite degree of Black!

And yet another fatal flaw —
Her tendency to rule of law

Biden's choice, such moral strength!

But don't examine her at length

Ah well, it might as well be said —
At least she's not as nearly-dead.

Voting rights are now abolished
No more wondering who's in charge

Donald Trump's beyond repentance
Count twelve lies in every sentence

States thirteen, of thee I sing
A president who thinks he's king

Fourteen senators acknowledge
Nailing the Electoral College

In the room there lurks an elephant—
Soon all votes will be irrelevant.

. . .

"CLIMATE CHANGE AND GLOBAL WARMING"

Traditional, Vancouver "Island" (former term for small landmass not covered with ocean).

Climate change and global warming!
See those super hurricanes forming!

Think that levels one, two, three
Were maximum velocity?
Now feel the gale at four, five, six

And though your house be sturdy bricks

It might as well be built of sticks

Climate change and global warming

Western fires so dramatic!
(Obviously Democratic)

How many gallons from a glacier
As the polar cap gets lacier?

Eight billion nine billion ten and climbing
Half-past Doomsday is our timing

Ice bergs calving in a series?
Eleven new conspiracy theories!

Climate change and global warming

Thanks to oil our days now seem dark
In an underwater theme park

Count twelve hundred days from when
You wouldn't listen to us then

And unlike those
Who called it "faked"
The planet now is—
Fully baked.

. . .

"CELEBRATE THE GIG ECONOMY"

Celebrate the gig economy
You can be whatever you wonomy!

Tinker, tailor, Uber, Lyft
Pick me up and make it swift

One minute order, two minute wait
Put my foie gras on a plate

Three minute swallow, four minute done
Indentured servitude is fun

AirBnB's inflated rents
Will put the rest of us in tents

Foreign condo owners hoard them
Might as well —WE can't afford them!

Celebrate the gig economy
Back at home with no autonomy

Six seven eight nine gigs on Fiverr
Fill the spare time of a driver

Ten short hours you worked this week
Those student loans are looking bleak

Part-time jobs? We gladly stayed for them
Praying one day

We'd get paid for them.

The Poor Get Poorer, the Rich Get Kardashian

Top of the news headlines on this day of mourning for decency and knowing our priorities: Kim Kardashian wore Marilyn Monroe's iconic Jean Louis "nude" dress to the Met Gala.

You know, the dress MM had to be sewn into before singing, and I use the term in its broadest sense, of including not singing, "Happy Birthday, Mister President" to JFK, as an invited crowd of Democrat males jumped onto tables to leer and wolf-whistle. Iconic, I guess, is thus defined as "facilitating the shamefully tacky but not unexpected."

Personally I don't know why she didn't just add a few patches of stretch Velcro to the side panels and gusset, but that's me, mister make-do-and-mend. Of course, there's also "Spanx".

Moving along, this decision, to wear, you know, Marilyn's JFK-Happy Birthday dress, has conservators of fashion furious, but quietly and covered with tissue paper in a dark, temperature-controlled room.

Wearing an iconic historical dress valued at ten million dollars can cause, for example, little microscopic tears in the fabric, maybe even the fabric of time at that price point, and Minerva help you if you're a heavy anti-perspirant user.

This sartorial slice of schlock history is currently owned by, believe it or not, Ripley's Believe It or Not, who assured everyone that Kim had to sign a contract not to perspire, sit down, lift her arms or breathe during the entire time she wore the dress on the red carpet, before rolling it off like a pair of used pantyhose and slipping into the replica she'd had made.

Did you hear what I just said? *The replica.* I would really appreciate your trying to be *more* attentive, *less* high-maintenance.

That's right. *She'd had a replica made of the ten million dollar dress,* using the money that, along with Jeff Bezos's money, and billionaire money in general, is not going to solve world hunger. Here's why:

There's a big, dark vault full of million-dollar bills under the Arizona desert where Kim and Jeff and Elon *et al.* go when life gets demanding. I'm sure you totally know this, and it just slipped your mind.

Once the six-foot-thick lead doors are bolted, they get naked—no funny business, either, sex is sex, animals can have sex, this is money. Animals do not have money, which is why we look down on them and generally show them disrespect by, for example, eating them—they get naked and smear themselves with almond butter and roll around and around and around in the million dollar bills, and whoever has the most bills sticking to them when the timer goes off gets to use that money, but, and here's the relevant bit, thanks for your patience, it has to be for something "fun".

Giving food to dark-colored people in third world countries, like Somalia or the US, is not "fun," in case you hadn't noticed.

Well, do YOU think it's fun? Is that how YOU spend your Saturday nights, you who hail from Des Moines? Right, so, put down those pearls, Little Miss Vera Virtue-Signal. Puh-*leaze*.

Anyway. Sarah Scaturro, chief conservator at the Cleveland Museum of Art and formerly a conservator at the Met's Costume Institute, was frustrated by Kim's decision of what to do with her win of the subterranean almond-butter money.

"So my worry," she said to the LA Times, "is that colleagues in historic costume collections are now going to be pressured by important people to let them wear garments."

Which is odd, because *my* worry is that Russians will rape more Ukrainian babies before shooting their mothers in the back of the head, and maybe Putin nuking New York City, but that's probably because you get crankier as you get older. I probably should just chill more.

KIM WORE THE REAL DRESS, THE DRESS that touched the sweaty, acetone-scented skin of Marilyn Monroe, and only changed into the replica once the damage had been done.

Why? For the same reason that Elon Musk bought Twitter and that Jeff Bezos flew his own spacecraft into not-quite-space-enough.

She wore it for the same reason the Kardashians have their own private fire department, or why the conservative members of the US Supreme Court are banning abortions, and are ordering an enquiry into that decision being leaked, did they think we wouldn't notice if it was Friday instead of Wednesday? Were they saving it up for Christmas? "Hey, ladies, guess what? Our surprise present to ourselves is *your* bodies!"

Or the same reason why Ron DeSantis and Greg Abbott are leading the now worldwide campaign vilifying and virtually outlawing gay men and transgenders.

Because, first of all, gay men are out to recruit your kids, a program which has been a dismal failure in the implementation. Now, this is just empirical evidence, but as far as I can tell without having done a controlled, randomized study followed by peer review and publication in "The Annals of Grooming," the continent is not *noticeably* awash with ten-year-old boys mincing around like tiny Bette Davi,[1] waving their arms like airplane propellers and screaming, "What-a-DUMP!"—well, except in Florida, where every adult not from Florida tends to participate in that critique.

Secondly, transgender persons can't really recruit your kids, at least, as much as they'd like to, because they're too busy avoiding being murdered, which involves a lot of staying inside, or running, or killing themselves. By the way, all this patriotic help rates not even an honorable mention from Abbott for saving him part of his budget.

I call that ungrateful.

Transgenders are getting the axe because, you know, they're just weird. Let's face it.

Not weird like Texans saying that non-existent wind mill farms forced on Texas by the non-existent Green New Deal is the cause of Texas' failure to cope with snow, and not weird like getting your neighbours to report you to the Gazpacho Police if you drive someone to an abortion clinic in your taxi, so they can collect a bounty of ten thousand dollars. Not even close to that kind of weird.

It's the kind of weird that doesn't cause any harm whatsoever to anyone, even accidentally. *No harm caused to anyone.* To a Republican, who uses the formula *effort expended ÷ harm caused = value*, now, that's weird.

Kim Kardashian wore that dress—by the way, I said "wore" but actually she couldn't shoe-horn her bootyliciousness into it, even after dieting; she had to leave it unzipped, and cover her *hashtag-dress-fail* with a white fox stole, which is certainly *my* preferred strategy—she wore

---

[1]   Bette Davi = plural form of Bette Davis.

the original just long enough to make the five people who care, but they really care, upset.

She wore that dress for the same reason Ontario Premier Doug Ford, whose psychotic, mirthless grin is so nightmarish he had to order dentures that wrap around three hundred and sixty degrees, is ramming his unnecessary highway through a section of Toronto's vulnerable green belt, or digging up Duffin's Creek wetlands in Pickering, contrary to all the advice he hired advisors to give him.

They're all doing it to say, "Fuck you. We can do this. Go ahead, stop us."

Their entitlement and arrogance, spread stinking-thick like manure on the fertile ground of their self-regard grows them from business persons and celebrities into royalty. Kim, Doug, Elon, Jeff—anyone with billions can buy their own bespoke feudal society and paper over the cracks of late-stage capitalism, as we kiss their toes and slouch back to Walmart serfdom.

This is our idea of leadership, these are the people we want to emulate as we throw public money at them like handfuls of Smarties.

These are the people who embody inequality, dogs eating dogs, instead of the baseline of equality that's so desperately unexciting to us.

How can we exult in others' wealth, the pot of gold at the end of the rainbow, without believing that at least some of us will always have to be miserable? Lazy slackers to the man, if we felt safe and secure we'd lie in bed all day, just not the same way our safe and secure heroes lie in bed all day.

We don't want democracy. We want the promise of the American dream, even if we're eating alfalfa sprouts in deepest Alberta. We want to dream about making a cartload of money, bucking the system, and disengaging from society because it's hard work dealing with all these other people who have the gall to say they want their rights, too.

Rights? What we really want is *handouts*. Unlike the *entitlements* our heroes get, as they lie in bed all day.

THESE MOUTHY MOGULS MAY talk and behave like the world's new royalty, but the proof that they're from the same beer-barrel as us is the contents of their wish lists, a crass collection of the tacky, the juvenile, and the ridiculous.

Kim's prezzie to herself we've dealt with: that pathetic ten minutes in a ten-million-dollar antique gown, worn once by a legendary star who, sixty years dead, still effortlessly outclasses her; the highjacking of a fragile artefact from a forgotten age that she forced onto her pampered frame, destroying it without a moment's thought or regret.

Jeff's toy was a B-movie rocket ship, into which he crammed his thuggish bald head, and maybe some McDonald's hash browns and a rich friend or two, in order to celebrate the most wasteful, unnecessary, immoral flight in history, while forest fires raged below and millions spent another wretched day scrabbling through garbage dumps for sustenance.

Elon's playpen is a segregated factory that's like a bubbling, roiling yogurt culture of racism, a *de facto* prison in which his demoralized employees are tasked with manufacturing loopy "autonomous cars" that drive like your Great Aunt Ruby after she got the drops in her eyes at the optometrist, except *she* didn't kill anyone.

We nod sagely as Musk pontificates about "freedom" and other topics with the trenchant insight of Readers' Digest Magazine and trolls users on the social media platform he now owns. They think government is like a business, civil rights your "free gift" if you send in proof of purchase.

We've been sold a replica of democracy, a souvenir of some place we did the guided tour of, but never truly appreciated.

It's bait and switch, a scam, like when I used to ask my parents for money so I could buy them gifts, which meant they effectively bought themselves that walk-in closet's worth of silk-polyester squares and enough bottles of Old Spice to marinate a whale, or, actually, Dad.

Kim and Jeff and Elon are the royalty we crave and detest, and they are all mentally ill, deeply, deeply mentally ill.

They are sick for attention, sick for power, sick with the sickness only money can buy. They are inhuman. They are zombies of money. They crave attention like a gay man craves a pirated Maria Callas recording or a Tiffany lamp, like a heroin user craves another penetration of his vein.

Maybe they can all put on dead Marilyn's dresses, climb into Jeff's space dildo, and Tweet something snarky about transgenders from a little higher up than Mount Everest, and maybe, just maybe this time they'll realize there's no need to hurry back.

Like, don't worry about the litre of milk.

WE ARE ALL CAPITALISTS in the same way that we're all racists: by default, out of sheer intellectual and moral laziness.

Conservatives are capitalists who get rich from our passivity, our cowed belief that "the market will decide" (well, yes, it will, but what decisions!) and our terror, which they instilled in us, of altering the outcomes.

"Deficits must be reconciled! Lower your expectations! That Jeff Bezos! Bless his cotton socks, he doesn't pay tax!"

And do we balk at his refusal to give back at least a bit of what he stole? Yes, stole. It wasn't Jeff who slogged in the warehouses!

I admit that Jeff Bezos doesn't break the law by paying workers as little as possible or timing their bathroom breaks or accepting government handouts or taking advantage of perfectly legal tax loopholes. He merely milks the system for every toxic drop he can get.

Morally broken people naturally create, espouse and benefit from morally broken systems. The perfect synergy helps them continue to believe in themselves as cutting-edge entrepreneurs and innovators, glamorous role models, the beautiful people, when they're really just banal, modern-day Scrooges, baleful vampires with smartphones.

Really, could the outcome of taxing Jeff until he only had, say, one billion dollars be worse than the outcome we have now? Tax Jeff until his pips squeak, he'll still be fine. I *promise* you.

If he claims to make no profit then close the loopholes or create legislation to claw back revenue and enforce decent living wages for workers.

Jeff and Elon and Kim and Mark, our kings, queens and jesters, all use our common infrastructure: the highways, railways, airports and staff, clean water, electricity, police and the courts of justice, banking systems and supply chains, vast telecommunications networks, world wide web and government subsidies, all of which support their grandiose schemes and frat-boy lifestyles.

They're like boorish guests who park their limo in your flower bed, use up your data plan and polish off your entire liquor cabinet, all the while complaining how mistreated they are. It's high time we were compensated for their goofy narcissism.

You'd think we'd proposed rearranging the planets to spell "Things go better with Coke!" but it's really very simple: *If you wouldn't let your five-year-old do it, don't let billionaires do it.*

Would you let your five-year-old take all the toys from all the other kids and hide them in his corner?

Of course not! You'd give him a little smack on the bum, tell him he'll die alone and wretched in a trap house if he continues being so fucking selfish, then make him give the toys back.

Would you let your five-year-old pee on the floor then not clean it up?

NO way! You'd force him on his hands and knees and hit him with a belt while he cleaned it up, then dock his allowance! Same with companies who pollute!

Would you let your five-year-old come into the living room at two AM and interrupt your grown up conversation with "I think Mummy and Daddy are a couple of stupid cocksuckers!"

Of course you wouldn't endure even a *second* of that before explaining to little Johnny that just because you can say it doesn't mean you should, and that nasty talk is kind of intimidating and anti-social. Then you'd hold his head in the toilet bowl while flushing it until he remembered.

Now, wasn't that easy? Just friggin' do it! Punish cheaters and liars and sneaks and criminals who steal the profits we created and pollute our common resources and throw their weight around.

Distribute wealth until no one's in poverty and everyone has the basic comforts of life. If any of us want more, we'll have the safe space to be inventive in and earn more.

Do you really think the only thing driving achievement is suffering and poverty? Bullshit.

Why do we care what conservatives think? They'll think it anyway! If the truth isn't cooperating, they'll lie! Just tax the rich, get rid of poverty and

you'll realize that we've been fighting over crusts of stale bread when we could have had waffles and ice cream.

Finale

The Pivot Chord

In Zen Buddhism there's a parable of being in a boat. All around you is the circle of water, and you believe that's all the water there is. But it's not; it's merely the water that is visible to you.

The water extends farther than you can imagine in all directions, beyond the horizon, and becomes the ocean: vast, sublime, an uncountable infinity of water. Another universe.

You think you see everything, but if the ocean were suddenly revealed to you, you'd be ashamed of your foolishness.

Perhaps your foolishness is a protection. Perhaps your mind couldn't cope with the ocean, at least, not yet.

What you see as the whole truth is merely part of the truth—the part you can handle.

At any moment, believing that what we see is the complete truth is a delusion.

. . .

GREETINGS TO ALL OF YOU AT peacehacks dot com. Mark Landry, your usual host, invited me, David Roddis, to write a guest article for you fine people, and my first thought, after being flattered, was: Why on earth would any of you be interested in my thoughts and opinions?

This is partly my natural diffidence. I have been at certain odd times in my life the sort of guy who writes a one-man show, complete with original songs, takes it to the Edinburgh Festival Fringe, then spends the entire day of the opening praying nobody will turn up.

It's not that I don't have interesting and engaging thoughts and opinions. Pay me a surprise visit one evening when you're in my neighbourhood and you'll almost certainly find me regaling myself with interesting and engaging thoughts and opinions by the cartload, until my roommate says something like, "You know, David, I've heard that talking to yourself is one of the first signs of madness."

And I'm old, pushing sixty-four, though studiously avoiding the Tilley hat and wrap-around sunglasses, and once you know my age, and because you are good people, you'll automatically pay me a little bit more attention. Skeptical, at first, but certainly polite.

Americans aren't throwing around the respect like it was oxygen. I get that. You didn't dump all that tea in the harbor to pay respect where it isn't due, after all.

But now that my world is composed of "Young People" and me—in fact, I think of all of you as "millennials," it saves time—you may just allow that I've had a few close calls, fallen in and out of love, lost a few people dear to me, made countless mistakes, done my share of laughing, crying and dancing; also hanging out in those cheap joints, doing that thing you do with less clothes on, and, ta-da! I'm still here to talk about it. That's not, as they say, nothing.

So feel free to make with the slightly forced and polite but in the end reasonably sincere respect.

I'm Canadian, and what we don't know about polite could be laser-engraved on the head of a pin, with room left over for a couple of dancing angels and the Lord's Prayer, in a display font. If someone punches us in the nose, we say, "I'm sorry, Madam, it appears that you wanted to fully and rapidly extend your right arm while clenching your fist—and I'm just guessing, here, but did my nose get in your way? My sincere condolences!"

I once bumped into a phone booth, apologized to the phone booth, and no one batted an eye.

Revolving doors defeat us. It's just one big, hot, Canadian mess, all of us standing around chirping, "After you!" "No, after you, eh?" and so forth, which is why we wear so many layers and always make sure we have a light snack handy—a sandwich and maybe some vegetable soup in a Thermos flask—because you never know when the next Canadian Stand-Off will rumble in like the polar vortex and play havoc with your statutory lunch break.

We do things a little differently. Our political system goes like this:

First check if there's a Person Called Trudeau (PCT) hanging around. Then, find out what party he's in—probably the Liberal Party, formerly exactly the same as the "Progressive Conservatives," dressed in nicer suits, but times have changed.

Now you must be careful to check: "Remind me, are the Liberals the ones with the human rights or….?" And your friend goes, "Yes, but then there's the deficit." And you go, "Hmmmmm, tough one…."

Anyway, if there's a PCT, then you must vote for the PCT, and then right afterwards be instantly disappointed at his every move.

Who does that PCT think he is, anyway, goldarn it? Putting on airs! That—tall poppy!

And we have no rules about term limits. You could vote for the same PCT, election after election, until the Trudeau kids had their own kids and Sophie-Grégoire had a mid-life crisis and ran off with the Cirque du soleil, and the person who makes lunch for the Trudeaus retired and wrote their tell-all insider story, and it wouldn't matter. We could keep voting for Justin, as long as he was alive and Leader of his party, basically, forever.

The British Monarchy figures in our government. Queen Elizabeth, that doddering papier-mâché puppet dressed in eye-popping colors, was laid to rest this past year, and another doddering papier-mâché puppet, her son, Charles III, has taken her place as our symbolic Head of State. His representative in Canada is called the Governor-General.

When we pass laws, King Charles has to give his assent. He probably will, especially seeing as the first King Charles lost his head when England decided it was fed up with kings and queens, and had a hissy-fit called the Civil War. Also, and more kindly, we like the royals to feel needed.

Hey-presto—fully up to speed on Constitutional Monarchy.

What else? I live in Toronto, Canada's largest city, which is on Lake Ontario. If you stood on the Toronto waterfront and lobbed a rock across the lake, it would skip overland and end up in Buffalo. Or maybe Rochester. So that's Toronto. Moving along!

Then there's Québec. Their slogan is *"Je me souviens,"* which means: "I remember." And when they say they *souviens*, hoo-boy, do they mean they *souviens*!

Québec was ruled by the iron fist of the Catholic Church from the very beginning in the seventeenth century through the 1950s, at which point they wearied of the abuse and the backwardness and the hypocrisy and the misogyny—you know, "Catholic Outreach"—and then came the Quiet Revolution, *la Révolution tranquille*.

At first this simply meant that Québecoise (that's the women) could legally leave the house during daylight and were entitled to take a few hours off after the tenth kid, I think that's right, and a definite improvement.

But sure as God made little green apples and Charles de Gaulle, it soon meant the Front de libération du Québec (FLQ), a Marxist-Leninist separatist group, and their subsequent terrorism, bombs, murder and a failed attempt at a coup d'état.

Oh, those French Canadians! Not a flicker of humor in an ice-castle full of them!

That whole FLQ terrorist episode, known as the "October Crisis," happened in 1970, and it was serious stuff. The current PCT's dad, Pierre Trudeau—yes they are kind of like the Kennedys, well done, guys!—invoked the War Measures Act, which put Montreal in a state of war-time martial law.

Troops in the streets, all civil rights suspended, detention without cause, search and seizure: in total, police arrested nearly 500 people suspected of belonging to the FLQ. This brings us to Pierre's most famous quote. In the midst of this crisis, with Canada under siege and two government officials taken hostage (one of whom would eventually be murdered), he was asked by a CBC reporter, "How far are you willing to go with this?" and Pierre, clearly peeved, pirouetted on his heel and snapped, "Just watch me."

Now, this does not, admittedly, have the noble ring of, say, "We hold these truths to be self-evident..." It's not quite cracking that glass ceiling of, maybe, the Gettysburg Address. But it's what we've got.

This is the pinnacle of Canadian temperament, our sharp-intake-of-breath moment. "Just watch me."

I invite you to try it out, should a suitable opportunity arise, and see if it doesn't fill you with snippy, ineffectual Canadian-style defiance:

> PARTNER ONE: Just how far are you willing to go with this leftover tuna casserole thing?
>
> PARTNER TWO: Just watch me.

Whoa, you guys! Settle down!

At any rate, ever since the FLQ, Québec has gone quite passive-aggressive. She teases, acts the coquette: "Maybe je stay, pffffft! Maybe je go!" Québec bats her eyes, lifts her petticoats so we see more than the usual amount of ankle, then exclaims, "Oooh la la!" in a way that's flirty and very *Moulin rouge*, but still makes you wonder.

I've left out all the Maritime provinces, British Columbia and the prairies, the territories of Yukon and Nunavut, but that's par for the course for someone from Toronto. Those of us from Canada's most populous and most important city sometimes forget other areas of Canada exist.

You know, like Americans sometimes forget that the rest of the world exists...

Now, this is all very well, but quite obviously I've been putting off the moment when I admit that my initial hesitation had to do with common ground, or more specifically, my inability to find some.

This is when I reveal myself as not just a Canadian, but a gay, nearly senior, liberal, snowflakey, radical left-winger Canadian who loves his country for all its faults and who is unabashedly atheist.

Not Dawkins-level, screaming at everyone atheist, but that's about as much cushioning as I can do. I've tried using "humanist," because I like to be something rather than not-something; a believer in the human spirit instead of a non-believer in the Holy Spirit. It flickers on and off.

And you are, many of you, good, friendly, welcoming-but-not-tolerating-fools type Americans, passionate, a little dramatic at times, but loyal to a fault, and many of you are also evangelical Christians, who are, and correct me if I'm wrong, here, a little stressed.

A little stressed that the American Dream no longer means what it used to mean, stressed that your values are under attack—good values like life, liberty and, not happiness but the pursuit of happiness—a little stressed that you no longer seem to be masters of your own domain.

You're a lot like Québec separatists, in fact, and if you don't believe me, check this out:

"Now or never! Masters in our own house!" says this poster from 1970s Québec.

Does that not ring true? Masters in your own house. That's all you want, yet everywhere this simple desire, which is really the desire to be left alone, seems under attack. I get that.

And I get that you have been—we have all been—lied to, lied to by bald-faced liars who run the corporations that are the de facto rulers, the rulers of the rulers we voted for in our respective countries; lied to by the politicians who promise anything to get into power; lied to and surveilled and spied upon until actual rational, intelligent people not unlike you or I form Facebook groups claiming the earth is actually flat and it's all a conspiracy.

I get how people can believe the world is flat, because what have we *not* been lied to about? They said the wealth would trickle down, and it didn't, and they said they had our interests at heart, and they had only their own. After a while, being lied to, day in, day out, makes a person crazy.

When you think about it, we've all been gaslighted on an epic scale.

America has been a kind of monolithic culture, so it stands to reason that the assumption has been that your values are Western values, your religion is Christianity and the rule is—play by the rules.

This is not a criticism; the world has turned upside down. America has been the shining city on the hill, and now a bunch of people are rattling around your borders who want what you've got.

And not just people: desperate people.

You have something that I don't have: you have the comfort of your religion. That is something eternal and rock solid, and you can take comfort in the beliefs you have in common with other Christians, beliefs that date back two millennia.

Belief in the redeeming power of Christ's sacrifice, certainty that the awesome sacrifice he made brought us back to God.

Christians believe in Original Sin, which is not just bad thoughts or actions, but eternal separation from God. Sin is the pain of that separation, pain that humans and God suffer equally.

That's how I understand sin. We weren't content to be with God, we were arrogant and restless, we had to find out for ourselves. So we ripped out God's heart and found ourselves alone in the wilderness we had created.

To be separate from God is to be in the place called hell, and it doesn't have to be a physical place. Buddhists suggest that when you are filled with anger that boils over, when you're filled with hatred, or ravenous hungers and desires, you are at that moment in hell.

You have these spiritual truths to sustain you. I was brought up Anglican, which is the church Henry VIII started when the Pope wouldn't annul his marriage to Catherine of Aragon due to its non-consummation, because Henry was, and it's hard to sugar-coat this, lying.

He fired the Pope and made himself head of the church. That's why Anglicans never mention "the Lord" or "God." It's considered at least irrelevant, definitely confusing, and probably in poor taste. So I was at a disadvantage right from the start.

But you are mostly evangelical Christians, which means that you want to spread the word. You want everyone to know this good news and share in Christ's redemption. Perhaps that's where the frustration sets in, because there is going to be a brick wall that you hit where your desire to spread the word, your passionate belief, is blindsided by someone else's polite refusal, blank stare or cry of outrage.

This bumping up against each other place is where we learn interesting things about freedom and rights, and what the difference might be between those two concepts, in a democratic—a pluralistically democratic—society. Freedom and rights don't occur in a vacuum to one set of people only and they are not absolute. One must be weighed against the other.

How we decide which freedom, which right, is to prevail at any moment is the crux of every head-butting impasse, and there are potentially myriad instances in a day.

But even if you don't agree with me, if you believe some freedoms are absolute and there's no debate possible, that's when we must keep talking.

This is life or death. The point at which you most want to stop talking and working this out, to throw up your hands in utter exasperation and cry "Liberals!" and where I want to do the same but with "Conservatives!" is the point where we absolutely must keep talking.

I'm going to call this Roddis's Law because it just occurred to me and the guy it first occurs to gets first shot at the naming.

How we decide what right or freedom gets precedence can be one of two things, I suggest: What is best for me / my group; or What is best for society as a whole, society being everyone that we bump up against, whether or not we like them.

Here's a rather trivial example: The guy who refused to bake the wedding cake for the gay couple's wedding. The court ruled very narrowly that he had the right to refuse on that occasion.

I don't like that decision, mostly because it seems to de-legitimize equal marriage. But far more clever legal minds than mine pondered this important cake question and ruled for the baker, narrowly, for this one occasion.

I'm a big boy of sixty-four and I will live with it. Seriously, are we going to stand beside the guy with a gun to his head, "Bake the cake, dude!"?

Meanwhile, at the reception:

> "This cake tastes weird, and I'm getting a headache."

> "It's Resentment Cake with Intolerance Icing, garnished with sprinkles of pure Homophobia."

"Ahhh, nice! Have you choked down a piece yet?"

I don't aspire to this. Who am I to say he can't express his disapproval? And was this battle worth it? Do we have a baker more sympathetic to equal marriage? Is there a way both sides can express their beliefs and enjoy their rights without this being so difficult and bearing so negatively on society?

I don't know the answer.

But it was still worth making the point, because more people are talking about it and working it out.

The bigger issue, at least in Canada, is resolved, and cake doesn't even come into it.

ONE THING I HAVEN'T TOLD YOU about myself is that I trained, early in my life, as a classical musician. I was going to be a concert pianist. I ended up being a piano teacher who played some concerts now and again, and I didn't play for years—something about rebellion against parental wishes, weird, right?—but nevertheless, music, especially Beethoven's music, is like my blood and my oxygen.

There's a concept in music called modulation. If everything's always in the same key it would get rather boring, so we need a way to make a transition from one key to another, a way of smoothing the path.

That's what modulation is. You approach a chord as though in the original key but follow the chord as though it had been in the new key.

It's the musical equivalent of that special effect with the revolving doors, where you enter in your t-shirt and jeans, and leave two seconds later in a business suit.

All you need to do is find the pivot chord.

And our pivot chord, yours and mine, is called "compassion," in my world, and in yours, "grace." I can enter your world with your pivot chord of grace; you can enter mine with compassion. This is our spiritual modulation.

Grace means to be granted the forgiveness that we don't deserve, the unconditional love that we didn't earn. Grace means we will never give up on each other, that we'll keep talking, listening, working things out. Grace means to embrace with all our heart those who we think we have every reason to reject.

Compassion means *to feel with*, to understand that men and women and children cross deserts because they are a family desperate to survive as a family, and have not yet lost all hope. Compassion means to recognize ourselves in them, to realize *this could easily have been us.*

We all know what family means. We all know what it is to love someone, to be afraid for our children, to have our hearts broken, to want our lives to have meant more than a churning of foam.

There is no one in the world, in the whole family of humanity, who doesn't feel these things.

...

YOU SIT IN THE BOAT, CONTEMPLATING the circle of water. Then sensei —or God—strikes you on the shoulder.

You receive the blow with a gasp, and you wake up from the long sleep that has been your life. In the middle of your life you awaken, returning to the ordinary world with new clarity.

You view the weed that pokes up through the concrete with the same astonishment as the rose from your garden; you see the wretched poor at your door as your own mother, father, child.

You realize that everything you experience is calling for your full attention, that there is nothing to be despised.

A famous Zen phrase puts it more bluntly: *"There's no place in the world where you can spit."*

www.ingramcontent.com/pod-product-compliance
Lightning Source LLC
Chambersburg PA
CBHW060107170426
43198CB00010B/806